The Phoenix Agenda

The Phoenix Agenda

POWER TO TRANSFORM YOUR WORKPLACE

John Whiteside

with Leatrice McLaughlin

omneo

An imprint of Oliver Wight Publications, Inc.

85 Allen Martin Drive, Essex Junction, VT 05452

Published by Oliver Wight Publications, Inc.

Oliver Wight Publications books may be purchased for educational, business, or sales promotional use. For information, please call or write: Special Sales Department, Oliver Wight Publications, Inc., 85 Allen Martin Drive, Essex Junction, VT 05452. Telephone: (800) 343-0625 or (802) 878-8161; FAX: (802) 878-3384.

Library of Congress Catalog Card Number: 93-060675

ISBN: 0-939246-47-3

Text design by Irving Perkins Associates

Printed on acid-free paper.

Manufactured in the United States of America.

2   4   6   8   10   9   7   5   3   1

The Phoenix Agenda is dedicated to:

my loving wife, Holly

and by her request
to all souls
with the courage
to face transformation

Contents

Contents

Contents

Preface

The Book at a Glance

The mythological phoenix arose from its ashes every 500 years. In this era of revolutionary change, corporations must get on a faster track to rebirth. *The Phoenix Agenda* provides that track.

For hard-pressed managers desperately seeking new skills that will enable them to aid in the rebirth of their corporations, *The Phoenix Agenda* offers an exciting choice:

You could work like this:	*Or this:*
Administer bureaucracy.	Manage for action.
Resist change.	Show courage.
Crave comfort.	Take risks.
Collapse the business.	Renew the business.
Follow the rules.	Be a master of possibility.
Be a prisoner of fixed assumptions.	Create new assumptions.

Preface

Exist in fear.	Live in freedom.
Manipulate and control others.	Attract and empower others.
Perpetuate pain.	Forgive enemies.
Conduct business as usual.	Start a whole new ball game.

The choices on the left reflect the old way of managing. Those on the right embody the new way. In *The Phoenix Agenda,* readers will learn how to manage in the new way by following a step-by-step program for corporate rebirth. They will:

- Learn a powerful new management approach in "Mindsets at Work."
- Gain new action skills in "Tools for Transformation."
- Design and implement grand strategy in "Advanced Strategies for Workplace Transformation."

Acknowledgments

Perhaps a thousand people's contributions are expressed in this book, which has been 10 years in conception. With many of you, a kind of electricity has passed between us, an excitement and a sense of shared purpose. This may have occurred as we sat next to each other on an airplane, worked together, interacted at a professional conference, met at my office or home, or participated in a seminar. You know who you are, and you will see your contribution in the pages that follow. Thank you so very much for taking the time to interact with me and thereby influencing the course of this book.

Leatrice McLaughlin brought an extraordinary and unexpected perspective to the message of this book. We met by chance, in April, 1992, at the retirement party of a mutual friend. A conversation over refreshments led to my mailing Leatrice an early copy of the manuscript for *The Phoenix Agenda*. She read it and as conversations ensued, we agreed that she would join me as a full partner in my new management consulting firm, Industrial Revolutions, Inc. Leatrice saw, in the early draft, resonance with her own interests in Asian philosophy and applicability to women's issues. Leatrice has edited every word of this manuscript and has taught me her craft of writing. When necessary, she also conjured up for me the confidence to continue the project when all seemed hopeless. As we continued our collaboration, it was clear that her perspective and thoughts were becoming totally enmeshed with my own in the

Acknowledgments

manuscript, so the only appropriate course of action was to acknowledge her on the cover as a true collaborator in the creation of *The Phoenix Agenda*.

Many other wonderful colleagues have worked intensively with me in the development of the ideas here. The main catalyst for all this work is John Bennett, my friend and collaborator of a decade. John says quiet words that can change your life, if you listen. He spoke to me in such a way in 1984 at a professional conference in Loughborough, England, sparking my interest in contextualism and the possibility of workplace transformation. Since then he has been my collaborator in teaching and writing, as mentor and coach, and has contributed enormously at every level and every stage of this book, especially in the areas of sensitivity to language, high-level design, and crafting of details. We have remained best friends even though separated by the land between coasts.

Dennis Wixon, my friend and associate, helped in many ways, most especially in working out the theory of common workplace mindsets. The idea of workplace mindsets is probably the most intellectually original material in this book, and discussions with Dennis over twenty years helped clarify this notion and bring it to life.

Sandy Egli, who works miracles at American Express, has also worked miracles on this book. She was an early supporter and understands the theory of the book thoroughly. Sandy has contributed original insights to the underlying theory.

Lou Cohen has also been an inspirational and guiding influence in my corporate life. Whenever corporate life and politics seemed without merit or purpose, I would talk to Lou and would see, afresh, the dignity of work.

Peter Conklin and Russ Doane were enormously influential in working out the ideas in this book, as well as being very supportive of me personally as we were experimenting with and honing these approaches in various corporate settings. Peter's area of mastery is operational excellence and he has been my coach and teacher in this and other areas of business. Russ taught me many things, but most especially he helped me see the power of acknowledgment.

During my corporate career, I was fortunate to have managers

Acknowledgments

who were gracious and generous in sharing of themselves and who acted more as partners and coaches than as bosses. Bill Zimmer was enormously influential in my corporate growth and education and was always selfless about giving acknowledgment to his people, me included. Tom Harris, a gifted and visionary manager, helped me build a world-class research and development group. He supported and funded me in innovative projects at risk to his own career. Corporate America could use more people like Tom. Ron Schaefer, a manager of great courage, befriended and believed in me at a difficult time in my career, when I was trying to promote the ideas in this book to an unreceptive audience.

Patti Anklam, Julie Farr, Ron Schaefer and I worked for David Stone, then vice president of software engineering at Digital Equipment Corporation, for two heady years. David was a masterful manager, brilliant in every respect, and a gifted teacher. During these years we honed many of the ideas in *The Phoenix Agenda* by putting them into practice in a large organizational setting.

Bob Shearer, Karen Force, and John O'Leary, all management consultants, gave totally of themselves to teach me, over a period of two years, that philosophy and ethics could be effectively applied in business.

William Keating, Lou Cohen, Nancy Reiss, Christine Bullen, David Marca, Linda Wells, and Marcus Wilson were all most helpful in reviewing early versions of the manuscript. Later drafts benefited greatly from thorough reviews and discussions provided by Patti Anklam, Walter Birge, Tony Della Ferra, John Fergeson, Lionel Fray, Claudia Mueller, Stephen Young, and Peter Conklin. Applying the ideas in practice with Marcus Wilson, Nick Montoya, and their associates at Intel has also been most helpful and has improved the book.

Trust, decency, professionalism, and desire to help create a successful book were accorded me by my agent, Michael Snell and my editor, Jim Childs. And comparing notes with other authors has convinced me that Mike and Jim are the best in the business. Every author should be so lucky as to have fine people such as these to work with.

Acknowledgments

Apple Computer and Microsoft Corporation have worked together to create fabulous tools to aid people who are writing books, and when doing many other computer-supported activities. What a joy to have lived to see the age of word processing, desktop computing, spreadsheets, and advanced telecommunications.

The most special thanks of all are due to my wife of 20 years, Holly Whittelsey Whiteside. This has been a difficult book to write and, at times, the cost to the family has been high. Holly has been unswervingly supportive and I owe her an unpayable debt of gratitude.

The Phoenix Agenda

Introduction

A Great Day at Work

I wrote this book because I care about those of us who work for a living. The book is about sharing with you a vision and the tools for a productive, caring, and constructive transformation of your workplace. We spend over 80,000 of the hours of our lives at work. Our work is a constant theme, perhaps even preoccupation, in our lives. We all deserve work that is deeply rewarding, allows us to accomplish and learn, and brings contribution and satisfaction.

Yet, as we strive for rewarding, meaningful, and profitable work, all around us the rules of the workplace are shifting. The U.S. and multinational corporate world of today is in considerable turmoil and faces declining profitability, the breaking of implicit "lifetime employment" contracts, ever-increasing rates of change in technology, and relentless corporate downsizing. Top managers are, in MIT professor Peter Senge's term, "bewildered," and their salaries are under scrutiny by government and the press. Middle managers, including many of my associates and friends, sense a loss of corporate leadership and vision. They are scared, and don't know what to do. At the same time, tremendous opportunities come with the current broad business movement away from hierarchical management by authority toward cross-functional teamwork, flat and fluid corporate structures, and management by mentorship, coaching, networking, and positive, open persuasion. This is unsettling, and also exciting.

The fact of these changes, as is true of any crisis, presents tremendous opportunities for us all. The decentralization of corporate authority also means the possibility of greater autonomy, productivity, and self-expression for individuals in the workplace. Unprecedented numbers of us have it within our grasp to transform our workplaces into environments that bring large portions of accomplishment, learning, and satisfaction, for everyone. The purpose of this book is to provide you with the insights and tools to create, for yourself and those around you, a workplace of significance, meaning, accomplishment, contribution, growth, and happiness.

Three Keys to Transformation

TRANSFORMATION MEANS THE SHIFTING OF ASSUMPTIONS, VIEWPOINTS, AND MINDSETS

The phoenix is a mythical bird, with a melodious song and magnificent red and gold plumage, that repeatedly transforms itself. It does this every 500 years by burning itself on a pyre of flames. Out of the ashes arises a new phoenix, even more magnificent than the one before. Thus the phoenix is an ancient symbol for death and rebirth, for the endless cycles of change and transformation.

In *The Phoenix Agenda*, what dies are old ways of thinking, old assumptions, and old mindsets. Transformation is each individual shifting to a mindset that empowers and enables reconstruction of the workplace.

Introduction

THE PRICE OF WORKPLACE TRANSFORMATION IS NOT MONEY.
IT IS PERSONAL COURAGE.

Anyone who has lost a career, and has later discovered a new and better one, understands and has lived through the cycle of the phoenix. People who have been through this transition understand the fear, the reluctance, even the grieving that accompanies putting to rest a tired way of doing business, yesterday's opportunity. They also know the new possibilities on the other side of the cycle. Yet, the fear of the fire traps tens of thousands of bright, capable people in companies that are obviously in profound business difficulties and that are laying off employees in sickeningly monotonous waves.

Part I of the book, "Mindsets at Work," begins the shift of mindset necessary to use the tools of The Phoenix Agenda powerfully. This part introduces the core concepts and promises of the book—how to use language to shape reality, how to create new assumptions and mindsets, how to drive progress through the deliberate creation of crisis, and how to overcome the ever-present danger of crippling addiction to one's own beliefs and forms of organization. It also shows that the cost of realizing these promises is not counted in money, but in courage—the courage to openly and honestly question deeply held beliefs and assumptions.

Part I can be read on at least two levels. On one level, it presents concepts and background necessary to use the material in parts II and III effectively. At another level, part I is designed to actually produce a shift of mindset. This shift, this "Aha" experience, happens in different parts of the book for different readers. For some, it occurs while reading part I. For others, it occurs later in the book. But in order for there to be a chance for this experience to happen for you, I recommend that you read part I at least once in a spirit of exploration and openness.

Chapter 1, "The Phoenix Burns," starts with the recurring theme of eyewitness accounts of great corporations in periods of decline. It shows, through poignant and true incidents, that poor business results, such as the loss of 80 percent of one corporation's market value over a three-year period, are ultimately traceable to self-imposed restrictions on deep and difficult freedoms: the freedom to question yesterday's success formula; the courage and freedom to redefine core philosophy, mission, and political structure; and the ability of responsible individuals to redefine the meaning of their corporations.

Chapter 2, "Mindsets in the Workplace," shows, by many compelling examples, that most of us live out our business lives following assumptions and rules that we neither invented nor understand. It develops a theory of mindsets in the workplace that gives insight into why everyday events within corporations occur as they do and where the leverage point for deep change is. The chapter gives a systematic way of understanding management practice. Most modern management is invisibly and deeply rooted in 18th-century philosophy, is handicapped by ignorance of this, and consequently has only limited access to more modern alternatives. It is time for a transformation to modern, productive ways of thinking and acting.

Chapter 3, "Workplace Transformation," gives you the key to altering your workplace reality. Though the rest of the book can be profitably read as a set of "how-to" instructions for coping with changes in the business assumptions and workplace directions around you, this chapter goes beyond "how-to" toward mastering the art of creating new assumptions that improve business results. Even without reading this chapter, it is possible to become an apprentice or journeyman in this art of transformational management—with it, plus the tools in parts II and III, you can become a master.

LANGUAGE IS POWER

The insights and lessons in *The Phoenix Agenda* will show themselves in your life, not as some difficult-to-define and evanescent motivational change, or as some hard-to-measure attitude shift. Rather,

Introduction

The Phoenix Agenda will be manifested in your everyday use of language in the workplace. This is not a book on how to write and speak correctly, however. It is a book on how to speak with integrity, power, and influence. It is a book on how to speak to alter the mindsets of others in the workplace. It is a book on how to communicate as if your success depended on it, which it does.

Practical ways for using language to achieve superior business results are presented in part II, "Tools for Transformation." Chapters 4 through 7 in this part guide you through the 12 facets of The Phoenix Agenda. The Phoenix Agenda is a set of design guidelines for creating powerful business dialogues in virtually any situation ranging from a brief phone call to the redesign of a corporation. Part II can be read independently, though reading part I either before or after part II greatly enhances your ability to use effectively the tools in part II.

Chapter 4, "Language for Transforming Reality," develops the grammar of transformational language; that is, it addresses using language in new ways to impact and alter your circumstances and environment.

Chapter 5, "How to Launch and Sustain Projects at Work," contains the four facets of The Phoenix Agenda for managing and altering, with their full knowledge and permission, people's conventional wisdom about situations. This part of the Agenda guides you in creating for people an empowering reality in which effective action flows with precision and grace.

Chapter 6, "How to Drive Action and Achieve Results," teaches you a powerful way of speaking that acts like an irresistible force for business accomplishments in organizations.

Chapter 7, "How to Make Work Rewarding," shows you how to complete projects in a way that supports learning, enables people to move gracefully to the next project, and generates a sense of personal satisfaction.

Introduction

YOU MAKE THE DIFFERENCE

Part III, "Advanced Strategies for Workplace Transformation," presents, in a "how-to" fashion, critical knowledge and skills for individual and group success in the hierarchically flat, constantly changing, team- and empowerment-oriented workplaces of the 1990s and beyond.

Many business books are written for "the organization" or "the corporation." This book is written for you, an individual who wants to increase your effectiveness in your workplace. Many of the business examples in the book are firsthand accounts and interpretations from my own years of experience in high-technology research, design, management, and management consulting. During this time, I worked with individuals from all levels in the workplace, from CEOs to employees in the ranks. Other examples are taken from conversations with colleagues in various industries. Some of the examples involve high-ranking managers, responsible for the fate of thousands of employees, millions of customers, and $100 million budgets. Some examples concern individuals in the workplace who work at more modest levels. Still other examples are from individuals in turmoil and transition, either recently laid off and attempting new careers or recently promoted to positions of increased responsibility. The business stories and the ideas in the book also cut across corporate functions: administration, marketing, manufacturing, engineering, finance, sales, and administration. Whatever your position in the workplace, The Phoenix Agenda is for you. Your use of language to produce worthwhile results is not limited to your hierarchical position nor corporate function.

Chapter 8, "Turbocharging the Agenda," tells you how to use multiple facets of The Phoenix Agenda simultaneously to solve real workplace issues. It presents a portfolio of transformational tools that can be applied to many common workplace situations.

Chapter 9, "Transformational Scheduling," discusses how to use transformational management to achieve radically faster time-to-profit and other desirable business results. It explains how the authoritarian, control-oriented view of time is inherently self-limiting and how a transformational view creates time when none seems available.

Chapter 10, "Transformational Coaching," deals with how to elicit ultra-high performance from individuals and teams. It also explains the critical relation between coaching, freedom, and permission. Managers can issue orders without first gaining employees' permission—coaches cannot. All the power of the coaching relationship depends on gaining permission and trust, not exercising authority.

Chapter 11, "The Dark Side of Transformation," discusses the various problems and difficulties that can arise from inappropriate or exploitative use of transformational management. Empowerment, for example, can lead to burnout. Language can be used to deceive and cause harm. Overpreoccupation with any approach, including The Phoenix Agenda, can lead to addiction. In addition to warning of these dangers, the chapter concludes by emphasizing the critical role of coaching in avoiding them.

Chapter 12, "The Phoenix Rises," supports and empowers those who want to be agents of change and want to improve their workplace.

How to Read *The Phoenix Agenda*

The design of the book borrows heavily from workshops, talks, and consulting engagements I have conducted for managers and employees over the years. As with these activities, I have designed The Phoenix Agenda to make an unmistakable and lasting difference for you and your workplace, in achieving superior business results through empowering yourself and others. If that is what you would like, I recommend a certain way to approach the book for maximum value. It will be helpful to consider what you want from your work and to relate this to the ideas and examples as you read.

Introduction

Perhaps you have high aspirations and want to make a significant difference in the world through your life's work. Perhaps you would be content to survive, to achieve your fair share of happiness and security in a turmoiled and uncertain company. Perhaps you face a specific and immediate problem with another individual at work or with another group that you see no way to resolve. In these pages are insights and new directions for all these concerns. To discover them for yourself, it will be helpful to keep your particular project or concern in mind, and do the work of relating that to the material as you read it. Try, initially, to read in an expansive, open-minded way, using whatever method you use when you are being creative. The whole point of the book is to give you a new perspective on your life at work that will lead immediately to you taking new actions— actions that are, perhaps, not accessible to you today.

Most books are designed to present information. This book is not about information. It is about you making a difference for the better in your workplace. It is not a book of handy tips and techniques, though you will find some of those. If the book succeeds for you, the way you speak and act in your workplace will shift. People will notice a difference. Your ideas and requests will have a greater impact. You will be able to conduct business and make progress more easily with difficult people and groups. You will notice an increased creativity, a new insight into why the people around you are acting as they do. You will be better able to listen to others, to see and extract value from what they have to say.

Read, enjoy, and apply these pages. It is not the book that is important. The important thing is that the reading of this book enhances and enriches your days at work.

PART I

Mindsets at Work

In physics today, so far as we know, the galaxies that one studies are all controlled by the same laws. This is not true of the worlds created by mankind.

—Edward T. Hall and Mildred Reed Hall, *Hidden Differences*

The Phoenix Burns

Today's structures were designed for controlling turn-of-the-century mass-production operations under stable conditions, with primitive technologies. They have become perverse, action-destroying devices completely at odds with current competitive needs.

—Tom Peters, *Thriving on Chaos*

Corporations in Crisis

Something desperate is happening in large corporations, especially American ones. As Andrall Pearson writes in the *Harvard Business Review*:

> Seven deadly sins—the corporate equivalents of sloth, pride, envy, anger, covetousness, lust, and gluttony—are laying waste a whole class of once dominant giant U.S. corporations. Today global U.S. companies in nearly every major industry find themselves tormented in a competitive purgatory largely of their own making.[1]

Imagine yourself as a powerful business leader. Perhaps, indeed, you are one. Imagine that you have $2 billion in cash, a thriving business with over $12 billion annual revenue, and 120,000 superbly educated and dedicated people who are fanatically loyal. Could you create profound and lasting success with these blessings? Virtually anything money can buy is yours for the asking. Surely, with the best available in physical resources, access to innovative ideas, people, talent, and global communications, you would be able to achieve almost any goal.

Does it seem even within the realm of possibility that two years later, your corporation would be in serious decline, and the board of directors would be replacing you? Market value is down 80 percent. The company has dropped 300 ranks on *Fortune*'s list of admired corporations. Workplace morale is terrible. Tens of thousands of people have left, voluntarily or by firing, including many of your best and brightest. White-collar workers are staging strikes.

Though it seems incredible that assets could be wasted to such a catastrophic extent, scenarios like the one described are happening over and over again. The company could be IBM, Digital Equipment Corporation, American Express, General Motors, Sears, Wang, or any one of dozens of once proud and dominant organizations.

Despite access to resources that would be the envy of emperors, many of our finest corporations are facing severe difficulties. When a large organization loses four-fifths of its market value, employees get bitter, suspicious, and hostile or withdrawn. They feud with rivals over the dwindling pool of jobs, and curry favor with anyone perceived to have power. An air of gloom, a pall, hangs over the workplace. Efforts turn from the productive to the pointless; in one originally successful company that went sour, those remaining after many rounds of layoffs turned their attention to competing with each other for possession of floors full of empty, dusty offices.

Customers look elsewhere, careers are wrecked, secure retirements are shattered, mortgages are foreclosed, and economic loss hurts communities worldwide. Most importantly, the possible contribution that the organization could have made to the world shrivels.

The Phoenix Burns

WHAT IS IT THAT ALLOWS INTELLIGENT, WELL-SUPPORTED, AND POWERFUL LEADERS TO CREATE SUCH FIASCOES?

Part of the problem may be that the leaders responsible for these defeats refused to heed warning after warning about the need to rethink, in fundamental ways, the consequences of their words and actions as commitments to themselves and others at work. It is now too late for many of them and for the good soldiers who unquestioningly followed them. Perhaps it is not too late for us.

BRUTAL BACKGROUND

Digital Equipment Corporation is the second-largest computer corporation in the world, and by 1990, the people in it were experiencing intense pain. Once ranked among the very finest, most humane companies anywhere, and as a model of excellence, Digital then entered a time of loss of direction and loss of profitability. This period was marked by destructive incidents such as these:

- It was widely rumored that two rival vice presidents attacked each other with fists in a company parking lot.
- Employees with up to 20 years of loyal and continuous service came to work one morning to be greeted by security guards, who supervised them as they cleaned out their personal belongings. They were ushered out the door without even a chance to say good-bye to friends.
- Stress-related illness, including heart attacks, high blood pressure, ulcers, and attempts at suicide, increased markedly in the employee population.

And yet the men and women on whose watch these events occurred were, I am convinced, honorable and virtuous souls doing their jobs as best they could within the world of work as they understood it. Circumstances plunged them into a changing world for which they were simply unprepared. As you read this, many other companies in North America, Europe, and Japan are now evidencing similar symptoms.

People, for example, in the financial services, automotive, banking, oil-field services, and semiconductor industries are reporting similar experiences to me. These are a holographic microcosm of a far more general crisis and change systematically affecting the world of organized work.

FLAWED MANAGEMENT MOTIVATION

If you gain the trust of managers in a large corporation and ask them to speak honestly about what drives them, most will confess that their own survival, their own skins, is at the heart of their motivation.

Never mind my colleagues, employees, and customers—if the chips are down, I'll take care of myself first and foremost,

one senior executive says, confidentially. Yet this is a very strange statement to make since the whole purpose of belonging to an organization, one would think, is to gain the benefits of cooperative enterprise, to achieve more than you could achieve on your own. This manager's philosophy does not even work, for after years of playing it safe and protecting his own interests, he now finds that all his projects have been canceled and his survival in the organization is uncertain.

A VICTIM SAYS FAREWELL

Statistical reports of large layoffs and corporate restructuring depersonalize the circumstances. We relate to them as abstractions, not as involving real human beings who might well be us, or whose suffering we have caused. To make the abstractions more real, here is a note from a low-level manager to his people just after he was informed of his impending layoff.

The Phoenix Burns

From: smith@server3.corp.gp
To: "group"
CC:
Subj: So long

I spoke to Barbara Immodesto this afternoon. She informed me that I am a "High Risk." This means I will be part of Monday's layoff. I will not beback to the plant. I will meet Barbara Immodesto Monday morning and signthe appropriate papers.

I want to thank each of you for the honor of working with you. I have learned a great deal from you all. I hope your lives and careers farewell.

Thank you again for all that you have done for me.
Stan

Consider the context in which this note was written and read. One day, this man was a manager. The next day, he simply disappeared. This note, sent out to an anonymous distribution list over electronic mail, was the sum total of his good-bye. As is true of most electronic mail, the note is hastily written and has numerous typing errors. The manager walked out of his office, leaving the items in it as though he were simply leaving for the day. His calendar, books, project sheets, plans, yellow Post-its, phone messages, and appointment schedule were simply left, suddenly stripped of meaning and relevance. Now, they are a disposal problem for his former supervisor. Perhaps she will call the facilities people, but they will claim it is not their job.

This note is a man's final statement about a burned-out career. His people are left to wonder who is to give them direction, what is to become of them. They have no idea. The Monday he refers to is December 7, Pearl Harbor Day. The layoffs occur just before Christmas. The note reveals much about how the layoff was handled. People are told, by powerless supervisors, that they are "High Risk." But "High Risk" is a euphemism. It actually means that he is certain to be laid off, come Monday. He has no idea who actually decided to lay him off. No one does.

We know something about the background of this manager. He thought he was doing the right thing, throughout his career, by controlling his people so that they worked to meet what he thought were the expectations of his higher-ups. He discouraged unorthodox, innovative thinking. He managed knowledgeable workers, people of incredible backgrounds and talents far richer than his own. For example, one of his people, an American educated in Japan and fluent in written and spoken Japanese, was highly regarded throughout the organization for her vision and ability to relate to customers. She even received a rare monetary reward for excellence in organizational impact. Yet, this manager consistently gave her mediocre tasks and projects that marginally utilized her talents. But what choice did he have? He thought that the purpose of his job was to keep his people's noses to the corporate grindstone, to crank out products. Never mind that few customers cared about the products and fewer still would ever use them. That was not his concern. The supervisor was dutifully operating within a framework of assumptions that, unfortunately for him, had itself lost touch with the essential purpose of the business.

Now consider that this scene, with variations, was repeated 2,000 to 3,000 times during those few days, in just one company alone. Even this is nothing. Peter Drucker, the philosopher of management consultants, predicts that wholesale flattening of middle-management ranks in major corporations during the 1990s will eliminate over 50 percent of current middle-management jobs and redefine the rest.[2]

MANAGEMENT, AS IT HAS BEEN KNOWN FOR MOST OF
THIS CENTURY, IS DYING.

The Cost of Rigid Workplace Mindsets

BUSINESS AS USUAL

Business-as-usual management that does not question its own underlying assumptions can create self-destructive practices that slowly strangle the breath from an enterprise. Consider the following business story.

A software group is facing cancellation due to customer lack of interest in their product. Committed to understand why this is happening, the group, on their own initiative, interviews customers and seeks advice from the company's sales and marketing people. A brilliant business solution emerges—shift the computer operating system on which the product depends. But this is a novel, unorthodox, and politically unpopular step in this organizational context. The middle managers oppose it. However, a young engineer has spent weekends and evenings experimenting with a version of the product on the new operating system. Now, exploiting his guerrilla work, the software group is able to gain crucial support from the head of U.S. sales and from marketing to transform the product. It ships and customers love it. The group is saved and their product is transformed from sure cancellation to a several-million-dollar business opportunity. But this is not the end of the story.

When it comes time to write the young engineer's performance review, the supervisor gives him a dismal evaluation. A colleague asks him,

What are you doing? Do you realize this young man has saved the project and probably your job?

The supervisor replies,

Yes, I do. But nothing in the performance review manual covers this. I

feel terrible about it, but my manager is pressuring me to follow the rules.

The colleague urges him to apologize to the engineer and submit a new review, which to the supervisor's credit he does, but the damage to trust is irrevocable and the young engineer leaves the company.

Months later, the managers who initially opposed the project successfully work to have it canceled, even though it is now profitable. More key team members become discouraged and leave the company. On hearing of the cancellation, a major customer calls the company:

If you cancel this software, you can come collect all your computers, remove them, and throw them in the lake.

The project, now minus its key people, is immediately reinstated.

This incident illustrates several points. First, the supervisor feels himself beholden to a set of assumptions called "the rules" or "business as usual." For some unknown reason, he is not free to do what he himself realizes is the right thing. Second, he exercises his bureaucratic authority in a way that deeply hurts the young engineer. Third, the middle managers are more interested in maintaining their control than they are in creating profits.

THE ENTIRE SYSTEM OPERATES AGAINST ITS OWN
BEST BUSINESS INTERESTS.

Everyone loses. Even apart from the loss of valuable engineering talent in the group, the incident has a lasting, chilling effect on other engineers' aspirations to do their creative best. A key customer feels threatened and makes plans to switch vendors. The middle managers win their immediate turf battle, but many themselves get laid off within the year. Is this not an example of corporate madness? Yet, each participant was acting in a way totally consistent with her own mindset, his own framework of assumptions.

The Phoenix Burns

What could bring about a transformation of whatever it is that holds such self-destructive systems in place? What if the courageous young engineer had been empowered to stay? His vision, hard work, and insight into the competitive software marketplace were so compelling that he was immediately snapped up by an aggressive young company. Why could the old company not adapt itself to prosper from the young engineer's talents?

DISTURBING BUSINESS EXAMPLES

In his dismal view of the future of corporate America, William Lareau writes:

> American management generally assumes that business practices and traditions are the way they are simply because that's the way it was meant to be; as if the current system is somehow mandated or preordained by the fundamental order of the universe. Nothing could be further from the truth.
>
> . . .
>
> Most practices of traditional American management are perpetuated much like the practice of wearing neckties; on any objective basis it makes no sense, but it's been part of the business world for so long that it's expected without question.[3]

For example, a senior manager, when asked, confides that he holds to the assumption that the nature of management in his company is "survival of the fittest." He sees himself and his fellow managers as locked in a death struggle over success, dollars, head counts, resources, and other accoutrements of managerial prerogative and power. Conversation with this individual reveals that "dog eat dog" and "survival of the fittest" literally *are* the reality of the management world for this person—these are not simply phrases that describe, they *are*. Other managers see the spark of a different possibility but do not know how to transform it into a new reality. One says (referring to the first man),

Mindsets at Work

I know what must be done for the good of the company but the system won't let me. In particular, manager X is after my budget and will use any sign of weakness or cooperation on my part to bring about the cancellation of my project so that he can take over a share of the funds.

The senior manager is asked if he would consider any styles, approaches, or mindsets toward management other than the one he employed. He said,

No, absolutely not! I refuse even to consider any alternatives. What I do now has worked well for a long time.

By his statement, this manager excludes even the possibility of new assumptions and alternatives for himself and his people. Within a year of this interview, profitability had disappeared from this manager's once profitable organization and he resigned. In his wake, he left 1,000 stunned and helpless people, who had believed in his absolutist dictums. He and his fellow managers had done a thorough job of imposing rigid thinking on their people. And the word got out to the wider community. A sign on a regional employment agency's notice board reads: FORMER MEGACORP EMPLOYEES NEED NOT APPLY. Unfairly, this employment agency was spreading the word that managers from this company were inflexible in their thinking. From the agency's perspective, it simplified their screening process.

In an entirely different type of workplace, a major university, the chairman of the physics department is horrified to discover that one of his older, tenured professors has been teaching physics to undergraduates for over 20 years as though Einstein had never existed. Twenty generations of introductory physics students have been led to believe that physics ended with Newton. The security of his tenured position has meant that for 20 years, he has not had to stretch himself. He has successfully avoided learning difficult new ways of thinking that threaten the very basis of what he thought he already knew.

Many managers today are in a similar position. The state of the art of management has advanced profoundly since the invention of bureaucracy, the assembly line, and the hierarchical organization chart. Yet, many of us are more concerned with maintaining our comfortable and familiar mindsets, and the assumptions that support them, than we are with taking the risk to learn and try something new.

As of this writing, GM's CEO has been hospitalized following his ouster by his board of directors. *Time* magazine wonders, on its cover, if GM can even survive as an entity.[4] For years, GM has been criticized for insularity and a failure to take a long, hard look at itself. There has been no lack of warning for its current plight. Absolute, steadfast refusal to consider alternative business assumptions seems to be the common thread through the criticisms of General Motors. Today, GM is faced with closing many of its North American plants and firing tens of thousands of workers. Why did they not take these warnings to heart? Even Ross Perot, who is not known as a shy, retiring person, could not make a dent in the mindset at GM.

The Mindset of Control

One of the common denominators of the corporate form of organization is the unquestioned assumption of the value of control-based management.

ANY ORGANIZATION BASED ON CONTROL ACTS TO MAINTAIN THE STRUCTURE OF CONTROL ABOVE ALL OTHER ENDS.

For example, in one department in a large corporation, three senior engineers are so desperate over the mismanagement that is hurting people, profits, and business that they organize a mutiny. Their idea is to march into their senior manager's office and tell him that from that moment on, he is no longer their manager. They approach the department's human resource director, who agrees that, while the department is indeed terminally ill, mutinies are things that happen in the movies, not in her department. In fact, she coldly says,

If you think you can stage a mutiny in a business, you are smoking dope.

The mutiny never happens. As the mutineers predicted, the entire department is disbanded by higher authority within a year. Many people lose their jobs, but the management hierarchy remains intact until the very last minute of the department's existence.

What kind of desperation would drive well-educated professional people to turn against their management and plot to forcefully remove authority? And what kind of breakdown in communication is so complete that force appears to be the only "rational" solution to the problem?

By 1990, it was clear to perceptive people in a number of *Fortune* 500 corporations that things were badly askew. In one company in particular, profits, sales, and market share were all dropping and senior managers were engaged in a costly turf war with each other. Out of concern, 50 of the company's most senior contributors draft and distribute an emergency call to action, carefully detailing the problems. They propose constructive solutions, including asking top management to attend a meeting on teamwork to set aside their differences and to work more constructively together. This call to action receives wide circulation via the corporate-wide electronic mail system. Shortly afterward, the senior vice president for personnel meets the leaders of this group in his office. He testily says,

I wish you hadn't done this. It's a bad time to stir up the soup.

He adroitly deflects the proposal, saying that he will consider sponsoring a meeting on top-management teamwork only if the proposers can prove to him with absolute certainty, in advance, that the outcome will be positive. Consequently, the meeting never happens.

We will never know if the proposal might have helped or how many jobs it might have saved. Perhaps none. But can leaders afford to be so threatened by ideas that question their authority because they come from underlings? What are they afraid of? Peter Senge, the management consultant, says that in an organization of 100,000 people, there are at least 100,000 ideas for corporate salvation.[5]

This same company is now in the process of terminating 20,000 to 30,000—eventually, perhaps, as many as 50,000 to 60,000— employees. Thousands of the top innovators and contributors have left. The people who remain suffer from poor morale. Not one of the top managers has publicly admitted responsibility for poor management. We have to ask, when General Motors lays off 70,000 employees, IBM 50,000 employees, and Wang 25,000 employees, could these business disasters have been avoided?

CONTROL CAUSES DELAY

The requirements for control in a large organization are often at odds with the need for getting new products to market quickly. As an illustration, a product development team in a large corporation is committed to reducing the time it takes for its new product to get to market from the customary five years in its parent organization down to one year. To get started, this team needs a $500 item of equipment, which they order. Six months later, the item has not arrived and a team member investigates why. She discovers a de facto purchasing system requiring 12 approval signatures for completion. Each approval signature follows the previous one, up and down three separate management hierarchies. Each individual in the approval chain is adamant that his approval is a necessary part of the process. Justifications vary with position and power. One candid administrator confides,

Well, I hope the system makes sense. Doing this provides my livelihood.

Another person in the signature chain, a manager, hints at deep misgivings over loosening up the purse strings to allow people at lower levels to approve minor purchases.[6]

The 12-signature-long approval chain that evolved in this particular organization had the effect of placing a higher value on control than on rapid time to market. The cost of involving a large number of people in minor financial approvals (the time value of the 12 people to process the approvals) far exceeded the cost of a $500 item. Worse, in the industry from which the example is taken, a six-month delay in getting a product to market wipes out, on average, all potential profits, with the result that there is no longer a reason to build the product. This means that the requirements of the purchasing system had the effect of insuring that the planned product never came profitably to market. A heavy price indeed to pay for control.

CONTROL COSTS MONEY AND HURTS MORALE

A mindset that values control often has negative business consequences. As an illustration, after months of painstaking effort at crossing organizational boundaries, two marketing teams (who report to different managers) discover that they can more than double the payback of their efforts by joining to form a single team to produce a single campaign with a single theme. They are thrilled with this team-oriented approach and clearly see how to make it a marketing success. With naive enthusiasm, they arrange an impromptu meeting with one of the managers. Brimming with excitement at this business breakthrough and hungry for approval, they begin their presentation to the manager. He stuns them by storming out of the meeting, loudly asserting,

Your logic is flawed!

The team interprets his subsequent actions, which serve to delay the new work initiative, as classic middle-management opposition to people working across organizational boundaries. To the team members, the manager's control of his own domain appears more important to him than profitability and teamwork.

The Phoenix Burns

At another company, the leader of a manufacturing team decides to impress his manager and run a breakthrough project. He invents innovative ways of working, inspires his people, takes big risks, and succeeds in delivering his product six months ahead of schedule. When he presents his achievement to the staff, the manager says,

You've done a really poor job of managing to schedule. Early is no better than late.

Humiliated and furious, the leader makes plans to leave the company.

In these two cases, we see the tension that is generated by different people approaching a problem with different mindsets. The project teams were close to their customers and understood the product space in which they were operating. In both cases, they had received strong exhortations from top management to do whatever was necessary to improve profitability. In both cases, middle management saw their efforts as disruptive to orderly, well-established processes.

ALTERNATIVES TO CONTROL

A large organization, faced with a cyclone assault of new technologies and new markets, will have difficulty surviving with inflexible and slow-to-change organizational forms and power structures. Rigid hierarchies offer control and are marvelous for delivering consistent results in a steady state, an unchanging world. Are rigid hierarchies and orderly, predictable procedures the best form of organization and power sharing in a rapidly changing, chaotic world?

Questioning Old Assumptions

In the examples discussed, individuals were sincerely trying to serve their corporations by questioning old assumptions and ways of doing business. Such questioning requires the courage to ask once unaskable questions, to open up areas for examination that others feel are closed. To respond productively to innovative approaches requires the courage to admit the limitations of one's own viewpoint. Productive inquiry for business involves freedom to find and make change at the points of highest leverage for profitability and service—the fundamental processes of the corporation itself and the constraints that limit the evolution and improvement of process.

> EVERY LOST BUSINESS OPPORTUNITY IN THIS CHAPTER WOULD
> HAVE HAD AN ENTIRELY DIFFERENT OUTCOME IF, IN EACH CASE,
> KEY INDIVIDUALS HAD SHOWN THE WISDOM AND THE COURAGE
> TO QUESTION THE ASSUMPTIONS AND MINDSETS THAT WERE
> DRIVING THEIR ACTIONS.

The distribution and exercise of political power inside corporations are held in place by deeply entrenched and heavily defended assumptions. The largest businesses today are the size of entire countries; Exxon's sales exceed the gross national product of Indonesia and General Electric's revenues rival the entire productive output of Greece. The quality of daily life of millions of employees and customers is more profoundly affected by corporate than by governmental exercise of authority and power. Yet, the typical employee or customer has infinitely more freedom to choose, influence, and ask questions of her political leadership than of her corporate leadership.

Effective leaders in a changing world have the option, if they choose, to empower inquiry for their people.

The Phoenix Burns

INDIVIDUALS, ORGANIZATIONS, AND INSTITUTIONS CAN BE
EMPOWERED TO CREATE *FREEDOM OF INQUIRY* AND *FREEDOM OF
RESPONSIBLE ACTION* WITH RESPECT TO THEMSELVES, THEIR
MANAGEMENT, THEIR SOCIETY, THEIR SKILLS, THEIR PROCESSES,
AND THE PRODUCTS AND SERVICES THEY PRODUCE.

FREE QUESTIONING AS A PATH TO TRANSFORMATION

To say that "Such and such is the way things *are*" kills all possibility of examining and experimenting with consequences if things *are not* that way. The manager who viewed his workplace from a "dog eat dog" mindset severely limited the possibility of working with a supposed rival who actually wanted to support him.

The great power of freely questioning once valid assumptions and viewpoints is, of course, that it can open vast new domains of possibility, ideas, and innovations that are simply not accessible any other way. Questions we might ask at this level include:

Are the other groups in the company truly our adversaries?

What sense does the mission of my company make?

Who are my customers and how may I best serve them?

Why do I eat three meals a day, not two or four? Why can I not eat four meals a day and put all four on my expense report?

Why do I have to follow this particular set of bureaucratic rules?

Why are you, as manager, the best possible person to be manager?

Clearly, asking questions at this level in a business setting could, in a control-oriented workplace, get people into a lot of trouble, and has. However, we are clearly *not* in the "ordinary scheme of things"—providing stock business-as-usual answers to questions such as those listed on page 29 is proving to be an international business disaster in the long run.

Both freedom and open inquiry are essential to the operation of a free-market economy. Consider assembling a stock portfolio, for example. The investor is free to invest or not in any security. Further, detailed inquiry—in the form of asking tough questions of the investor relations people and other information sources—is not only expected but is key to successful investing. How strange that some of the most fundamental aspects of business and free markets vanish when one enters the world of corporations. Outside their walls, corporations demand freedom to function, yet inside their walls, they grant little or no freedom to their people. The popular phrase *mushroom management* means management by keeping employees in the dark and shoveling manure over them.

EMPOWERMENT THREATENS CONTROL

Empowerment is a fashionable concept in business. But underlying this notion taken seriously, not just mouthed as a management buzzword, is this truth:

WHEN PEOPLE ARE EMPOWERED, THEY MAY NO LONGER ACCEPT THE CONTROL OF THE MANAGERS WHO EMPOWERED THEM.

In *The Virtual Corporation*, authors Davidow and Malone offer a vivid picture of corporations of the future.[7] They project that by the end of the decade, the authoritarian corporation as we know it will have all but disappeared, to be replaced by loose but fluid networks of individuals and groups who work together by free choice and reorganize as they interpret changed conditions. In part, this is made both necessary and possible by the incredible advances in information technology.

Change of this order of magnitude requires fundamental and profound change on the human side of the business equation. It requires changes in the basic beliefs about human nature on which all management activities, decisions, and progress are based. It requires change in the assumptions underlying corporate politics, the corporate power structure, and the corporate belief system. Sadly, many now in power will oppose these changes, even if the price is the collapse of the business that they are chartered to serve.

The mindset of authoritarian control behind the current business practices of most large organizations is based on a set of implicit assumptions. If we look behind the pressure to follow the rules, the assumed reluctance to cooperate, and the refusal to give up authority, we see belief in the assumptions that workers need constant direction and that power once attained must at all costs be maintained. In the past, the ranks of middle management have swelled primarily because of such assumptions.

These assumptions may be too costly to afford today. Vastly improved information and storage technology has created the infrastructure for a massive decentralization of power in organizations. Further, the rapid rate of change in technology, markets, and consumer preference has meant that corporations must get new products to market more quickly than ever. This need for rapid product-cycle times leads to a need for a basic transformation in ways of working. To understand how we may accomplish these changes, we need to examine the frameworks of assumptions and interpretations in the workplace.

2

Mindsets in the Workplace

Place a monkey in a cage, and it is the same as a pig, not because it isn't clever and quick, but because it has no place to freely exercise its capabilities.

—From *The Book of Leadership and Strategy: Lessons of the Chinese Masters*, translated by Thomas Cleary

Why Shift Mindsets?

Creating fresh mindsets provides the magic that enables basic transformations in the way we work together. A practical knowledge of workplace mindsets, and their relationship to business results, gives unusual insight into the behavior of others. It can lead to a way of speaking to people so that their actions go beyond merely being effective to becoming extraordinary.

Operating within the viewpoint of business as usual, only business-as-usual results are possible.

Assumptions and mindsets, as we currently understand the idea, lie behind human interpretations of reality itself. Since our assumptions are tightly linked to our actions, techniques for first uncovering and then actually shifting our own and other people's assumptions are the most powerful noncoercive ways of effecting change. For example, if you can masterfully shift mindsets, you can:

- Solve seemingly impossible business problems.
- Generate ultra-high productivity.
- Create sustainable, renewable profits.
- Continuously renew meaning, contribution, and zest on the job.

This chapter inquires into workplace mindsets, and shows you how to recognize and take advantage of them. Chapter 3, following, introduces the art of creating and sustaining major shifts of mindset in the workplace.

What Is a Workplace Mindset?

In formal, abstract terms:

A workplace mindset is a consistent but unexamined framework of assumptions and viewpoints about the nature of reality as it pertains to business.

In business terms:

Any company that could continuously shed old workplace mindsets and create powerful new ones would be in business forever and would be impossible to compete against.

Mindsets in the Workplace

In terms of an analogy:

A MINDSET IS A LENS OR A FILTER THAT CONTROLS YOUR MIND,
YOUR THOUGHTS, YOUR PERCEPTIONS, AND YOUR ACTIONS.

MINDSETS IN SCIENCE

Mindsets in science are called paradigms. Current usage of the term "paradigm" in business books and articles stems from the work of science philosopher Thomas Kuhn. For Kuhn, a paradigm shift is a major change or revolution in scientific thinking about the nature of truth and evidence. Contrary to the popular view of science as progressing incrementally by amassing more and more facts and observations about the world, Kuhn realized that scientific facts themselves only have meaning and validity in relation to a preexisting set of assumptions that themselves could not be proven scientifically. The history of science, according to Kuhn, is a history of mental revolutions or paradigm shifts. Each shift signals that previously accepted assumptions have to be reinterpreted in the light of new viewpoints. Einstein's theory of relativity triggered a major paradigm shift in physics that led to a complete revision in the interpretation of scientific "facts" gathered, over centuries, under the influence of a Newtonian paradigm.

Thus, the "truth" of scientific discoveries is relative to the mindset within which the scientific investigation was conducted, rather than absolute. Scientific revolutions occasionally occur in which the entire fabric, the paradigm, the conceptual framework itself, is overthrown.

WHEN A PARADIGM SHIFT OCCURS, MUCH OF WHAT WAS
PREVIOUSLY REGARDED AS PROVEN FACT BECOMES
CONSTRAINING AND OBSOLESCENT. NEW INTERPRETATIONS
EMERGE, AND ENTIRE NEW AREAS FOR INVESTIGATION
ARE OPENED.

Also, because a paradigm shift challenges a person's existing belief system, many people oppose new paradigms, holding on to old beliefs for most of their lives, if not until death.

For example, the phlogiston theory of combustion, popular during the late-17th and 18th centuries, held that all burnable material contained an unobservable substance, called phlogiston, that was given off in fire, leaving ash, or dephlogisticated matter, as the remaining substance. Experiments with gases in the mid-18th century led Joseph Priestley to the threshold of the discovery of oxygen, but he insisted on interpreting his discovery within the phlogiston hypothesis. Antoine Laurent Lavoisier, performing very close to the same physical experiments, chose a different interpretation and "invented" oxygen. His conceptual reformulation started what is called the chemical revolution and formed the basis of modern chemistry. For the rest of his life, Priestley opposed Lavoisier's interpretation. Today, Lavoisier is known as a father of chemistry. Priestley is consigned to the second rank.

Even in hard science, it appears that assumptions, viewpoints, and mindsets can exert a powerful influence in attaining or not attaining outcomes that scientists value highly. Reputation is precious to scientists, as important as profitability is for business people. If mindsets play this role in science, the discipline that we all look to for answers and certainty, then surely they must play an even larger role in the less ordered and less certain worlds of personal life and of the workplace.

MINDSETS IN PERSONAL LIFE

Mindsets are involved in the application of conventional, if unarticulated, wisdom to virtually all areas of life. Once we become sensitized to underlying beliefs, assumptions, and viewpoints that operate in everyday life and business, we notice them everywhere.

Most of what we do is driven by concealed assumptions rather than as the result of deliberate thought.

Mindsets in the Workplace

A story is told of a new housewife who cooked a ham for her husband. He noticed that she cut off the end before baking. When he asked why, she huffed and said that was simply the way it was done. The issue came up every Easter, for years, as a ritualistic, slightly annoying topic of conversation. One year, the woman's mother was at dinner with them, and her daughter happened to ask why the end of the ham should be sliced off. The mother thought for a minute and said that Granny had always done it that way, so she assumed it was for a good reason. Now interested, the pair called Granny, who explained, "Oh, because my baking pan was too small to hold a whole ham."

Now, what if virtually everything we do that we have never actively inquired into or questioned has the same property as slicing off the end of the ham? Grandmothers aside, perhaps what has the most sway over the actions and beliefs of our lives are hidden assumptions. Assumptions permeate the scaffolding of our lives and minds. Some assumptions we are simply unaware of. These we can uncover through disciplined inquiry. Other assumptions we refuse to examine or acknowledge, perhaps because we are addicted to them.

OUR FRAMEWORK OF ASSUMPTIONS INFLUENCES, INDEED DETERMINES, WHAT WE HOLD AS REALITY AND WHAT IS BEYOND QUESTION. THE FRAMEWORK ESTABLISHES NOT JUST HOW WE EVALUATE EVIDENCE, BUT WHAT WE HOLD TO BE EVIDENCE ITSELF.

For example, people entering the country are not merely classified as aliens or citizens by the Immigration and Naturalization Service; they *are* aliens or citizens with all sorts of profound consequences as to the possibilities open to them on arrival in the country. Or consider the seemingly innocent activity of classifying people as male or female. Most of us are given over to the belief that there *are* males and females. That *is* reality. So say the government forms that classify us. But certain events can jar this reality, as in the case of a Spanish athlete who looked like a woman, was raised as a woman, thought she was a woman, and had the anatomy of a woman. Imagine the effect of being told by Olympic officials, at what should have been the high point of her life, that she could not compete because their testing showed the presence of an (inactive, as it turned out) Y chromosome—meaning she must be a man. The incident sparked a worldwide controversy that has yet to be resolved.[1]

MINDSETS IN THE WORKPLACE

In challenging or uncertain times, managers will always react in a way that is consistent with a larger, all-pervasive, and mostly invisible set of assumptions and principles that are indicative of that time and of the individual. According to Gregory Bateson:

> All human beings (and all mammals) are guided by highly abstract principles of which they are either quite unconscious, or unaware that the principle governing their perception and action is philosophic. A common misnomer for such principles is "feelings."[2]

The words that people speak and resonate to, the actions they take as well as those never considered, the acceptance of success and failure, and the perception of the very rules of business itself— all of these things derive in large measure from unexamined assumptions. In a large part, such assumptions are derived from cultural interpretations and past learnings, the origins of which are unavailable to most of us. Just as the wife's slicing off the ham reaches back to Granny's long-forgotten short baking pan, so, too, may the traditional manager's treatment of his people as quantifiable resources reach back to René Descartes's 17th-century mindset of a world in which all matters could be dealt with mathematically.[3]

Applied to the workplace, the word "mindset" is roughly synonymous with "conventional wisdom" about business practices. Naturally, if the conventional wisdom shifts, so do the business practices. In The Phoenix Agenda:

Mindsets in the Workplace

THE WORD "MINDSET" MEANS A DEEPLY HELD SET OF
ASSUMPTIONS AND VIEWPOINTS CONCERNING THE NATURE OF
BUSINESS REALITY. THESE ASSUMPTIONS AND VIEWPOINTS, WHILE
TYPICALLY HELD AS SACROSANCT AND UNQUESTIONABLE, CAN, IN
FACT, BE MODIFIED. WHEN INDIVIDUALS IN THE WORKPLACE
CHANGE THEIR ASSUMPTIONS AND VIEWPOINTS, THE
ENTIRE RANGE OF ACTIONS AND RESULTS AVAILABLE TO THE
BUSINESS TRANSFORMS.

Here are some examples of major business shifts that require re-thinking and transformation at the level of mindsets:

○ Transforming an engineering-driven business to a market-driven business.

○ Shifting a major corporation from the mainframe business to an as-yet-undefined new business.

○ Moving from a hierarchical organization to empowered teams.

Though historically difficult in practice, such shifts are entirely possible. The key is an appreciation of mindsets and the art of shifting mindsets. Shifts at this level require massive rethinking, reorientation, and reskilling within organizations and include the possibility of massive economic dislocation. But the nature of today's competitive, technologically driven world with its incredible rate of change means that companies without the skills to create and design such shifts will enjoy, at best, only a brief moment in the sun—a moment briefer than the average working life of an individual. On the other hand, the corporate citizen with insight into the mindsets of colleagues and customers can be instrumental in devising strategies for success. The change agent skilled in the shifting of mindsets holds the keys to corporate destiny.

The Six Laws of Mindsets

To summarize, mindsets in the workplace operate according to the following six principles:

1. The range of possible actions available to us is completely determined by our current mindset.
2. Our currently held mindset is largely hidden to us. To shift mindsets always requires the help of other people.
3. All of us display resistance to switching mindsets.
4. Mindsets are untestable and unprovable; multiple, mutually contradictory mindsets may exist simultaneously within organizations and societies.
5. All mindsets eventually become ineffective in a continuously changing world.
6. When we shift mindsets, we alter the entire range of business actions and solutions available to us.

Taken together, these principles imply that mindset issues account for many lost business opportunities and that constant openness to examining our own and others' mindsets holds promise for lasting business success in changing times. The next section introduces four specific mindsets commonly found among individuals in organizations.

Four Common Workplace Mindsets

This section develops a picture of common mindsets in the workplace. To familiarize yourself with these, imagine you are a manager facing schedule pressures. Perhaps your organization has a history of being consistently late in getting products to market. Or perhaps you are faced with the problem of creating dramatic reductions in your production schedule in order to remain competitive. How do you deal with the problem? As you read about the following four alternative approaches to this common business problem, try to notice the extent to which you personally identify with each approach. Do you favor one of the approaches or does one seem to characterize a noticeable tendency among the people you work with?

APPLY PRESSURE

You could, as a first approach, decide to apply pressure to people. Suppose you wanted your people to show up for staff meetings on time. You could simply command them to do so. You might even threaten to write up their tardiness in their performance reviews. What if you wanted your production team to design a product in half the time originally planned? You could threaten and cajole them. You could use project management and planning software to plan, in micro-detail, exactly what everyone is supposed to be doing when and then monitor their performance with close scrutiny.

All would know, whether you explicitly said so or not, that your approval or displeasure depends on their attaining a schedule that they suspect is unattainable. They know that if they fail, their group is likely to be censured, if not openly, then in hallway scuttlebutt. They also suspect that their jobs and careers are on the line. So the group adopts various strategies for survival. They put in extra hours and work like maniacs. In addition, they are not completely truthful or open with you about how long things will really take. They inflate their estimates in order to cut themselves some slack and come to resent you poking into their activities too closely. The entire organizational mood becomes dominated, fear-laden, and adversarial. But you keep up the pressure because you know:

That's the only way to get things done around here.

ACCEPT THE STATUS QUO

As an alternative second approach, you could simply not take the problem seriously. Perhaps you have met people like this. The existing orderly processes and procedures are set up to take whatever time they take, and nothing can be done about it. Imagine a simple problem such as getting reimbursed by petty cash for your travel expenses or persuading everyone to start meetings on time. The petty cash officials are likely to tell you that the reimbursement system is fixed and a matter of official policy. The people who arrive late at meetings might say that everyone comes late to meetings, that's simply the way it is in the corporate culture.

Now imagine a more complex problem, such as coordinating a major product announcement. Everyone knows that signature approval is necessary from six different department heads, each of whom is usually unreachable on short notice. Further, they will only speak to you if you have made appropriate overtures to their subordinates. The system for product announcements—while you might consider it to be a stereotype, and while it might be slow—has evolved over the years to ensure that all interests are served and that all the appropriate precautions are taken. Therefore, circumventing the system is unthinkable.

UNDERSTAND THE ENVIRONMENT

Some managers take a third approach. They assume that performance is not so much a function of pressuring people, or of simply following fixed procedures, as it is a matter of providing a supportive environment, tools, and infrastructure in which people, as a matter of their basic good inner nature, do their best. For example, W. Edwards Deming says that 95 percent of the problems and difficulties that beset companies are not the fault of the people doing the work, but rather are the result of the system in which they find themselves.[4]

As a manager taking this approach, you pay close attention to the broad system of production and seek to modify it. If you do this, you will find yourself dealing with ever-larger issues and with the interdependency of the issues on each other. For example, you might decide that the nature of the reward system is critical and switch from a system of individually based performance reviews and raises to one that rewards the team as a whole. This might immediately put you in conflict with the corporate personnel organization or cause other groups to wonder why they are being treated differently. Your superiors might view your efforts as tangential and not oriented directly enough toward the bottom line.

SHIFT THE CONTEXT

A fourth approach would be to rapidly and radically redefine and restructure the entire situation so that the original problem simply disappears. Take the case of trying to get a product designed in half the time originally planned. The task is to produce a workable design in a year, a feat perhaps never before achieved in the organization. Instead of telling people what to do, or micro-managing their efforts, you might ask the following questions:

Why are you doing this project at all?

Does it make any sense?

Do the customers want it?

Does the current organizational structure make sense in terms of the project?

Is doing this particular project the best and only way to achieve business success and also serve your personal needs?

Is there some completely different and more profitable activity you could do?

Could another group do your project better than you?

Given a fixed amount of calendar time, what of all the possible things that you might do would likely produce the greatest business success and profits?

After penetrating and rigorous self-examination, including extensive consultation with customers, the team members come up with a transformational solution of abandoning their project entirely and adding their efforts to another project. This turns out to be a greatly preferable business solution.

IDENTIFYING THE MINDSET IN YOUR WORKPLACE

In reading about these four approaches, did one or more seem to describe the preferred type of problem solving in your workplace? Do people in other groups that you encounter seem to fall into one or more of the categories? The next section further explores the idea of mindsets in the workplace and contains some practical advice about how to deal effectively with each of them.

Exploiting Workplace Mindsets

Each of the four approaches, *apply pressure, accept the status quo, understand the environment,* or *shift the context,* follows naturally from a well-established and coherent mindset.[5] Each is related to a specific mental orientation to reality itself that has been handed down for generations. Each of the four approaches derives from a bedrock view of the nature of our world, of which the world of business is a part, and what is admissible as evidence. The mindsets behind the four approaches are:

Apply pressure.   The mindset for authoritarian control.

Accept the status quo.   The mindset of orderly stereotyping.

Understand the environment.   The mindset of broad understanding.

Shift the context.   The mindset for continuous transformation.

In applying this framework to the workplace, one of the most important things to remember about mindsets is Law 4:

MINDSETS ARE UNTESTABLE AND UNPROVABLE; MULTIPLE, MUTUALLY CONTRADICTORY MINDSETS MAY EXIST SIMULTANEOUSLY WITHIN ORGANIZATIONS AND SOCIETIES.

As a corollary:

PEOPLE WITH DIFFERENT MINDSETS HAVE DIFFICULTY COMMUNICATING.

Not only will people with different mindsets disagree, they will disagree on what disagreement is. Their conversations may make little sense to each other, and each person may, in extreme cases, decide that the other is acting in bad faith. This makes for difficulties in business because all business involves dialogue; for example, dialogue between co-workers, dialogue between managers and subordinates, and dialogue between salespeople and customers.

The classic difficulties between members of line and staff organizations, or between individuals in corporate operating organizations and corporate purchasing, can be attributed to mindset differences. Managers in an operating organization typically are action- and results-oriented. They want needed supplies and equipment tomorrow. Corporate purchasing typically has a different charter, which is to standardize procurement across the entire corporation, to see that responsible rules and procedures are followed, that proper audit trails are left, and that the corporation as a whole pays a responsible price for goods and services. The urgency of immediate action can be a hallmark of an authoritarian mindset, whereas a concern for orderly procedures is more in keeping with a stereotypic mindset. Members of the different organizations have different goals and look at the world from different viewpoints. Both mindsets are valid and necessary. The possibility of productive dialogue between people with different mindsets exists when each party makes the effort to understand and appreciate where the other person is coming from. For example, a manager from an operating unit might apply pressure to speed a particular order, which will probably meet resistance, or the same manager might choose to work with central purchasing to devise a new general procedure that both speeds delivery and is also orderly.

The fact of multiple, contradictory workplace mindsets at first seems strange or logically impossible. If only a single reality exists, why do people have such different views of it? Perhaps multiple business realities exist simultaneously. Perhaps the simultaneous holding of contradictory mindsets on matters of practical significance in our lives also can be the source of enormous creative action. It is not that one mindset is right and the others wrong. Expecting a right and a wrong answer in every situation may itself reflect an assumption about reality rather than being a natural absolute.

People who have different mindsets, then, have profoundly different assumptions about the nature of life, meaning, time, business, relationships, ethics, evidence, science, and virtually every other important aspect of human existence. Further, they can never resolve these differences through evidence, experiment, or argument because the differences include profound disagreements on what assumptions and viewpoints it is legitimate to discuss. What is bedrock, unquestioned axiom from one point of view is entirely open to question from the other viewpoints, and vice versa!

An example of a fruitless dialogue between people operating within different mindsets is the current barrage of attacks and counterattacks between Japanese and American business interests. In most of these skirmishes, the Japanese tend toward the mindset of continuous transformation, whereas the Americans tend to rely on the mindset of authoritarian control. In one incident in this prolonged war of words, when an entourage of U.S. automobile executives visited Japan with President Bush in early 1992, they were told by their Japanese counterparts that "American industry needed to transform itself radically."[6] The Japanese were pointing to a host of mindset issues, inviting the American executives to start a searching self-inquiry into questions of the nature of the corporate hierarchy, inflated levels of executive compensation (including their own), continuous improvement, and total quality.

However, the American executives, whose purpose had been to strong-arm the Japanese into opening their markets, became angry and hostile. The photographs accompanying the story show an uncomfortable and scowling Lee Iacocca, with his arms folded in front of his chest and his eyes downcast, sitting between the chairmen of Mitsubishi and Toyota, who are wearing sanguine—almost smug—expressions. Mr. Iacocca is reported to have left the meeting visibly angry. Another photograph shows Iacocca together with his counterparts from Ford and GM, disconsolate and bowed. The attempted dialogue was later widely described in the press in both countries as a fiasco. And, yet, both America and Japan clearly have their successes; history reveals great progress and power within different mindsets.

The next four sections explore the four common workplace mindsets and provide hints about how to speak effectively within each and from one mindset to another.

THE MINDSET FOR AUTHORITARIAN CONTROL

The mindset for authoritarian control is the most common in hierarchical corporations. Its central metaphors are the machine, force and action, and cause and effect. Authoritarians tend automatically to favor explanations based on cause and effect mechanisms, action and reaction, analysis of complex situations into their component parts, and the characterization of objects by quantifiable properties. Measurement, mathematics, and metrics are strong themes. Engineering is a profoundly authority-oriented discipline; corporations that are driven by engineering will reflect this leaning in all their activities. In facing schedule pressure, for example, the authoritarian will apply force to his or her people to get them to work faster. They react, predictably, with resistance. An extreme form of authoritarian management is dictatorship, in which absolute power is exercised by an individual or a junta.

HOW TO APPEAL TO AUTHORITARIANS

In business, authoritarians are often traditional managers with an intense preoccupation with their own authority. Any conversations that question that authority, even obliquely, are dealt with harshly. Requests and proposals that acknowledge that authority may be well received, as in:

We've analyzed this proposal six different ways, boss, and need your final decision.

Much of modern management is rooted in the mindset of authoritarian control. This view lends itself naturally to management by hierarchical authority, in which the preferred tools are control, prediction, force, specification, and metrics. The scientific management of Frederick Taylor is a prime and pervasive example.[7] Under its precepts, managers analyze tasks in great detail and prescribe optimally efficient actions for workers.

Mindsets in the Workplace

THE MINDSET OF ORDERLY STEREOTYPING

Orderly stereotyping, which has a strong affinity to authoritarian control, is the view that coping with reality is largely a matter of sorting things into categories and giving them names. Classification and finding prototypical examples of things are typical activities. Stereotyping is a typical view in well-established bureaucracies. It is crucial that everything be unambiguously ordered and labeled.

For example, in the stereotypic way of thinking, one assumes that there exists an unambiguous, correct, and fair amount of taxes that each tax payer owes. To the consternation of the IRS, every year *Money* magazine asks 50 professional tax preparers to analyze the same return. Many years, no two preparers come up with the same answer. In fact, the range between the top and the bottom amount is always many thousands of dollars. Does this suggest that there actually is no such thing as a correct amount of taxes—that the tax

---

HOW TO APPEAL TO STEREOTYPERS

Stereotypers are often found in bureaucracies, governments, routine administration, and support services such as finance, accounts payable, auditing, and the legal department. Requests made to these people must respect their view of the world. That view reflects a world whose complexity must be organized into orderly, preexisting categories. Any attempt to question the validity of the categories themselves will meet with resistance. An everyday example is filling out expense reports. These must be accurate and with expenses sorted into proper categories. It is easier to manufacture terms designed to fit into preexisting categories than to create new categories.

For example, one manager wanted to buy T-shirts and baseball caps for his department. His initial requisition was rejected by purchasing. He submitted a new requisition for "upper body covers and lids," which was accepted, since it did not trigger the negative category of "frivolous expenditures."

---

codes actually were inherently ambiguous? But if the tax codes actually were inherently ambiguous and indeterminate, that would violate the fundamental mindset premise upon which the tax code is based; namely, that there really exists an actual amount of taxes that each person owes that can be determined impartially.

THE MINDSET OF BROAD UNDERSTANDING

In this mindset, we see a holistic, systems approach. Outcomes are the consequence, not of isolated causes, but rather of complex and integrated systems. Systems thinking and systems modeling, beautifully presented by Peter Senge,[8] typify ideas consistent with the mindset of broad understanding. The whole is greater than the sum of its parts, and the output of a system is the result of complex interactions of large numbers of variables. Complex econometric models are also examples that emerge from the approach of broad

---

HOW TO APPEAL TO UNDERSTANDERS

The mindset of broad understanding is often found in academics, economics, and soft science. In the workplace, it is found in the organizational development, and human relations departments. Conversations designed to appeal to this audience need to emphasize high-level meaning and broad understanding of situations that take into account a wide range of fuzzy variables. Richness and depth of the model is a major criterion. Conformance with evidence is important but secondary.

Understanders favor systematic, orderly, well-articulated change. They will favor a large proposal that addresses many issues simultaneously, as in:

We could solve this particular problem, or we could take the time to study the general issues that cause this problem to come up again and again.

---

understanding. Such models are descriptively very rich and provide many insights. They are, however, poor at prediction and at determining courses of effective action.

In corporate life, it is common that the value system and approaches of human relations and organizational development professionals have roots in this mindset. Authoritarians tend to label them as "soft."

THE MINDSET OF CONTINUOUS TRANSFORMATION

In marked contrast to the other mindsets, especially the mindset for authoritarian control, is the mindset for continuous transformation. Operating under the transformational mindset, individuals seek to uncover and shift the background context in which an event occurs. Specific events are never analyzed independently of their context, indeed, could not be, for it is the context that defines the event. Cause-and-effect, as an explanatory principle, is foreign to the transformation mindset. Events do not have causes; rather, they

---

HOW TO APPEAL TO TRANSFORMERS

The mindset of transformation is most often found in inventors, entrepreneurs, the creative departments such as design or marketing, and among leaders. In general, these people respond poorly to detailed analysis and to evidence. Instead, they look for novelty, boldness of conception, daring, willingness to take risks, innovation, fast action, and personal commitment.

Transformers have little patience for established procedures and will react negatively to pressure. They respond positively to bold visions for the future, as in:

Let's take an entirely different look at the problem. What if we completely revised the executive compensation scheme?

---

occur inevitably in concert and harmony with the surrounding context. Many forms of marketing are highly transformational activities, with the context provided by rapidly changing customer needs and wants. The market-driven company seeks to be in harmony with the market context, and even to take a leading role in shaping it.

COMPARING THE FOUR COMMON MINDSETS

Both authoritarian control and continuous transformation are active mindsets. When we act within them, we impact the world directly. Both are powerful in their potential for impact on the workplace, though in different ways. Authoritarians operate through manipulation of people and objects, direct force with measurable outcomes. In this mindset, objects and people have an existence independent of the context in which they occur. By contrast, transformation operates on the context that surrounds people and objects, not on the objects themselves. Both approaches have monetary, visible, audible, and felt consequences on the human world. Both approaches are ethically neutral, in themselves. One tends to have strengths where the other has weaknesses and vice versa. In geopolitics, for example, military activity is the principal example of an authoritarian approach, whereas diplomacy and negotiation tend to be transformational. Both certainly are capable of stunningly successful or disastrous results.

One of the most compelling points of difference between authoritarian control and continuous transformation is the nature of evidence that each accepts as reasonable. Authoritarians, with their emphasis on prediction and control, tend to feel that past events and past results are, in fact, the best evidence for the genuineness and soundness of interpretations. By contrast, a transformer will always be oriented toward possibilities for the future. Transformers are apt to be visionaries. For them, evidence *is* the extent to which ideas and approaches hold possibilities for the future. In part this is true because each incident, every historical episode, is unique and will never be repeated exactly. Consequently, the generalization from past experience to future outcomes is uncertain. We can see the tensions created by these basic disagreements in, as an illustration, discussions between venture capitalists:

What is this person's track record? Where is the evidence that the business will succeed?

and entrepreneurs:

Why can't they see my vision for my new company?

Orderly stereotyping and broad understanding are passive and reactive mindsets. Stereotyping can be complementary to authoritarian control—putting things into orderly boxes and categories makes it easier to dominate them. Similarly, understanding and transformation can complement each other. A broad understanding of a situation can give clues as to where most effectively to apply the power of transformation.

For the authoritarian, the known world *is* a conglomerate of cause-and-effect machines, each with measurable inputs and outputs. For the stereotyper, things *are* what they are named and classified to be. For the broad understander, the world *is* an indivisible whole whose parts cannot be studied in isolation. For the transformer, the world *is* fluid and flexible and completely relative to the context or viewpoint from which it is perceived. These mindsets represent fundamental, culturally-inherited commitments about the architecture of everyday reality.

People are not always consistent, of course. They may tend toward one or another form of explanation in different areas of their business and personal lives. However, it is possible to develop an acute sense of hearing, not just for what people say, but also for what assumptional, bedrock framework must underlie what they are saying.

One strategy for exposing the underlying workplace mindset that people use is to engage them in a conversation on a topic about which they care deeply—something close to what they hold themselves to be as human beings. Then ask for reasons why they hold particular views and positions on the matter. It is not so much the particular reasons that give mindset clues; rather, it is what class of things, what sorts of logical and illogical argument, they raise.

For example, ask committed managers and employees about the "reasons" for declining profits or business failures. The answers often relate to underlying mindsets. Authoritarians might identify specific causes, such as insufficient capital or heavy competition. These explanations often focus the blame on external causes. Stereotypers might explain the behavior by naming absolute categories such as poor managers or unmotivated employees. These explanations place the blame on the inherent properties of the thing being blamed. Understanders favor systemic explanations, such as deeply rooted flaws in the corporate culture or maturing markets. The locus of blame tends to be something overwhelming. Transformers might identify a failure to seize the moment or adroitly to define the context as in: "We acted too late" or "We didn't succeed in creating the market." The locus of blame tends to be more on their own actions rather than on external causes. Over time, if you listen to conversations of concern in this way, you will gain a great deal of insight into and predictability concerning the way in which the other persons are apt to react, especially in crises.

The Transforming Workplace

Of the four common mindsets, only continuous transformation, as a mindset for change, is ideally suited to the rapidly evolving, flexible, and fluid business environment. From the perspective of the other mindsets, a workplace based on continuous transformation is incomprehensible and threatening. For the authoritarian, a transforming workplace means an end to permanent authority and privilege. For the stereotyper, the transforming workplace contains no fixed categories. For the understander, the transforming workplace is literally not understandable because it is always shifting and changing. Who on earth would want to work in such a place, viewed from these perspectives?

Each of us can make a personal decision, freely and by choice, as to what kind of workplace and what kind of work experience we want. In terms of human values, the transforming workplace has one property shared by no other workplace mindset: freedom. It offers the best opportunity to create a workplace in which people can achieve the fullest possible expression of their humanity. In the transforming workplace, people do not leave their hearts and minds at the factory door.

From a business perspective, the transforming workplace can offer the advantages of speed, fluidity, and deep commitment to customers. In current times, it may be the only mindset worth adopting, assuming we have freedom to choose. Control takes too much time and alienates those not in control. Stereotyping never quite fits a rapidly changing world. Broad understanding is always oriented toward making sense of past events, not toward creating new ones.

The transformation mindset treats people as autonomous, self-generating, and creative.

CHARACTERISTICS OF THE CONTINUOUSLY TRANSFORMING WORKPLACE

Reality created through expression	Correlational, systemic
People as possibilities	Contextual
Management by open persuasion	Appreciative
Management by permission	Generative
Creative	Empowerment-based

In the transformation-based workplace, people speak in such a way as to create an organizational setting or background against which powerful action shows up naturally with precision, grace, and inevitability. The direct or indirect application of force, coercion, punishment, or manipulative recognition of people has no place in the transformational workplace. In everyday terms, a leader in such a workplace operates much as the leader of a purely volunteer organization. Transformational management depends almost entirely on the power of open, honest persuasion.

Mindset Shifts and the Phoenix

Transforming the workplace requires shifting of mindsets. Nothing less is required than this profound level of change. A major mindset shift is an abrupt switch of core assumptions and values that affords the opportunity to examine afresh all historical data, knowledge, and practice. Like the death and rebirth of the magnificent phoenix in ancient mythology, from the death of the old springs forth the glory and promise of the new.

Mindset shifts in science are times of wrenching reappraisal, new directions, and creative discovery. What was chaotic becomes ordered, and what was ordered becomes chaotic. At a personal level, a major mindset shift feels like a bolt out of the blue that shakes one's long-held beliefs to the core and yet also contains the seeds and energy for the creation of an entirely new future. Mindset shifts in business have similar properties, exaggerated in intensity by the urgency of immediate economic impact.

Yet, all accounts of mindset shifts and mindset shifting are written by bystanders or retrospective observers, commenting on what has happened. Still to emerge is a theory and practice of actual mindset shifting—how to do it, how to do it constructively, and how to do it quickly. In the following chapters, we explore an avenue of inquiry and a basis for action. We address the question:

WHAT IS REQUIRED TO EMPOWER FUNDAMENTAL SHIFTS OF
MINDSET IN THE WORKPLACE?

3

Workplace Transformation

*Nothing is real beyond the imaginative patterns
men make of reality.*

—William Blake

Mindsets and Workplace Reality

A high-ranking manager in a world-class, multinational corporation graciously shares with me, on the occasion of his retirement, the central defining episode of his life that had solidified his management style. That event was witnessing the decline and fall of NCR in Dayton, Ohio, as technology shifted from mechanical gears and wheels to integrated circuits. He saw the careers of craftspeople, their skills at machining brass passed down for generations, destroyed, and saw the impact on family and community. As is true of all good leaders, this complex and reflective man achieved many successes but also lost many significant opportunities. For the episode in Dayton had persuaded him to be extremely conservative in investing money that was not immediately and directly related to core business of his organization. In one sense, this style was driven by determination to avoid repetition of the despair of Dayton, but in another sense it was a re-creation of it. Without realizing it, he repeated in a different form his Dayton experience. By starving investments in new technology, he locked out innovation. He was indeed masterful at squeezing every last dollar of revenue out of his organization. And after he left, his people found themselves with outmoded technology, loss of competitive position, and declining profits in a furiously changing market and many lost their jobs, just as had the women and men of Dayton before them.

You will meet many people, such as this vice president, whose actions, reactions, and feelings—the totality of how they conduct themselves in management—are ruled and governed by a particular interpretation of reality that they place on events.

CONSIDER THE POSSIBILITY THAT ANY INTERPRETATION IS ALWAYS
ONLY ONE POSSIBLE CHOICE AMONG MANY.

Given the Dayton saga, an equally valid interpretation is that an organization should invest resources in leading the march of progress, not defending against it. In fact, Andy Grove, the CEO of Intel Corporation, despite his own modest early beginnings, comes to an entirely different conclusion. He believes that massive reinvestment in new research and products holds the key to lasting business success. His picture on the cover of *Fortune* magazine in early 1993 bears the caption "Invest or Die."[1]

RIGIDIFICATION OF MADE-UP REALITIES

Consider the possibility that reality is always and only defined, made up, and made possible by our assessment, construction, and interpretation. Perhaps when we were children, an interpretation was laid out for many of us, handed down and given to us by parents, teachers, books, and social customs. When we join the workplace, other people, such as managers, the personnel department, the controllers of the reward system, the press—indeed, all those around us—enforce their particular view of the world on us. These people indoctrinate us with a mindset that gives us a set of relatively adequate (in the sense that I am still around to write this and you to read it) rules and procedures for living.

> PEOPLE MAY ENFORCE MINDSETS TO SERVE THEIR OWN
> INTERESTS AND NOT YOURS.

Each of us has had a greater or lesser degree of success in living within a framework of particular assumptions, procedures, and interpretations. Other people invented, evolved, and enforced these rules in the context of, and to serve the needs of, times, ages, and conditions that no longer exist. Or we may have invented them to bring a temporary coherence to events in a particular context, such as the layoffs in Dayton. In an earlier time, when the pace of change was slow, living out of a handed-down set of rules, living out of yesterday's viewpoints and assumptions, might have allowed us a degree of comfort and predictability in life, barring unforeseen circumstances. Those times no longer exist, especially in swiftly shifting industries.

BLINDNESS TO OTHER VIEWPOINTS

In vast areas of life, most of the people we meet have difficulty adopting a new viewpoint.

> MOST OF THE TIME, OUR ASSUMPTIONS AND VIEWPOINTS ARE
> NOT ACCESSIBLE TO US AS SOMETHING MADE UP AND AS
> SOMETHING WE COULD CHANGE.

Many people do not have a free relationship to their own viewpoints and assumptions, nor do they realize that these represent only one of many possible ways of relating to the world. In fact, many people would rather die and bring misery to others than question their core assumptions and fixed viewpoints. The father of a friend of mine steadfastly believed, all his life, that doctors are charlatans and hospitals are charnel houses. When he became painfully ill, he clung to this belief and refused to seek treatment. My friend and his mother endured many months of watching him waste away in agony in his own bed. After he died, an autopsy revealed that a quick and painless treatment would have spared his life and all the pain.

People can, but rarely do, make up a new reality, not as a defensive reaction to past events, but rather to support them in achieving a vision for the future.

> FOR MOST GROUPS IN THE WORKPLACE, "BUSINESS AS USUAL" IS
> THE ONLY POSSIBLE REALITY.

The difficulties in successfully shifting mindsets are revealed in the following episode. A vice president and his staff meet, on executive row, to transform the basic business mindset of their organization. A month and many vice presidential memos later, how is the message being received by the product groups? Have people grasped the urgency of improving time-to-market, running the organization as a business, and encouraging entrepreneurial actions? Three levels down in the organization, a manager of one product group tells his people,

> *Well, let's not let any of the changes being bandied about affect our ongoing work.*

It is as though the vice president's staff and the product group live on different planets. The people in the product groups have an iron-clad commitment to the continuation of their ongoing work, to business as usual. They respond to everything they hear, every new idea, and every change initiative by minimizing the impact on what they are already doing. They simply do not hear the vice president's message. Similarly, the vice president's staff speak about and design their program as though unaware that the fundamental commitment of people in their organization is to business as usual. This is more than simple miscommunication. It reflects the influence of viewpoints, assumptions, and mindsets on business reality itself.

The range of actions, experiences, and even thoughts available to the groups were all closely coupled to a particular perspective, a particular viewpoint on reality. The team members could not grasp the idea that they could actually redirect their ongoing work, that they could invent a new product venture rather than continue to support old ones with declining market share, and that they could actually take the vice president's message seriously and at face value. They may have suspected a hidden agenda (note that such a suspicion itself stems from an assumption), or been fearful (also a result of an assumption). Each of us has, as a result of life experience, a vast array of assessments, opinions, judgments, automatic ways of thinking, things we like and do not like, impressions, interpretations, stock critiques, and expectations about almost every known topic. Collectively, this array constitutes our perspective on life, our mindset, and it correlates perfectly with our ongoing actions and experiences.

FILTERS AND SIEVES

Filters and sieves protect us from information that might contradict our already existing interpretation of ourselves. Some filters are even explicit and quantitative. For instance, scientific experiments are explicitly and mathematically designed to filter out all discoveries except those that meet certain rigid statistical criteria. These criteria have nothing to do with the value of the discovery, commercial or otherwise, nor do they even pertain to the relevance or impact of the discovery on scientific theory itself. In other words, society may lose many relevant and valuable discoveries as a result of the conservative filter built into scientific practice. The cost of these lost discoveries is not factored into the tests. Science is by design conservative, biased toward reserving judgment and delaying actions until a result is proven beyond a high, but arbitrary, level of statistical certainty. In the case of experimental AIDS drugs, for example, this means that the research establishment withholds drugs that people with AIDS are quite willing to take a chance with. People with AIDS and scientists are playing by different rules.

FILTERS AND SIEVES KEEP FIXED MINDSETS IN PLACE.

The same phenomenon shows itself in the case of various information filters designed to keep irrelevant information away from busy people. An executive secretary serves this role, shielding the executive from time-wasting, bothersome people. Of course, vital information from unexpected or unorthodox sources will also be lost.

The *Wall Street Journal* interviewed me about my use of an electronic mail filter—a sort of artificially intelligent secretary.[2] At one point, my volume of electronic mail amounted to a backlog of 1,000 unread messages, with 50 more arriving each day. I could program the computer-based filter to scan the contents and to file or even discard messages according to rules that I could specify. For example, I could ask the computer to delete, unread, any messages from certain individuals, to file messages from other people in a low-priority file, and to alert me immediately to messages from yet other selected people, such as the vice president.

What I found after using this system for a while was that the information getting through was simply a reflection of the world as it existed in my mind when I originally wrote the rules. I missed interesting and valuable messages from new people that the system did not recognize. I also missed messages from people who changed interests or jobs or who, despite a past record of sending useless messages, suddenly changed their ways and sent something valuable. For example, my rules did not recognize the name of the organizer of a meeting to design a new campaign to launch innovative, revenue-generating consulting services. I missed the meeting, and consequently the consulting services I had designed were not included in the campaign and their potential revenue was forever lost. Eventually, I stopped using the mail filter in favor of a more thorough, flexible, manual screening of all the mail.

NEGATIVE ATTITUDES TOWARD OTHER REALITIES

From any viewpoint, say the viewpoint of accounting, the viewpoint of gardening, the viewpoint of gold futures, the viewpoint of the funeral industry, the viewpoint of mathematics, or the viewpoint from the water cooler, a rich range of invented nuance and variation exists. Operating masterfully from a particular viewpoint is a matter of becoming attuned to the subtleties and niceties that the viewpoint reveals. For the uninitiated, an unfamiliar viewpoint reveals little. To the novice in investing, the viewpoint of stocks, bonds, no-load mutual funds, and zero coupon bonds appears at best fuzzy and indistinct. To the experienced investor, that same viewpoint reveals exciting opportunities for action.

In a tragic and recurring failure, human beings tend to overlook and disparage the richness and potential relevance of unknown viewpoints. Explorers of an earlier age routinely dismissed as primitive and barbaric the people that they encountered. Similarly, the remaining rain forest today is to many as featureless as a field of overgrown weeds. One common symptom in many large companies is the obvious and ill-concealed disdain that different functional departments have for each other.

ARROGANCE TOWARD OTHER VIEWPOINTS IN THE WORKPLACE
EXTRACTS A TERRIBLE PRICE IN LOST BUSINESS RESULTS

In one *Fortune* 500 company, an engineer has invented, and completed the advanced development for a new product. She receives overwhelmingly positive reactions from prospective customers, including vice presidents from Delta, Alcatel, Transamerica, British Petroleum, and John Deere. In a state of early and naive enthusiasm, she arranges a presentation to one of her company's marketing groups to solicit their encouragement and support. To her surprise, even before she opens her mouth, the audience is nasty and hostile, and the people will not let her finish the presentation. Since she has never met these people, nothing personal appears to be involved, so she does some background investigation.

What emerges is a long history of mistrust and broken relationships between the entire engineering and marketing organizations. Engineers drive the company and invent products and product lines and then, as the expression has it, "toss them over the wall" to marketing and sales. The marketing and field arms exist, from engineering's perspective, as a second-rate service organization that has to execute the mundane task of bringing engineering visions out into the world. For their part, the marketing people feel they have no effective input into what engineering builds, and they have organized themselves to do the best possible job they can in reacting to what, from their perspective, are engineering's whims. So the mindset of individuals in the organization has engineering and marketing in a basically hostile and suspicious stance, rather than a cooperative and mutually supporting relationship.

It takes her some time to realize and personally recover from the implications of this. Meanwhile, other large companies as well as numerous start-ups create successful businesses from the basic product idea. The company where the idea was invented gains no benefit from its investment.

The prevailing attitude in the company where these events took place is best summarized by the following public comment from an extremely high-ranking engineering manager to his marketing executives:

Your work isn't worth a piss hole in the snow.

Imagine yourself as a marketing executive listening to this statement. What would be your reaction? Are such statements the best way to insure quality of life and quality of products in the business world? Would a more empowering interpretation of reality be that both engineering and marketing are incredibly rich domains, filled with elaborate and powerful nuances? Are the possibilities for both engineering and marketing richer in an organizational relationship based on respect and appreciation?

FIXED MINDSETS LIMIT INNOVATIVE ACTION

What do people in your organization do if they walk in late to an important meeting? Typically, they will offer an excuse. Excuses and reasons always derive from underlying assumptions and viewpoints and change if the assumptions change:

I'm sorry I'm late, but my car broke down.

On the face of it, this is a reasonable excuse. Many managers would be satisfied and let the matter drop. What if you pursued the following dialogue?

Q: Why did your car break down?
A: The oil was low.
Q: Why was the oil low?
A: Well, I forgot the scheduled maintenance.
Q: Would you like some help remembering your maintenance schedule?

At this point, the person probably thinks you are being pushy and rude. However, notice that the initial excuse (my car broke down) has the effect of getting her "off the hook" for being late. Excuses reveal a person's viewpoint and level of commitment. Here is a list of possible excuses for missing a meeting, ordered, roughly, from weak to strong.

○ Didn't feel like coming.

○ Had something more important to do.

○ Was exhausted.

○ Car broke down.

○ Had the flu.

- Dog died.

- Child was in an accident.

- Was diagnosed with a fatal disease.

- Died.

For some people, the excuses near the top of the list are sufficient reason to break their promise to attend a meeting. Would it be possible, though, to organize your life in such a way that none of the listed events, even the last one, would lead you to break your word? Some people take their commitments so seriously that those commitments will be met even after they themselves die. Physically, that level of commitment is not hard to arrange. All that is required is a mindset shift from focusing on excuses to focusing on possible actions. If a meeting were sufficiently important to you, would it be possible to arrange, in advance, to have someone else prepared to attend and honor the commitment even if you could not attend due to some tragedy?

Contrast this level of possible dedication with that revealed in this example of a standard "business as usual" meeting. At a meeting of a vice president and his staff, the topic is the status of action items. All the action items are late. As turns move around the table, each manager gives an excuse as to why his (they are all men) item has not been accomplished. The excuses all pin the responsibility on some other organization—never on the person speaking. The vice president's scowls grow darker. Each person "in the barrel" comes up with even more watertight reasons why his item could not possibly have been finished. No one offers any new ideas or assistance. The meeting ends after three hours with no accomplishments at all. Meanwhile, a group of junior people, convinced that they have new answers to the compelling business and technical problems facing their organization, are once again put off to next month's agenda, because this meeting, as it always does, runs late due to the length of time devoted to excuse making.

These incidents are examples of a pervasive and pernicious assumption common to large, bureaucratic organizations:

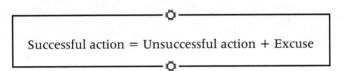

Successful action = Unsuccessful action + Excuse

It is as if we can make failure just as good as success by adding an excuse. When people focus on excuses, they limit the possibility of innovative action.

Breaking the Rules of Workplace Reality

A SUCCESS STORY

Many people give clues to their assumptions about reality in their language—especially the metaphors they use. This is vividly illustrated in the case of one product development group building an innovative new product within a large corporation. Members of this group are having trouble getting cooperation from other people in the organization. In meeting with the group, a visitor listens carefully for clues about the reality individuals in the group have constructed for themselves. Within 45 minutes, the visitor hears all the following expressions:

Go for the jugular,

Coerce, pressure, and twist arms,

Pulling chains,

Whip into shape,

Beat into shape,

Yank us around,

Bear down on them,

Beat them up,

Beat into submission,

Squeeze,

How can we force them to do that?

Clamp down on them,

Jerk around,

Kick us around,

Get him by the short hairs, and

Crucify him.

This list is striking in its underlying metaphor of violence and mutual coercion. The team members speak these phrases naturally, and the world they perceive themselves to be living in is, for them, peopled by obstructionist enemies. So, as seems natural, they deploy this combative attitude and way of speaking in all their communications with prospective allies, including their manager. And their project is going nowhere.

Most of the time people act out of, and reinforce with their communications, a particular, made-up interpretation of reality. Unfortunately, this interpretation is not usually accessible to us *as* a made-up interpretation; we unconsciously assume it to be the *only* reality—the way things *really* are. For this development team, everyone else *really is* a stupid, ill-intentioned jerk.

The members of the group live in a world of people going for each other's jugulars. Unfortunately for them, their product can not stand on its own but needs to be carefully integrated with many other products in order to be successful. Not only that, without cooperation from product management, product administration, marketing, and sales, the product will not succeed. Naturally, as in any large, complex organization, all the people from these other functions are busy with many projects and have multiple demands on their time.

The issue facing the product development group is how to attract the interest and cooperation of all these other people. When the visitor first meets the people in the group, they have experienced little success and feel the entire organization is against them. Fortunately, the team leader is a gifted and experienced engineer and manager with a burning vision for his product. After the meeting of the violent metaphors, conversation with the team leader reveals that the theme of competition and violence saturates his communications with everyone in the organization, including his management. He even explains how he shook with rage in his manager's office that very morning. As a passionate manager with a strong desire to see his product succeed, he knows no way to drive his project to success other than through acts of communication that spring from an underlying mindset of authoritarian control. Fortunately for his project, he accepts coaching from the visitor, who helps him alter his speaking so that his requests for help begin to reflect a polite and caring acknowledgment of the people he is dealing with, and so that he avoids destructive or threatening forms of expression.

The result is an almost overnight turnaround in the degree of cooperation and support he is able to garner from other individuals and organizations in the company. The product ships, successfully, six months later. The team leader thinks it is magic.

WHAT SHIFTED?

Helping move a group away from abusive language shows the basic mechanisms of mindset shifting in everyday practice. Whatever the "objective" circumstances, we can always find another interpretation that grants more freedom of action, greater integrity, and superior peace with ourselves and others than the interpretation we currently hold. Access to the new interpretation is through our forms of communication. The development manager actually shifted his reality—shipped a profitable product—by asking cordially, yet persistently, for help instead of issuing threats.

WHEN THE LANGUAGE USED TO DESCRIBE THE "REAL WORLD"
SHIFTS, SO DOES THE REAL WORLD ITSELF.

In the mindsets of authoritarianism, stereotyping, and broad understanding, the real world exists independently of the language used to describe it. The mindset of continuous transformation is unique in the view that language actually creates new reality. Our everyday forms of communication are so much a part of us that their relation to reality is usually concealed and obscure, as was the case for the combative manager. But under the mindset of continuous transformation, to communicate, we do not have to be mentally convinced, beforehand, of the reality of what we are communicating. It was actually irrelevant what the team members "really" thought of the organization. What was important to their success was what they actually said to the people with whom they worked, whether they spoke to them as hostile enemies or as potential partners. Interestingly, as their language became more positive, so did their appreciation of their workplace fellows.

ANOTHER SUCCESS STORY

Many large software companies maintain a distinction between the job of programmer and the job of product manager. Product managers are the link between the programmers who write the software and the customers. Product managers are responsible for administering the complex bureaucratic and political processes that let a software product be created and shipped. They coordinate and communicate between customers, marketing, and the engineering groups.

In 1991, in a large software company, the average time from

conception to revenue-generating shipment of a software product in one division was almost five years. During a typical five-year development cycle, there are numerous shifts in corporate and group strategic direction, numerous changes of hardware, which usually means that most or all the software written up to that point has to be rewritten. Meanwhile, changes in customer needs and marketplace demands also take place. Consequently, the product focus of the software is constantly changing during its development with the threat of cancellation always hanging over all products. The product manager's job is to make sense and expedite this vortex of change without explicit authority.

Software is problematic to develop. Its characteristics, as the user or customer sees these, are highly resistant to formal specification, but are instead shaped, on the fly, by the accumulation of daily micro-decisions that software engineers write directly into the computer code. It is as though the shape, color, engine size and placement, road feel, gas mileage, cost, and safety parameters of an automobile were literally determined in the heat of the moment by the assembly-line workers, rather than by preplanned design. The engineers, naturally, have great pride in their work, and one of the ways they express this pride is by jealously guarding the final say in what the product should look like, what customers it should appeal to, and what functions it should perform. And they do have the final say, since they are the only ones who understand and can alter the code.

Clearly, the product management job has its share of frustrations. When it becomes obvious that software profitability is declining and that this particular company has lost touch with customer needs, a vice president moves to empower product management to take a greater role in driving profitability. It is his wish that they should no longer play second fiddle to the engineers, as has been the tradition up to that point. To help deliver this message, members of the vice president's team design an event and invite 100 product managers from all over the company. The product managers' frustration and sense of disempowerment are obvious. One team member, an engineer, begins his remarks by saying,

On behalf of engineering, we wish to apologize to you for years of being arrogant and of thinking we had all the answers. You are experts at what you do, and we have been blind to that for a long time. Now we realize we are in trouble and we need your help.

People in the room gasp. Given the historical context, these are highly unusual and initially unbelievable remarks. Then follows a round of spontaneous applause. After this, many product managers are able to form collaboration-based, as opposed to subservient-based, relationships with their engineering counterparts, resulting in a dramatic reduction in time-to-market for projects.

What had been missing, for many years, was a lack of appreciation by the engineers for the difficulties and for the differentiation, depth, and value of the product manager's world. Engineering really needed product management to be successful, but did not realize it in an immediate way. Without anyone intending it, a technocratic elitism grew up in which the world was divided into technical people, the elite in this particular culture, and everybody else. "Everybody else" got less up-to-date equipment, funny looks in the halls, were often the afterthought on meeting invitations and minutes, and received other daily reminders of their nontechnical status. No one intended this; nor was it the result of malfeasance.

LEARNING TO APPRECIATE THE RICHNESS AND VALUE OF OTHER
PEOPLE'S WORLDS CREATES RICH OPPORTUNITIES.

BREAKING THE VICIOUS CYCLE OF REALITY AND ACTION

Any particular interpretation of reality allows only actions and experiences consistent with itself. It also cuts off access to actions, thoughts, and experiences outside its self-perpetuating frame. A new reality—someone else's or one that we invent—gives access to an entirely different range of possible actions and experiences, even in the face of objectively unchanged circumstances. People can always generate powerful access to new actions, experiences, and feelings, and new results, by making up a new reality—tinkering with the architecture of truth, especially truth about ourselves, as we currently understand it.

For most people, most of the time, action and interpretation are fused, mingled, melted together, combined, and indistinct from one another. This feels like day-to-day living on autopilot—being "thrown," closed off, covered up, concealed, in a state of tranquilized obviousness, safe, and spiritless. It is as though our spirit lives in a bounded world consisting of exotically tangled and interconnected actions, interpretations, rules, judgments, assessments, and beliefs—rather like the roots of a pot-bound plant or an overstocked and polluted aquarium. These rules are both defining and limiting. Everything inside the world defined by a particular viewpoint is exotically self-confirming. We are literally unaware of other possibilities.

> POSSIBILITIES FOR ACTION ARE LIMITED TO WHATEVER IS
> AVAILABLE WITHIN THE SELF-CONFIRMING RULES OF A
> PARTICULAR INTERPRETATION OF REALITY.

There are, of course, other realities. It is even a simple matter to break out into them. All you have to do is to identify and question your most cherished, hidden, and protected viewpoints and assumptions about yourself. Though simple, this is by no means easy. It involves what has been variously called the leap into the abyss, an act of deep courage, or a leap of faith. Since your particular interpretation of reality is *your reality*, leaving it is by definition venturing into the unknown. You may indeed fail, look foolish, or incur the wrath of others. On the other hand, you might also achieve your true greatness.

If you succeed in breaking out of a particular interpretation of reality, you will sooner or later discover that you are now in a new interpretation of reality—larger, perhaps, with more freedom of action—but still a closed system. The process of breaking out goes on forever, much like the never-ending quest for quality in an organization committed to continuous improvement and continuous learning. You find freedom, if anywhere, in the act of breaking out, not in the attainment of some ultimate and static state.

The Source of New Reality

INVENTED NUANCE

Nuance, subtlety, richness, and depth in any area of interest to human beings is always and in every case invented, manufactured, and created in language. The human world is created out of focused, articulated awareness. The unlabeled, undifferentiated world is flat and featureless, rather as Helen Keller's world appeared to her before she mastered language.

For example, for most of us, a page of text is simply a page of text, much like any other. But to the typesetter or typographer, any page is rich with complexity. Typeface, type weight and stress, white space, rivers of white space, justification, headers, footers, floating heads, pagination, paragraphing and paragraph style, hyphenation, widows and orphans—these are just a few terms from the rich world of typography. It is a highly articulated world and the product of centuries of evolution. Computer manufacturers who thought of text as primitive electronic information representable as simple ASCII computer codes historically underappreciated and even mocked this world as soft and arty. Consequently, far-reaching decisions were made about computer and software architectures that just ignored the production of beautifully printed pages as a goal. The result is that certain large, multinational corporations simply cannot compete in lucrative, multi-billion-dollar markets surrounding the small business, personal, or departmental desktop publishing arenas. At the architectural core of their massive, multi-billion-dollar arrays of hardware, software, and service, certain nuances are simply missing that render all of this vast infrastructure quite helpless in supporting a single user to produce a beautifully printed page.

The world of print is hardly a fixed, preordained world, set into being by forces outside ourselves. People invented it and brought it forth through acts of expression. What about the historical source of reality for companies now not competitive in the desktop publishing space? The source of that outcome was not some massive, well-funded strategy and deliberate plan. Rather, it was, at the origin, someone making this negative remark at a crucial staff meeting:

Who needs fonts? Those are just for nontechnical people, not for engineers like us!

History shows this to have been a costly negative remark, perhaps well intentioned at the time, and also made not only from lack of awareness of the richness of printing, but also from lack of any realization that this awareness is missing. The moral is to be extremely cautious about making negative remarks.

THE POWER OF TAKING RISKS

Questioning our own current interpretation of reality is one of the most courageous acts we can undertake, since it involves raising the question of who we are. It is also the most freeing action self-defining beings can take.

If we choose to invent and create, at some point we are going to have to take a risk. We will have to say and do things that are not reasonable, that make no sense within the fashionable framework of reasons existing around us at the time. And if we want to be surrounded by inventive and creative co-workers and employees, we must empower them and support them in taking risks, even and especially risks that could threaten our own current position.

Paul Hawken, the entrepreneur, writes about the moment of fear, the awful emptiness in the pit of the stomach, the self-doubt that accompanies the launching of a new venture. He says this moment is an essential part of launching a new business.

> THE WILLINGNESS TO FACE AND MASTER THE FEAR OF FAILURE
> IS A LARGE PART OF THE SECRET OF ENTREPRENEURIAL SUCCESS.

It is the same with any other groundbreaking, innovative undertaking. The creative act always requires a leap into the abyss of the unknown. This is especially true if we define success as breaking the boundaries of the expected and the predictable. We will not find the key to success by studying, in retrospect, the past actions and strategies of successful people. We find it in the state of mind of successful people *before* their success. To model and learn from successful people, we need to find them before they achieve their success, not afterward.

To see this, imagine that you want to support a start-up company. If you align with the company before success is assured, share the risk, and do everything in your power to help the company succeed, you will learn a great deal about entrepreneurship and business, firsthand. And if the business succeeds, you will be well rewarded. On the other hand, if you wait until the business is successful and only then try to jump on the bandwagon, you will miss the valuable firsthand lessons and will only get the rewards due a Johnny-come-lately. A friend of mine knows this well, to his everlasting regret. He turned down an offer to join a young, unknown company called Microsoft, as the third employee to be hired.

A Powerful Alternative Reality

A BRIGHT VISION FOR THE WORKPLACE

Imagine working in an organization where most of what people said in meetings, memos, directives, performance reviews, business plans, position papers, and in the hallway is thoughtless, confused, guarded, critical, negative, devious, not to be taken at face value, or self-serving. Conversely, imagine what would it be like to work in an organization where communication is explicit, cogent, well designed, supportive, contributory, and action-oriented.

IT IS POSSIBLE FOR ALL OF US TO ACHIEVE MEANINGFUL ACCOMPLISHMENT, ACCELERATED PERSONAL GROWTH, AND DEEP SATISFACTION AT WORK

Each day at work can actually be extraordinary. I visit a start-up software company of about 25 people. I cannot believe, at first, the degree of camaraderie and mutual respect between the sales force, the marketing people, the engineers, and the researchers. The experience is absolutely foreign to me, given my years of experience with large corporations—I had forgotten that it is possible for people to treat each other so well. The tenuous nature of a start-up venture makes everyone's dependence on everyone else's success highly apparent in a short time frame and leaves little room for elitism or for treating other people as less than full and respected team members. And the last time I checked, the company was turning great profits. A great day at work is indeed possible for everyone, at least in that particular company. Why cannot everyone have a great day at work, every day, in every workplace?

THE PHOENIX AGENDA

Peter Senge, an MIT Sloan School of Management professor and noted management consultant, interviewed many top business performers who told him that at one time in their careers, they had a "peak work experience," a time of profound teamwork, mutual respect, caring, and fantastic accomplishment. They added, wistfully and sadly, that the central quest of their professional lives was seeking to have that experience again.[3]

Consider the possibility that what we and our associates say and hear, what we and they communicate and observe, is the single most important factor in determining peak work experience—including a bottom line to be proud of. If that is so, it is critical to have a richly articulated framework and set of tools to allow us to always communicate with positive and forceful intention and to support us in not communicating destructively.

THE WORKPLACE CAN BE DESIGNED TO OFFER PEOPLE THE FREE CHOICE TO ACHIEVE FULL EXPRESSION OF THEIR HUMANITY.

The Phoenix Agenda, as outlined in the next four chapters, is a framework for transforming workplace communications that, when completely implemented, continuously creates a rewarding and satisfying workplace, by the free choice of everyone involved. The Phoenix Agenda consists of 12 language and communication tools designed to create:

A GREAT DAY AT WORK, ONE DAY AT A TIME, FOR EVERYONE.

Part II of this book, "Tools for Transformation," deals with each of the 12 facets of The Phoenix Agenda and shows how to put each one into practice.

PART II

Tools for Transformation: The Phoenix Agenda

Being a good human being is good business.

—Paul Hawken, entrepreneur

Language for Transforming Reality

Language is the house of being.

—Martin Heidegger, philosopher

The Language of Transformation

The power to transform is rooted in the way we use language. Language includes anything we are, say, do, or think that impacts the behavior or thinking of ourselves or another person. This includes nonverbal communication, actions, gestures, and expressions, as well as spoken and written speech.

According to this definition, it is an act of language to give a presentation, install plumbing, design a building, get married, found a company, or sell a car. The power in calling these "language" lies in considering them all as acts that affect the human world; that is, as acts that communicate understanding and experience from one human being to another.

Expressions in language can either reflect a particular interpretation of reality or they can be designed to alter it. The important thing to realize is that every language act influences reality. Through using language, it is possible to alter current business assumptions and create a reality that provides for the successful achievement of personal and organizational goals.

Take, for example, the engineering supervisor who is getting nowhere following the usual route of formal proposals to management committees to request money for a key project. His company has shown declining profits, but he has a plan that he thinks will create new customers and generate cash quickly. His managers have put him off for months and co-workers advise him,

> *Slow down, don't be so pushy. We get paid on Thursdays anyway. Why bust your buns?*

But this is no ordinary supervisor. He decides to jump five levels of managers and go straight to the vice president. Under the conventional assumptions and viewpoints of his organization, it is unthinkable to pass over five levels of management and to incur possible jealousy of co-workers, even in the interest of pleasing customers and generating profits. The supervisor is, however, determined. The problem is how to reach the vice president, who everyone says is unapproachable and inaccessible. He designs a strategy. Knowing that the vice president is planning a business trip, he learns the flight number and time, and drives two hours to the airport to intercept him in the departure lounge. Within five minutes of inspired and courageous speaking, painfully aware that his entire career is at risk, the supervisor persuades the vice president and gets the backing he needs. The result is a successful project that generates several million dollars for the company.

In the world of business, reality is simultaneously held in place and shifted through acts of language. Driving to the airport late at night, being present in the departure lounge at the right time, wearing a suit, and generating five minutes of persuasive and

Language for Transforming Reality

impassioned conversation—these are powerful language acts, carefully designed by a supervisor determined to make a difference.

THE LANGUAGE OF TRANSFORMATION IS THE LANGUAGE OF
COMMITMENT, CLARITY, AND COURAGE.

The view that language directly impacts reality is foreign to conventional thinking. The conventional view holds that a neutral, objective reality exists independent of our expression of it, and, therefore, the role of language is to reflect that reality. The continuous transformation viewpoint is that reality is created in the content and structure of language acts themselves. For example, in one case study, an elementary school class is randomly divided into two groups of children with equivalent learning abilities. Students in one group are told that they are in a remedial class. The students in the other group are told that they are gifted children in a special program. Both groups actually receive the identical curriculum. After one school term, the supposedly remedial group is performing poorly, and the supposedly gifted group is performing exceptionally.

THE KEY TO CREATING A NEW REALITY LIES IN BOLDLY SPEAKING
WHAT YOU ARE COMMITTED TO BRINGING INTO EXISTENCE.

In everyday conversation, we tend to categorize what we hear and experience in a way that enables us to relate it to what we already understand. In particular, we insist that we think before we speak. In meetings, for instance, many people are planning what they are going to say next, instead of paying full attention to what other people are saying. This view is closely related to Descartes's postulate: *I think therefore I am.*

The assumption is that *being* is dependent on *thinking*. An alternative view might be: *I will know what I think when I hear what I say.*

The assumption of this view is that *thinking* begins with *being*. While every person speaks spontaneously to some degree, most people preplan and prethink what they will say when they are placed on center stage, want to impress others, or need to make a presentation. Speaking spontaneously and speaking according to a plan are very different ways of communicating. Though both have their place, spontaneous speaking has greater leverage in the day-to-day business of workplace transformation. If you are not comfortable speaking spontaneously, select a familiar situation in which you can practice. Business meetings are a good forum for this. As the meeting goes on, instead of precalculating and preplanning your remarks, you might try generating your remarks on the spot, in genuine response to what is happening in the meeting.

Everyday conversation is prone to pettiness—to dismissing whatever we hear that is not immediately understandable. We demand, ordinarily, that what we hear, speak, or even think be understandable, at least to ourselves if not to others. Understandable means that we are able to assimilate it easily into the rules of our existing viewpoints and assumptions. Inventing a new reality demands letting all of that go.

> *UNDERSTANDABLE* MEANS ACCESSIBLE THROUGH OUR EXISTING
> VIEWPOINTS AND ASSUMPTIONS. THEREFORE, WHAT IS
> UNDERSTANDABLE IS BY DEFINITION NOT INVENTIVE.

In transformational conversation, we seek to invent a new context for understanding. A new reality is generated when we bravely and with commitment speak of a new future—not as an extrapolation of the past, nor as an understanding of the past, but as a vision for the future without proof. Since a new reality is in the future and has not happened, there can be no proof, since proof is by definition an assessment of the past. Leaders understand this way of speaking well. One needs only to think of Winston Churchill galvanizing the British Empire against the Nazis or John F. Kennedy boldly envisioning a man on the moon in order to understand the impact of such ways of speaking.

Language for Transforming Reality

THE KEY ACTION IN CREATING A NEW REALITY IS PROCLAIMING
A PUBLIC COMMITMENT TO THAT NEW REALITY.

The power to transform is rooted in the way we use language. To create the fulfilling workplaces that we all want, we need to learn, not just to speak differently, but to adopt a new mindset with respect to communication and language itself. The next section begins this path of learning by developing the building blocks for using language as a vehicle for transformation.

The Building Blocks of Transformational Language

Most of us operate under the assumption that language and other forms of expression convey information about reality. We speak in order to reflect an already existing world. To do this, we state facts and report on our feelings and understandings. Speaking in this way means that what we say is consistent with, and also locks into place, our current assumptions and viewpoints. The advantage to this everyday way of speaking is that we appear normal to the people around us. The disadvantage is that we rarely create anything new.

Consider the possibility of an alternative assumption about language and other forms of expression, namely that:

OUR USE OF LANGUAGE DOES NOT MODEL REALITY,
RATHER IT CREATES REALITY.

Our ability to create transformation depends on our ability to use language in entirely new ways. Everyday language, the rules of grammar we learned in school, is not concerned with transformation, but rather stems from the mindset of orderly stereotyping. The grammar of everyday language contains building blocks (such as nouns and verbs) and rules for using these correctly so that we can send messages and information to other people in a format that they understand. This new approach to language has different building blocks and different rules of usage.[1]

There are four building blocks in transformational language:

○ *Reality probe*—a question or inquiry.
○ *Status report*—a statement of fact based on evidence.
○ *Action request*—a precision request or promise for action.
○ *Transformational proclamation*—an inspirational declaration that generates the future.

These four building blocks represent four categories or ways of speaking that form the fundamental building blocks of any transformational communication. As with the grammar of ordinary language, there are correct and incorrect ways to use them.

The "correct" forms shape reality in desirable ways. They inspire courage, drive excellence, encourage discovery, and deliver results. The "incorrect" forms create a distorted reality that is inconsistent with transformation. According to this view, "incorrect" use of language can demoralize people, delay projects, make enemies, destroy organizations, and reduce profits. The examples in the Transformation 101 table further illustrate these differences.

Reality probes, action requests, and transformational proclamations are rare in the language of business as usual. Unlike status reports that mirror, describe, or reflect reality, these three forms all modify reality, in the sense of altering and impacting the world.

A FUNDAMENTALLY DIFFERENT WAY OF USING LANGUAGE TRANSFORMS REALITY, GETS RESULTS QUICKLY, AND PRODUCES EXTRAORDINARY AND UNEXPECTED ACCOMPLISHMENTS.

The next four sections define each of the four building blocks of transformational language in more detail.

Language for Transforming Reality

Expression	Correct Form	Incorrect Form
Reality probe	Are we building the right product?	What right do you have to question the manager's decision?
Status report	The computers are down.	The stupid system is down again. It *never* works right.
Action request	Let's meet at Joe's at noon on Thursday for lunch.	Let's do lunch sometime.
Transformational proclamation	We are committed to our customers' success.	Your work isn't worth a piss hole in the snow.

REALITY PROBE

New knowledge and fresh understanding are created by reality probes. Reality probes are designed to initiate dialogue and discover possibility, not to produce ready answers. This is true, for example, of the scientific method that, at its finest, starts with asking questions about the world around us.

The usual form of a reality probe is a question. It is not a confrontational question, but an honest and open one. A reality probe is a sincere attempt to find out about something that we do not know. The more open and free of presupposition the question is, the more we learn.

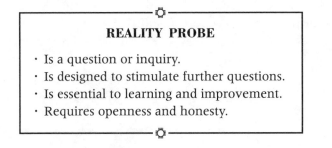

REALITY PROBE

· Is a question or inquiry.
· Is designed to stimulate further questions.
· Is essential to learning and improvement.
· Requires openness and honesty.

Probing is key to discovering and creating new realities, to learning, and to continuous improvement. For example, a company decides to develop a program that sends senior engineers and managers to visit customers. The idea is that customer contact and feedback at this high a level within the company will produce better products. Unfortunately, most of the engineers are not trained to ask the kind of open question that can help them learn what is important to the customer. So they ask questions such as:

What would you do with 60 MIPS on your desk?

A more appropriate type of question might be:

What do you need to know to be successful in your business?

The latter question produces a more fruitful dialogue. It is phrased in the customer's terms, expresses interest, and leads to a better relationship. When pursued, this line of questioning can produce a richer set of possibilities for products and solutions that will be of significance to customers.

STATUS REPORT

Most large organizations demand regular status reports from their employees. These consume much time and energy and may or may not provide a discernible result. In general, under nontransformational mindsets, all language is held to be an expression of information; in other words, a report of status. But using language only to convey information produces few if any results. A report of status simply conveys information and facts. While status reports are important in providing the information that a business needs to function, by themselves they are a weak and ineffective vehicle for transformation.

Language for Transforming Reality

STATUS REPORT

- Is a statement about reality for which the speaker is prepared to offer evidence.
- Corresponds to "information" as seen from the viewpoint of authoritarian control.
- Tends to lock in the existing circumstances.
- Is the weakest element in transformational language because status produces no change.

Stating facts tends to reflect existing viewpoints and assumptions and hold them in place. Thus, status reports are most useful in creating results that are predictable within the context of a particular mindset. The language of status reports is the language of business as usual. However, most common statements of fact have two major problems.

First, they can contain unwarranted and cynical overtones, as in the example in the Transformation 101 table on page 87:

The stupid system is down again. It never works right.

This is an expression commonly heard in computer-dependent organizations. It is never literally true, and it promotes an atmosphere of petty complaining that undermines an organization's higher purpose.

Second, often the speaker of such a "fact" is not willing to take responsibility for its accuracy, making it extremely difficult for others to act upon the statement. To state a fact strongly means that we are willing and able to provide evidence. To state a fact weakly means that we are not willing to put ourselves and our word on the line.

Weakly stated facts often take the form of rumors, scuttlebutt, murmurs, and hearsay. These forms of communication are always enormously destructive to organizations. A rumor is an apparent status report with a hidden purpose of transforming reality, often to negative effect. For example, suppose you hear and pass on an unsubstantiated rumor about another employee falling out of favor with the organization, as in

Sam is a poor employee.

As a status report, the words are irresponsible unless you can provide proof. As a transformational proclamation, it is a negative form that has the effect of hurting Sam's career. Of course, Sam can also spread rumors about you. Taken to extremes, this sort of communication destroys organizations.

As participants in a transforming workplace, a critical issue is the extent to which we are willing to provide evidence for our statements. For example, suppose we are selling a customer a new machine for his assembly line. Which statement will the customer find more convincing?

This machine might solve your problem.

or

I've studied your manufacturing needs and checked them against the features of this product. This machine will solve the problems you have.

This latter statement illustrates the productive and responsible use of status reports.

ACTION REQUEST

Action requests are expressions that state explicitly what is to be done, by whom, and when. When we request someone to do something, we are not reporting on status. Instead, we bring about an event that could make something happen. Precise requests are action requests that have specificity and clarity; imprecise ones do not. Imprecise requests generate confused and murky results.

ACTION REQUEST

· Is a precision request or promise.
· Always includes *what* is to be done, by *whom*, and *when*.
· Is the source of action.

In today's business, we see enormous lack of clarity and confusion concerning requests. It is possible to generate large and immediate productivity improvements for ourselves and the people around us simply by always stating our requests clearly. A clear request, also known as a precision request, asks a specific person to do a specific thing by a specific time. It may also include a statement of conditions of satisfaction; that is, the criterion that will determine that the request is done or complete. An unclear request leaves out one or more of these basic components: who, what, and by when. Simply listen for precision requests in business meetings to convince yourself that most people, most of the time, make confusing and unclear requests. When requests are unclear and poorly presented, the results they produce will reflect the same lack of clarity with unexpected and frustrating consequences.

TRANSFORMATIONAL PROCLAMATION

Transformational proclamations are forms of expression that create new futures by focusing on new viewpoints and assumptions. Because they generate the future, they are never based on evidence and cannot be comments about the existing state of affairs. Technically, a transformational proclamation is an expression in language that creates the possibility of a new future by virtue of its being expressed powerfully within a befitting context. In the continuous transformational view, it is an act of expression that through its expression alone creates the future.

☼

TRANSFORMATIONAL PROCLAMATION

- Always creates a new possibility for action and result.
- Is *never* supported by evidence.
- Depends for "truth" on personal integrity and commitment.

☼

For example, when you stand in front of the altar with your significant other, you have the opportunity to choose and create a dramatically different future. In that moment, when the question is asked, "Will you take . . . ," you actually have a free choice to create, based only on your word, an entirely new life and set of relationships for yourself and your partner. What if you said,

No!

You could. Realistically, you actually could. Serious consequences would result, people would be upset, and you might feel bad, but you could still say, "No." Similarly, you could say, "I do," and in speaking those two words create the future that follows from such a statement.

These moments, when we are in a position to radically alter the flow of future events based entirely on our word, are critical turning points, giving us major control over the future direction of our lives. At such times, we put ourselves and our word on the line.

For the workplace, transformational proclamations are the most potent tools of change. Using transformational proclamations skillfully is crucial to leadership and innovation.

IN THE TRANSFORMING WORKPLACE, EVERY PARTICIPANT IS COMMITTED TO EVERY WORD AS SERIOUSLY AS IF SAYING "I DO" BEFORE THE ALTAR.

When you speak with a commitment to transform reality, you have nothing except your word—no evidence, no information, no representation of the existing world—just your word.

The Phoenix Agenda

Under the continuous transformation mindset, events and results in business organizations do not simply happen; they do not simply appear out of a set of circumstances handed to us as a finished script. Instead, they are created, brought forth, fashioned, formed, fitted, and shaped to craft a world of our own design. The key to this crafting lies in how we choose to express ourselves in language. Access to desirable change, therefore, is through communication—that is, forms of expression that we generate to impact the experience of other people. Transformational communication uses the four basic building blocks—reality probe, status report, action request, and transformational proclamation—strung together in various designed ways to product maximum effect.

Such well-designed forms of communication can be a means of generating organizational and business environments that honor rapid innovation, sensitivity to customers, transcendent opportunities for *all* employees, contribution to the world, and sustainable prosperity. The Phoenix Agenda is a 12-faceted framework for designing empowering workplace communications. But please remember that we have adopted a different mindset with respect to communication itself. Communications based on The Phoenix Agenda do not communicate *about* the workplace. Rather, such communications shape, alter, and transform the workplace. Indeed, they actually *become* the workplace.

THE PHOENIX AGENDA

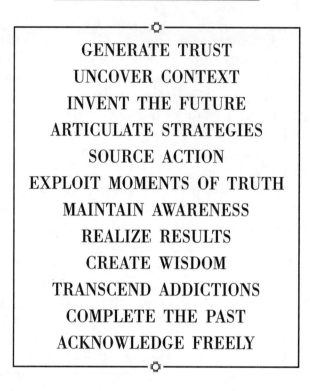

GENERATE TRUST
UNCOVER CONTEXT
INVENT THE FUTURE
ARTICULATE STRATEGIES
SOURCE ACTION
EXPLOIT MOMENTS OF TRUTH
MAINTAIN AWARENESS
REALIZE RESULTS
CREATE WISDOM
TRANSCEND ADDICTIONS
COMPLETE THE PAST
ACKNOWLEDGE FREELY

Projects at work will be productive, satisfying, and successful to the extent that all 12 ways of communicating are strongly developed in the workplace. Having all positive forms of communicating masterfully present and balanced is a significant step toward a great day at work, one day at a time, for everyone. Each facet of communication can be richly expanded, learned, practiced, and developed. We can master project participation and leadership by internalizing the empowering communications to the point where every action, every utterance, every contribution at meetings, every memo, and every report embodies all 12 ways of communicating in a positive rather than negative way.

SAMPLE USE OF THE AGENDA

Suppose that you absolutely must arrange a meeting with someone far removed from you in the organization, someone whom, by the conventional rules, it would take months of scheduling and re-scheduling to see. Using The Phoenix Agenda as a design aid, you could determine what form and content of communication would most effectively produce a meeting quickly. The following business note, designed in this way, successfully produced an "impossible" meeting:

To: Bob Bellman, Vice President

From: John Whiteside

Re: Meeting about new markets requested with you on March 31

Dear Bob,

Congratulations on your well-deserved appointment to vice president. All of us learned from watching you. Now we might be able to apply what you have learned to the challenge of a new market—we could double the projected profits. My people and I have prepared a plan, code named Omega, that calls out a honed strategy, allows for rewards for all involved, and has taken into account what is likely to go wrong. We're ready for your advice and counsel.

May we meet with you at 10:00 A.M. next Friday, March 31, to present this? The research people and the presentation specialists have put their heads together to create something slick that you'll enjoy seeing. Russ Farnsworth can give you a 30-second endorsement and preview, if you'd like. After the presentation, we'd like to take you out to lunch to celebrate your latest achievement.

Best personal regards,

All 12 facets in The Phoenix Agenda are used in designing this letter. In some of the sentences, three are invoked. As any letter, this one is written against a particular context, history, and setting. It would not be word-for-word appropriate in any other setting. However, you can use the facets in any situation to design any communication in a way that is appropriate, harmonious, and effective. This letter is written for a culture where electronic mail is in widespread use. It is addressed to a busy executive whose professional orientation is focused on the next action to be taken. Due to the press of his responsibilities, it is difficult to see this man, especially at short notice. Hence, the requested action is given in the header and repeated in an easy-to-find place in the text. Furthermore, the letter is designed to be less than one display screen in length as a convenience to the reader. The letter contains personal acknowledgment, the possibility of results, an indication that careful planning has been done, and a specific request for action, including a date. In the culture for which this was written, personal acknowledgment is rare. Acknowledgment, however, is essential to teamwork and trust. Sincere acknowledgment also tells the truth (notice that the acknowledgment in the letter refers to a specific, public, and verifiable achievement).

IMPLEMENTING THE AGENDA

The facets in The Phoenix Agenda are like design elements. The creative part comes in applying them to particular situations. By analogy, landscape architecture uses qualities such as line, form, contrast, balance, appearance, color over the changing seasons, and viability of the chosen plant material in the local climate. Knowing these does not design a landscape, but does provide an essential starting point of things to consider in the design. The facets identified in The Phoenix Agenda play a similar role in the design of productive and impactful communications.

The three chapters that follow present the 12 facets with examples for designing your communications. Descriptions also include organizational symptoms that you are likely to encounter when a facet is present or missing in any situation. For easy reference, these are summarized in a table at the end of the section for each facet.

Language for Transforming Reality

Use the table to help you identify whether the facet is missing or present in your workplace by comparing your situation to the descriptions of workplace climates in the table. For example, if you notice that the people around you anger easily and prefer to isolate themselves when working, look in each table for the type of work climate that reflects those characteristics. What may be missing is trust or acknowledgment. In the absence of these facets, the workplace lacks cooperation and is hostile; people refuse to talk and tend to isolate themselves in their work. To explore the possibilities of how you might change your work environment, use the list of practical strategies at the bottom of the table for ideas. Also notice which of the four elements of grammar are most impactful for creating a great place to work. These are provided in the table along with positive and negative examples of expressions.

The presence of all the facets, in an appropriate and balanced way, accompanies the peak work experience pointed to by Peter Senge[2] —a vibrant, vital, productive, growing, nurturing, learning organization hallmarked by profitability, service to customers, and the well-being of its employees. Each of the 12 facets is critical because its absence, or its presence in a negative form, will erode the enterprise. All facets must be present for meaningful organizational prosperity that lasts.

How to Launch and Sustain Projects at Work

Loose, dispersed organizations depend on people liking and trusting each other.

—Charles Handy, business author and teacher

1. Generate Trust

THE HIGH COST OF NOT TRUSTING

In the late 1980s, a major corporation launches a multi-million-dollar project—the largest single software effort the company has ever undertaken. The purpose of the project is to remake entirely the look and feel of the company's software from the older, traditional typed command approach into a modern, mouse-and-windows-based interface. The project involves contributions from diverse business groups in the company across continents worldwide. Two groups in particular are critical. One, from New England, is the company's premier software development organization, a group of great pride and achievement, with a long history of aggressive schedules and profitability. The other, from California, consists of brilliant researchers and inventors with an international reputation for their expertise and creativity in designing software for the new age.

Almost from the beginning, the interaction between these two groups is difficult. The principals from each group fly to a common meeting place and find themselves without introductions in a room together. Tempers flair and pencils are broken and hurled in anger within the first five minutes of the first meeting. Later, a team member asks the head engineer of the New England group if he would be willing to trust the California researchers.

No! Trust has to be earned. When these people learn to deliver on schedule and deliver their requirements in our standard format, then I'll trust them,

he exclaims.

For their part, the California people feel unappreciated and are convinced that the New Englanders do not understand and will not accept the power and brilliance of their inventions. This mutual mistrust and mutual lack of appreciation permeates the entire project, which consequently develops many of the aspects of a competition between the two groups rather than the necessary cooperation. The net result is that the project is delayed by at least 18 months. The final suite of products has a level of customer-perceived quality far below what it could have been and far below what the competitive state of the art demands. In time, the California researchers all leave the company and the project is not profitable. The New England group, what remains of it, goes on to witness declining market share and declining influence of their once proud organization.

How to Launch and Sustain Projects at Work

All of the people involved have a high degree of talent, credentials, track record, integrity, desire to succeed, preparation, and skill. No one acts in bad faith. However, what is missing is trust. No one takes the need for this into account, no one designs or crafts it as a quality or presence into the project. Trust is simply missing. What is present is distrust. The East Coast and the West Coast people have different sets of expectations from the outset. They express these expectations as absolutes:

Trust has to be earned.

and

Those people can't appreciate what we are doing for them,

as statements of fact about their respective fixed assumptions about trust, rather than as reality probes or questions, open to change and design. Nowhere in the project is the state of trust generated— expressed as a design element and carried forth through communication.

All kinds of things can be done to establish trust and nurture it throughout a project, some of them quite simply. For example, a series of dinners or other social events can be arranged prior to the crucial first business meeting. Someone can step forward, or be appointed, as responsible for monitoring and highlighting the manifestations of trust itself as an essential project quality. What is missing is not good will, desire for success, or the best of intentions. Rather, what is missing is trust itself as a necessary aspect of working together, and one that is amenable to creation and design.

WHAT TRUST GENERATES

A division of Intel runs operations across the Pacific. Its people in Malaysia possess backgrounds that include a multiplicity of cultures—Chinese, Indian, Malaysian, and American. This group is linked to an organization in the southwestern part of the United States. Obstacles to smooth functioning include a nine-hour time zone shift, a distance of 12,000 miles, and cultural and religious differences. Yet, the division is highly successful and profitable. In one meeting, a group of managers is discussing the role of trust:

We have to trust each other, we have no choice.

One participant, a Muslim, inspires the group by explaining,

I am hesitant to bring religion into our business discussions, and I don't intend to impose my views, but in my religion, it is a sin to mistrust others. So I trust all of you, even if I don't know you yet.

This man states the essence of trust. Trust at its core is a state of being, a state of possibility—not a result on a tally sheet.

TRUST IS GENERATED IN THE ACT OF PROCLAIMING IT AND IS
NOT SOMETHING TO BE BASED ON EVIDENCE.

Whenever people mistrust each other, it is possible for them to achieve together only whatever is allowed within the framework of their mutual mistrust. Similarly, the greater the degree of trust, the wider the scope of the project that can be attempted and the greater will be the magnitude of the future that can be created.

ONE HUNDRED PERCENT TRUST IS REQUIRED FOR
100 PERCENT SUCCESS.

GENERATE TRUST BY PROCLAIMING IT

It is possible to treat trust as a gift; something offered freely without expectation of reward. Furthermore, it is possible to offer trust even in the face of evidence to the contrary. This is trust viewed from the transformation mindset. From the authoritarian mindset, by contrast, trust is considered as a property, a result. Under the authoritarian cause and effect view, people search for evidence for trust, granting it only when the evidence is favorable, and withholding it when the evidence is missing or neutral.

Under the transformation mindset, generating trust in yourself for someone else is amazingly simple. You simply say it and then honor your word.

> TO GENERATE TRUST POWERFULLY, PROCLAIM IT PUBLICLY AND
> THEN ACT IN A WAY CONSISTENT WITH WHAT YOU HAVE SAID.

This requires no evidence, no decision, no weighing of pros and cons, and no interpretation. It simply requires saying it. The state of trust is made possible in the committed saying of the words

I trust you.

It may not seem that simple when you are standing in front of a microphone facing an unfriendly audience. It may not seem that simple when the person or group in question is interpreted by you to be untrustworthy and to have acted irresponsibly. But that is how it is done. In the example of the East and West Coast software teams, uttering those words in an appropriate and powerful way could have created an entirely different outcome for that project.

The cost of mistrust is far too great for any business to absorb in a world where cooperation and creative interdependency of people provide the competitive edge that companies need to survive. Without trust, cooperation and high-performance teamwork will always be missing. Without trust, the workplace cannot be healthy, productive, and rewarding.

> IT ALL BEGINS AND ENDS WITH TRUST.

VIOLATED TRUST

Why then, if trust is critical to high productivity and a healthful workplace, is it so pervasively missing in our work? What happens at work on a day-to-day basis that constantly undermines our abilities to generate trust openly and willingly?

Can you think of an experience in which you found it difficult or even impossible to trust someone with whom you were expected to work closely? Can you remember a circumstance when in trusting what someone told you, you made a fool of yourself or lost an opportunity? Such experiences are not easy to forget. They breed mistrust and a cautious temperament. It is therefore not difficult to understand how most mistrust can result from violated expectations and assumptions.

Assumptions are tightly integrated into how we act and what we say, so much so that we rarely examine the expectations that they generate or communicate them clearly to others. As the first example in this section showed, when expectations are not clearly communicated, the consequences are devastating. The East Coast team had expectations for schedule delivery and process control that did not match the requirements of the West Coast team for design quality. Each team expected that they would control the project and be the primary center of development. The West Coast team expected that their design work would dominate the schedule. When both sets of expectations were not met, each refused to compromise. The result was that together they violated a third set of expectations, those held by their company, which expected a fully collaborative effort that would result in millions of dollars in revenue.

Every day you live, you are setting expectations that potentially can be violated. That you trust and expect others to return your trust is an expectation that has the possibility of being violated. So why are we so angry when it happens? Ironically, it is the very fear of violation that feeds and contributes to our reluctance to speak our expectations clearly, that keeps us from putting them out there where everyone else can see them and know them. Realize that every word you speak is an opportunity to tell others what your expectations are, whether it is the simple expectation to be heard, to be respected for what you say, or to be given what you request. When you do not communicate your expectations clearly and precisely, you set the stage for disappointment and mistrust. You become as responsible for the anger, shame, and hurt that may result as the person who violated what you thought to be mutual trust.

A question often asked is:

If you give trust to someone and that person then fails you or uses that trust to deceive you, do you continue to trust them?

In actuality, this question is not about trust, but about risk. Are you willing to risk having your expectations violated again? If the person who failed you is your child, is there any doubt that you will give them another chance? So what is the difference between the way you trust your child and the way you trust at work? Do you have less at stake for the consequences of your work than you have for the growth and well-being of your child, spouse, or loved one?

COMMUNICATIONS TO GENERATE TRUST	
Intent:	Create a foundation for accomplishment.
Appropriate grammar:	*Transformational proclamation:* "I trust you."
Work climate when trust is present:	Strong relatedness, rapport, dependability, extensive support, integrity.
Inappropriate grammar:	*Reality probe:* "Why should I trust you?" *Status report:* "They're untrustworthy."
Work climate when trust is absent:	Suspicion, hostility, lack of cooperation, organizational collapse.
Practical strategies to generate trust:	Create close relationships with co-workers, be consistent and dependable, act in integrity with what you say, trust others.

Violation of trust is a painful experience. The pain alone prevents us from easily dismissing it as an accident or mistake. So how do you alter the communication or situation that generated the violation? Examine the context for the violation closely. Is it possible that you did not communicate the plan or strategy clearly and precisely? Perhaps you asked too much of people without providing the training or support they needed to do quality work? Or they may not have been willing to do it "your way" and had ideas of their own. Did you empower them to find their own solutions or did you dictate strategies that did not make sense to them? A breakdown could have occurred at any point in the communication. It is important to realize, however, that it can also be repaired after it is found.

To avoid the pain of violated trust, state your expectations openly and as clearly as possible, remaining in 100 percent support of each person for whom you set these expectations. Most of all, keep expectations and trust distinct and separate from each other. Do not weigh how much trust you give someone on the basis of how much risk you are willing to take for their meeting or failing your expectations. When you say you trust someone, say it in a way that communicates:

I trust you even in the face of violated expectations!

2. Uncover Context

GENERATE TRUST
○ UNCOVER CONTEXT ○
INVENT THE FUTURE
ARTICULATE STRATEGIES
SOURCE ACTION
EXPLOIT MOMENTS OF TRUTH
MAINTAIN AWARENESS
REALIZE RESULTS
CREATE WISDOM
TRANSCEND ADDICTIONS
COMPLETE THE PAST
ACKNOWLEDGE FREELY

HIDDEN ASSUMPTIONS

All of us operate under hidden assumptions. Even with 100 percent trust in our co-workers, these hidden assumptions twist projects in predominantly negative ways. Much of the power of the transformational workplace mindset lies in surfacing and then redesigning assumptions to support the task at hand.

One useful strategy to unearth the existing context and the hidden assumptions that hold it in place is simply to ask,

Why is that important?

whenever an issue is raised. This rapidly leads to a discussion about the underlying assumptions that lock in the current context.

For example, a manufacturing group is attempting the impossible task of building and shipping a finished product in one year. The norm for the organization is much longer. At the kickoff meeting, one of the section leaders explains why he is reluctant to take on such a risky endeavor.

Because we might fail,

he says. The group's manager asks repeatedly,

So what! Why is that important?

After discussion, it emerges that the section leader's core reluctance is not at all related to the manufacturing and distribution considerations of the project. Nor has his core reason anything to do with being afraid of hard work, for this man is a prodigious worker. His core concern is that he remain able to meet his mortgage payments should the project fail. The team members assure him that whenever he wants, they will hold a brainstorming session and generate a list of feasible ways in which he can meet his mortgage payments, none of which would depend upon the success or failure of the current project. This core concern addressed, he and the team go on (with the help of a lot more coaching and with a tremendous effort on their part) to an astonishing success in shipping their product in a fraction of the time usually taken for such efforts.

By uncovering their section leader's basic concern and addressing it, the group members empowered him to devote his full efforts to the project.

THE POLITICS OF CONTEXT

Shifting the context can be a political act in that it forces reassessment of the existing distribution of power and prestige. Consider the case of a massive software effort to create a new look and feel for hundreds of software products. Such a shift involves moving from the traditional computer interface in which users type mathlike coded commands to a graphical interface in which users point to pictures on the computer screen to indicate their intentions. The command interface is rooted in formal logic, mathematical expressions, and abstract representations. The graphical interface is more free flowing, more physical, more visual, and requires a developer to have artistic and visual design aptitude.

Over the years, an elaborate political, status, and reward system grows up around the formalistic school of software interface design that the old style demands. Suddenly, with more artistically designed interfaces required, the new style begins to threaten the older established system. The consequences are both interesting and disheartening to watch. Engineers who were "heroes" in the old style of design suddenly find themselves in a new context. Other contributors, such as technical writers and marketing people who were not as highly regarded in the past, suddenly blossom as they discover a new context in which to express their previously hidden creativity. Naturally, the established engineers take a dim view of this.

We've got to protect the purity of engineering!

becomes the rationale; new people who are flowering in the new context are, if not actively discouraged, at least told in subtle ways that their contributions are not sufficient basis for promotion. Predictably, the best of these people leave the company, and the transition to a modern and competitive style of interface is never fully realized.

The people involved on both sides are talented and honestly trying to do what they believe is best. Neither side can succeed without understanding and support from the other. Each shares a responsibility in making the shift happen. What is missing is an appreciation of the magnitude of change that can accompany a context shift. In general, people underestimate the constraints imposed by the political and reward systems of an organization. Maintaining positions of power and status too frequently take precedent.

> ASK WHAT ASPECTS OF YOUR ORGANIZATION ARE KEPT HIDDEN
> AND NOT OPENLY SPOKEN ABOUT. CAN ANY OF THESE BE
> SHIFTED TO ALLOW A LEVEL OF SUCCESS THAT IS CURRENTLY
> UNIMAGINABLE?

THE POWER OF A QUESTION

One practical strategy to raise context issues is to phrase concerns not as statements, but as questions. Questions create openings and invite reflection and inquiry, whereas statements tend to invite retort and opposition. For example, management is trying to shift the orientation of a creative design department to include business and profit issues as well as creative issues. Management attends a two-hour review of the merits of a proposed new marketing campaign. The material is engaging and well presented with abundant detail. However, no mention is made of prospective customers, pricing, or other profit and business-oriented issues. At the end of the meeting, the presenter asks,

> *Well, that's it. Is it worth the $2.5 million and two years of effort we are proposing?*

The visiting manager says,

> *Why are we making a business decision in the context of a creative review?*

There is a stunned silence. Later, the team organizes a program of extensive customer visits and market surveys, prepares a business and profit plan, and substantially changes the design content of the campaign as a result. The campaign succeeds.

When in doubt, ask a question.

THE POWER OF CONTEXT

David Stone, former vice president of software at Digital and later president of AT&T Network Systems, says,

> *The only unrecoverable error on a project is made in the first 15 minutes. That error is choosing the wrong context for the project.*

Assuring a powerful context for a project requires revealing hidden assumptions, through open and respectful questioning, and then either finding a new context or redesigning the existing one so that the project moves forward against a background conducive to its success.

✿ 110 ✿

How to Launch and Sustain Projects at Work

Intent:	Reveal the hidden assumptions that influence a project or goal.
Appropriate grammar:	*Reality probe:* "What is the core competency and philosophy of this organization?"
	Action request: "I request that everyone actively participate in this meeting and use this time as an opportunity to ask questions and explore a "next" step."
	Transformational proclamation: "The more we can learn from one another, the more productive we can be as a team."
Work climate when context is uncovered:	Rapid learning, strong customer awareness, new market opportunities, excitement, challenge, and discovery.
Inappropriate grammar:	*Status report:* "The market has changed."
	Action request: "Stop asking so many questions and get on with what you are doing."
Work climate when context is hidden:	Business as usual, humdrum and predictable, loss of customer's perspective, lost opportunities.
Practical strategies to uncover context:	Ask, encourage, and welcome questions, especially "off the wall" ones.

3. Invent the Future

GENERATE TRUST
UNCOVER CONTEXT
✿ **INVENT THE FUTURE** ✿
ARTICULATE STRATEGIES
SOURCE ACTION
EXPLOIT MOMENTS OF TRUTH
MAINTAIN AWARENESS
REALIZE RESULTS
CREATE WISDOM
TRANSCEND ADDICTIONS
COMPLETE THE PAST
ACKNOWLEDGE FREELY

VISION

A workplace without a future is a sad and depressing environment. Even with trust present and context understood and shaped to advantage, a workplace needs a bright future to be engaging, fulfilling, and productive. Having a bright future to look forward to feels great. Having a murky, uncertain, or dismal future feels terrible.

A future is communicated by a vision—a statement of an attractive state of affairs set forth as a possibility that has not yet come to pass, such as:

A WORLD WHERE EVERYONE IS NOURISHED

or

SHOEMAKER TO THE WORLD

or

A GREAT DAY AT WORK, ONE DAY AT A TIME, FOR EVERYONE.

Visions such as these capture the essence of an organization's purpose. These particular visions also express a desire to contribute to others. Some visions, while they point to a desirable state of affairs, lack a quality of contribution to other people. For example, the vision statements

GENERATE CASH FOREVER

or

RECOGNIZED WORLD-CLASS LEADER IN FIBER OPTICS

or

100 PERCENT MARKET CONTROL OF PIZZA FRANCHISES
IN OUR REGION,

while still powerful, are weak in their ability to attract others. The risk is that people outside of the organization will perceive such visions as self-serving and mercenary.

Sometimes, companies and even countries have no vision at all. When asked what the company vision is, one CEO of a multi-billion-dollar company says,

I have no idea.

Within two years, this company's board asks for the CEO's resignation. Shortly thereafter, 30 percent of the workforce is laid off. A United States president is sent packing by the electorate when he acknowledges his discomfort with "the vision thing."

A LEADER'S MOST CRITICAL JOB IS THE ARTICULATION
OF A VISION.

TRANSFORMING THE IMPOSSIBLE INTO THE POSSIBLE

To say that a project has a future means that the project is directed at a possibility that has the promise of becoming a result. Because it is not yet a result, there is no evidence whatsoever that it will ever be realized. A true future is not predictable and is therefore unknown and exciting. Once the future is assured, it becomes future viewed as though it were already past, predictable and dull, without the power to call people to greatness.

What is it that over time takes a project from being unimaginable to being imaginable, from being impossible to being possible, from being probable to being accomplished? Somewhere along the line suggested by the string of words in the Impossible to Possible table shown below, a shift occurs. Probably between being impossible and being possible, a state changes and a change in the quality of the project is experienced. What is halfway between impossibility and possibility in the generation of a project or an idea? Where is the boundary crossed between chimerical and down-to-earth? Is it something external that happens? Or could it be a shift, a change of mind, a change of perspective, and a change of mindset? What is the difference between impossible and seemingly impossible? Is the seemingly impossible the same as possible? Are seemingly impossible and seemingly possible the same thing? Could it be that all seeming possibilities were once seeming impossibilities to which something happened? What happened?

Time and again in business, the impossible becomes possible. Entrepreneurs turn an impossible dream into a profitable business that provides employment, delivers valuable products and services, and contributes to the economy. In the process, they confound all early critics, overcome objections of conservative bankers and critical observers, and succeed. A research team in a bureaucratic company develops a profitable product in one year instead of the usual four years. Before the accomplishment, the team leader could not get an appointment with her manager to present the vision and strategy for making this happen. Now her manager listens carefully to everything she says. Things that were previously considered impossible now appear eminently within reach.

What is the circumstance that accounts for the shift from impossibility to possibility?

How to Launch and Sustain Projects at Work

Unimaginable	Microsoft, 1960	Your dream, today
IMPOSSIBLE		
UNREAL		
CHIMERICAL		
FANTASTIC		
IMAGINABLE		
VISUALIZED		
POSSIBLE		
FEASIBLE		
PROBABLE		
PRACTICAL		
ACTIONABLE		
UNDERWAY	↓	↓
ACCOMPLISHED	Microsoft, 1993	Your dream?

IN EXTRAORDINARY ACHIEVEMENTS, SOMEONE ALWAYS BELIEVES IN
THE POSSIBILITY OF THE IMPOSSIBLE AND MAINTAINS THIS BELIEF IN
THE FACE OF CONTRARY EVIDENCE, IN THE FACE OF PRESSURE, AND
EVEN IN THE FACE OF HUMILIATION AND RIDICULE.

Often when an entrepreneur or visionary first announces an idea or plan, they are met with skepticism and occasionally vicious cynicism:

If you go out on your own, you'll starve.

Don't rock the corporate boat.

You? A success in your own right? Don't make me laugh!

Computers in people's homes? That's absurd!

In summary, anyone who is committed to the possibility of a new future must hold to that commitment even in the face of pressure to abandon it. For these people, the key to the future is in speaking it and then holding true to what they say.

CYNICISM DESTROYS THE FUTURE

Whenever you denigrate, criticize, or tear down an idea, be very clear about what you are doing. You may feel that you are acting responsibly by helping another person see an error. But consider that you also might be destroying a possible future. There is no guaranteed way to tell which beforehand.

PROCLAIMED FUTURES NEVER HAVE PROOF BEFORE THE FACT OF THEIR ACHIEVEMENT.

Proclaimed, visionary futures can seem reasonable or unreasonable under the framework provided by the current context, climate of belief, workplace mindset, and assumptional framework into which they are spoken. Of course, if the context shifts, then the possibilities shift also.

Let's consider the example of new management desperately trying to turn a business around. From the outset, they meet great cynicism and resistance from the employees. One cynic, when asked why he is always saying that the new programs will not work, responds,

Oh, I'm a professional cynic. It's my job to point out the flaws, not to fix them.

Your ability to effectively generate new possibilities for your workplace depends on the climate and mood that you yourself create through what you say. Killing off your own future and those of the people around you is easy. Simply speak critically at every turn, criticize and belittle other people's ideas, and decide in your own

How to Launch and Sustain Projects at Work

	COMMUNICATIONS TO INVENT THE FUTURE
Intent:	State the future in a way that is attractive and empowering to others.
Appropriate grammar:	*Transformational proclamation:* "We will promote in our company a pride of recognition for quality and productivity that keeps us on the competitive edge and increases profits."
Work climate when future is invented:	Commitment, new possibilities, sense of mission and purpose, freedom to invent and plan, leadership.
Inappropriate grammar:	*Reality probe:* "I wonder what the future will bring?"
	Status report: "People will never use a computer in their home."
	Action request: "Stop working on anything that won't help this quarter's bottom line."
Work climate when future is missing:	Lack of vision, hopelessness, discouragement, purposeless and mindless activity, cynicism and skepticism.
Practical strategies to invent the future:	Brainstorm, envision the future, remain open to new ideas, question basic assumptions.

mind, once and for all, that you see no possibility that things could be any better than the way they are. Adopt a rigid set of assumptions about the way the world is and never question them. Become cynical.

Alternatively, you could be a herald for the possibility of a future different from today, perhaps radically different.

YOU COULD ENCOURAGE NEW IDEAS AND NEW THINKING, AND
EVEN REWARD PEOPLE FOR THEM.

You could adopt the position that, at any given moment, an infinite number of actions and futures are possible, most of which are simply not accessible within the framework provided by your current assumptions, viewpoints, and mindsets.

Without a future, a vision, a prospect, there is really no point to business and to work. Are you making a difference by contributing daily to the business that provides your livelihood, or are you effectively destroying the business, and thus your own future, by speaking cynically and destructively in your comments?

If the human world is fixed and rigid, then cynicism may indeed be the best approach to living. If the human world is malleable, then an open, exploratory view may be best. What if the world is actually created by your stating your view, rather than your view being a spoken response to the world?

4. Articulate Strategies

GENERATE TRUST
UNCOVER CONTEXT
INVENT THE FUTURE
✪ ARTICULATE STRATEGIES ✪
SOURCE ACTION
EXPLOIT MOMENTS OF TRUTH
MAINTAIN AWARENESS
REALIZE RESULTS
CREATE WISDOM
TRANSCEND ADDICTIONS
COMPLETE THE PAST
ACKNOWLEDGE FREELY

SEPARATE STRATEGY FROM VISION

Communications that articulate strategy naturally follow communications to invent the future. However, the two types of communications need to be sharply differentiated. When communications about future and strategy are mixed, a team can feel hopelessly stuck without a path forward. Finding a way to move forward in such a situation may be merely recognizing the degree to which statements about the future are being interpreted as strategy by those around us.

An example of this is the product team that needs to reduce its scheduled delivery time by six weeks but in spite of intense management pressure has no idea how to do this. In the hopes of resolving the problem, they invite a consultant to attend their planning meeting. After listening for a few minutes, it is clear to the consultant that the group's communications for the future and for strategy are not working. The meeting goes approximately as follows:

CONSULTANT: Does anyone have any ideas about what we might do to pull the schedule in?

MARIE: Well, what if we didn't do regression testing? That would free up one afternoon per week of everyone's time.

TOM: No, we can't do that—quality will suffer.

CONSULTANT: Let's try to collect all the ideas we can without criticizing them.

CHARLES: What if we didn't hold the Wednesday staff meeting for a while?

STEVE: That's a terrible idea! We need that to communicate!

CONSULTANT: Tell you what. Let's make our goal for the next 30 minutes to come up with all the ideas we can about pulling the schedule in. Our goal is to fill the whiteboard with ideas. To do this, we'll hold off all criticism of each other's ideas for at least 30 minutes.

(Silence, then finally)

MARIE: We don't know how to do that. We always rip each other's ideas to shreds.

CONSULTANT: Okay, you can go back to doing that in 30 minutes. For now, just try to generate as many ideas as possible.

Slowly at first, then with increasing speed and enthusiasm, the group grasps the idea of creative brainstorming. At the end of 45 minutes, they ask for more time and generate more than 60 ideas about what might be done. The consultant says they can now go back to criticizing and leaves the room. Later, she hears that the meeting has gone on for two more hours and that the team has hammered out a workable plan for pulling in the schedule. They implement the plan, and it works.

Weeks later, the team's technical leader, the supervisor, and the manager call the consultant back and thank her for "breaking the logjam." She is invited to a celebration lunch marking the successful release of the version of the product. This is a great honor, as outsiders are not normally invited to such celebrations in this corporate culture. At $100,000 per year loaded cost per engineer, and a team of 10 engineers, with a five-to-one revenue markup expected over production costs, this breaking of the logjam, and the events that follow, are worth an estimated $500,000 in increased revenues over costs to the company.

RAISING AND HANDLING OBJECTIONS CONSTRUCTIVELY

Communications about strategy are directed at designing helpful and empowering plans to meet an objective. Devising strategies means exploring reasons for reluctance and hesitation and meeting them through planned appropriate actions. Most of traditional management practice and theory is directed at this issue.

Communications to articulate strategy depend upon the raising of objections within the framework of currently perceived reality and the devising of ways around those objections. The idea behind communications to create a new future is to raise, as possibilities, various futures for which there is little or no apparent evidence. Nothing destroys an unrealized future, a possibility, faster than assessments about its impossibility. Yet, speculative futures, possible things to do, are the raw material of innovation. By collapsing the possible and the practical we literally insure a future that is grounded in the present and that cannot transcend it, except by chance. By simply allowing for communication about speculative, even fanciful, futures, we widen the field of possibility. We probably also expose some of the unstated assumptions that leave us unable to move forward.

Future, in this sense, is never a mechanical extrapolation of the past. Instead, it calls for a quantum jump, a leap of faith, a search for a new context that makes a desirable new future possible. Strategy, by contrast, is grounded in the here and now and takes practical considerations into account.

IT IS A PROFOUND TRAGEDY FOR HUMANITY THAT MOST OF US, MOST OF THE TIME, RESPOND TO NEW IDEAS AND SUGGESTIONS IN A NEGATIVE WAY.

For those of us who are more comfortable focusing on the positive and the possible, negativism is distressing. It is helpful to treat the negative comments, not as attacks or criticisms, but rather as requirements that need to be addressed by the strategy, and to interpret criticisms as basically well-intended even when they are not crafted in an attractive and empowering way. For example, if someone says your idea is no good, ask why, and then why again when they answer. Done politely, this will reveal not only people's objections, but also clues and new possibilities as to ways those objections can be met and still have the project succeed.

Since criticism is heard by many people as invalidation, when criticizing someone else, it can be helpful to combine the criticism with acknowledgment and an offer of help. For example, instead of saying,

That's a terrible idea. It'll never work,

you might instead say,

I appreciate your vision and support the project you are trying to move forward. I'd like to help. It seems to me that if you could overcome problem X in your plans, you'd have a better chance of success. I even have some ideas about where you might look for a solution.

In this example, you have added acknowledgment to the communication for articulating strategy, thus making it far more likely that your concern will be heard and acted upon. Try something like this at the next meeting at which you review someone else's proposal and see what happens.

AUTHORITARIAN AND TRANSFORMATIONAL STRATEGIES

Traditional management practices are excellent at defining detailed strategies. Strategies provide direction, certainty, orderly procedures, and predictability. These attributes are highly valued in the authoritarian mindset. There are numerous, widely used tools and techniques for devising authoritarian strategies. Management by objectives, management by planning, impact analysis, and strategic planning are a few of the better-known approaches.

Traditional project planning is a highly refined discipline. It boasts mathematical theory, a large body of history and practical experience, and an impressive set of tools. One such tool, a software program called MACproject, allows managers to plan projects down to the finest detail using a computer simulation. Using it, managers enter all of the tasks and subtasks necessary to complete their project, including how long each subtask takes, which subtasks are dependent upon others, and how much money and equipment are required. You can even include allowance for holidays, people getting sick, turnover in personnel, and the estimated productivity of individual team members.

In its introductory manual, MACproject includes a sample exercise: organizing a barbecue. You specify to the software all of the tasks and subtasks everyone needs to accomplish in order for the barbecue to be ready at 7:00 P.M. Your wife, for example, must go to the store to pick up salad materials, drinks, and dessert. You go to the specialty meat market to select steaks. You need to phone ahead to your teenage son to light the coals by a certain time. Your teenager is unreliable, so you also call the neighbor to check that the coals have, in fact, been lit according to the plan.

The software program takes all of this information and prepares a detailed strategy showing exactly what everyone has to do and by when in order to have the barbecue ready in time. Some tasks are flexible, but other tasks, if late, jeopardize the whole undertaking. For example, if your son forgets to light the coals, dinner will be late.

The problem is that in the real world, plans always go awry and require modification, especially in, as now, rapidly changing times. Suppose, for example, that five extra guests show up for the barbecue at the last minute, or one of the guests turns out unexpectedly to be a vegetarian. In addition, focusing on the specific steps to prepare the barbecue distracts from transformational solutions that do not require a barbecue at all, such as going out to dinner or going over to a friend's house.

Authoritarian strategies seek to pin down every last detail about a project: the exact nature and order of steps, resources required, and precise deliverables. These strategies virtually never work out exactly according to plan. In one large software development group at Digital, a three-year survey reveals that not one single product out of hundreds was ever built on schedule and according to plan, despite prodigious management efforts at planning.

Transformational strategies look quite different. They involve defining and committing to a goal but leave maximum flexibility as to the means. Such strategies are common in entrepreneurial ventures, for example. The business plan may call for delivering $1 million worth of services in the first year of operation but does not specify exactly which services, in which order, and to which clients. Those details are generated day to day, as events unfold.

An analogy between authoritarian and transformational strategies can be found in the European and Micronesian approaches to navigation. The European navigator starts with a detailed plan to reach the destination and knows, with high accuracy, where the ship is supposed to be, and where it actually is, at any moment in the voyage. The Micronesian navigator likewise knows where he is

COMMUNICATIONS TO ARTICULATE STRATEGIES

Intent:	Lay out the steps to the future.
Appropriate grammar:	*Reality probe:* "What can we do to prepare the market?"
	Status report: "Our research shows the market is not currently ready for our product, so . . ."
	Action request: "I request, and you can say no, that you plan a path forward for the company that will give us recognition as the number-one leader in our industry by the year 1995."
Work climate when you articulate strategies:	Commitment, new possibilities, sense of mission and purpose, path forward, purpose, and vision.
Inappropriate grammar:	*Action request:* "You say you can do $10 million? I want $15 million or you're fired!"
	Transformational proclamation: "This project is a terrible idea. What idiot thought this up?"
Work climate when you have no strategy:	Lack of direction and vision, slow demoralization and paralysis, mistakes, rework, and poor quality.
Practical steps to articulate strategy:	Separate strategizing from brainstorming, raise objections respectfully, be open to others' ideas, use crises creatively, work together to overcome obstacles.

going, but not the detailed steps of how to get there. As each stage of the journey unfolds, he responds to tides, wind, and drift. He cannot at any moment say exactly where he is, but he always knows the next step to take in relation to his destination.

Authoritarian strategies, true to the mindset from which they derive, seek maximum control in advance by specifying actions to the smallest detail. Transformational strategies likewise have a goal in mind but are more flexible and trust the individual with greater creativity and freedom in the moment.

TRANSFORMATIONAL STRATEGIES PROCEED IN THE ABSENCE OF EXACT KNOWLEDGE ABOUT HOW TO REACH THE GOAL. TRANSFORMATIONAL STRATEGIES RELY INSTEAD ON THE POWER OF HUMAN COMMITMENT AND CREATIVITY IN THE FACE OF WORTHWHILE AND EMPOWERING OBJECTIVES.

6

How to Drive Action and Achieve Results

The business of America is business.

—Calvin Coolidge, President

5. Source Action

PRECISION REQUESTS

Elegant and powerful strategies accomplish nothing in themselves. Action is what gets results and moves projects forward. Unfortunately, everyday conversation often lacks the precision and focus to initiate powerful action. It is possible, however, to speak in a way that consistently leads to accomplishment and results. One powerful way to make something happen is to ask someone to do something. If you ask someone to write a report by Friday at 3:00 P.M., and the person accepts and delivers that report as asked, then by making your request, you initiate action and empower. To give your request maximum impact, it is important to speak your request with clarity and precision.

Requests that suggest action and requests that openly and forthrightly specify the action are vastly different. Compare the following two ways of speaking a request:

Let's do lunch sometime

versus

Will you meet me for lunch at 12:00 noon at Chez Fred's tomorrow?

The first statement is murky, like a car with a gummy carburetor that will not start. The second statement is clean and direct. It makes clear what is to be done, who is to do it, where it will happen, and when the action is to take place.

Asking someone to do something in this clear way is called making a precision request. In the grammar of transformational language, it is the most powerful form of an action request.

PRECISION REQUESTS ARE SPECIFIC ABOUT WHO, WHAT, WHEN, AND WHERE.

A precision promise is an agreement to complete a precision request, and in this sense is the mirror-image of that precision request. For example, the statement

Yes, I will meet you at Chez Fred's at 12:00 noon tomorrow for lunch

is a precision promise.

ONE HUNDRED PERCENT PRECISION REQUESTS ARE ESSENTIAL FOR 100 PERCENT WORKPLACE EFFICIENCY.

BUSINESS CONSEQUENCES OF VAGUE REQUESTS

Reluctance to use precision requests or to make precision promises is common in many business cultures. In business, people prefer to use vague requests and make statements that are ambiguous about an intended result. For example, a manager says,

Please handle the overdue equipment matter,

omitting any reference to time. The employee does nothing for two weeks. At their next meeting, the manager complains that the matter has not been handled:

I told you to do that two weeks ago! What's the problem?

Well, I was busy with other things.

Later, at review time, the manager criticizes the employee for not following up on instructions promptly.

Imagine, instead, the following interaction:

Tom, please handle the overdue equipment matter.

Sure, Anne. What would you like me to do?

Talk with Susan and get the latest invoices, then call the supplier and find out what's happening and when they plan to get it to us. Also, check with Jack to find out what his last date is before he runs into problems on the shop floor. It's Jack's priorities that are the most important here. And I need you to work closely with the supplier to get that equipment here fast.

Sure, I can do that. When would you like me to have this done by? Um, how about by five today?

That's tight, would tomorrow morning be okay?

Yes, thanks.

In this example, Tom asks the right questions to get the information he needs in order to turn an imprecise request into a precision request. Tom now knows what Anne meant when she asked him to "handle" the matter. The date is arrived at by negotiation so that both parties are now clear about what is to happen, how, and by when.

For whatever reason, there is enormous confusion and ambiguity in ordinary business conversations concerning explicit commitment to due dates for action items. People are reluctant to state due dates, yet become upset when, after making a request, nothing happens. Why is this surprising? How can someone complete a task on time if the assumed due date is never stated?

In a rapidly moving business world where profitability depends on creating and shipping quality products quickly, such ambiguity and confusion in everyday business conversation simply does not work. People have wildly different assumptions and expectations about due dates for action items when actual dates are not specified or negotiated. This creates inefficiencies and costly delays, especially in globally distributed corporations where communication is already hindered by time zone differences that require conversations outside of normal workday hours.

In one transnational company, where 60,000 employees are able to send electronic mail to each other each day, a survey showed that the range of time over which people expected to receive answers varied from immediately (within two minutes) to two months! Furthermore, people were astonished to learn about each other's unstated expectations. In this type of work environment, it is common for someone from sales to send a message to someone in engineering. The sales person expects, but does not say explicitly, that he requires an answer in 24 hours because he is trying to close a deal. The engineer, ignorant of the time pressures under which sales people operate, simply assumes that the answer can wait for two weeks. Over time, such misunderstandings, repeated over and over, create tension across the entire organization. People come to make statements such as

How to Drive Action and Achieve Results

Engineering is simply not responsive to sales' needs.

Sales people are pushy.

Multiplied over thousands of people, these stated sentiments can create such dissension in an organization that communication between sales and engineering grinds to a halt. The sales people never get the information they need and appear uninformed to the customers. The engineers are cut off from insights into customer needs that the sales people could be giving them. Customers stop buying, and engineering becomes increasingly isolated from customer issues.

These misunderstandings could be minimized by using precision requests:

I'm from sales, trying to close a deal with DuPont. It would really help if you could get me the following technical information within 24 hours. . . .

In the world of business as usual, the hierarchical structure of management actually makes it possible to make a request without really making requests. CEOs and company presidents are held in such regal status and authority that their every word carries immense influence and power. This is not a new phenomenon. Since ancient times, titles have been bestowed and used as badges of authority, enabling the bearer to influence, demand, and command without the need to make requests. But, like in the story of the emperor's new clothes, regal status has its drawbacks.

Take, for example, the visit of the general manager for European operations to one of his Paris offices. A man of considerable warmth with an outgoing personality, he prides himself on his close working relationship with his people and his ability to work with them as a peer. He does not anticipate, therefore, that a casual remark could be so completely misinterpreted. As he enters the main lobby of the Paris office, he happens to glance upward to the ceiling. It is an elaborately decorated ceiling in the style of the French high baroque and painted a greenish-yellow color that could not be mistaken for anything except bad taste. His next reaction, though casual, is immediate: "What an ugly ceiling!" That evening, a workman stays on late into the night to paint the entire ceiling white. The general manager is shocked when he walks in the next morning to find the ceiling freshly painted and the tired workman cleaning his brushes. He had no idea that his casual remark had been heard so absolutely as a request.

HANDLING OBJECTIONS TO DIRECT REQUESTS

Precision requests are the essence of productive cooperative enterprise, the lifeblood of business. As a manager or individual contributor, your impact and effectiveness at work is directly correlated with the number of precision requests you generate. Yet, in the culture of everyday business, people are confused and reluctant to make requests. The reasons people give for not making precision requests are interesting. They include:

- It's rude.
- The person might say no.
- The person is too busy anyway.
- They should know what I want without my having to ask for it.

Requests can be designed so as not to raise these objections and nonetheless be clear. For example, some people might consider the statement

I request this report by five o'clock

to be rude. Its social interpretation depends on many contextual factors, such as the relative authority status of the people involved, the urgency of the report, workload, and other considerations. The English language is, fortunately, rich with synonyms for the formal term "request" that can be used in designing questions appropriate to any situation. A few of these are:

How to Drive Action and Achieve Results

Urge	Take care of
Suggest	Call for
Advise	Charge
Recommend	Invite
Handle	

There is also an abundance of words and phrases that add politeness to requests, such as:

Please	I'd appreciate it if
Kindly	It would be helpful if
Would you be so kind as to	If you don't mind

In short, there are numerous ways in almost every language to design requests that are both precise and appropriate to a wide range of common business situations.

REQUESTS AND EXPECTATIONS

If you expect people to know what you want without telling them, you court disappointment. Only a clairvoyant or someone with whom you spend a great deal of time can know what you want without you asking for it. Today's business climate requires that people explicitly state expectations and needs. Fast-forming and fast-dissolving teams, fluid management structures, and ethnically, racially, culturally, and generationally diverse workforces depend on clear and precise communication in order to function.

Precision requests and promises are the language of business. The core of operations of any successful enterprise consists of a set of requests and promises that are specific about what is to be delivered, by whom, when, and how the adequacy of the deliverable is to be determined.

IMPROVING THE SPECIFICITY AND CLARITY OF REQUESTS
THROUGHOUT AN ORGANIZATION IS THE SINGLE MOST DRAMATIC
AND LOWEST-COST PRODUCTIVITY ENHANCEMENT
THAT YOU CAN MAKE.

COMMITMENT TRACKING

Much academic research, entrepreneurial activity, and evaluation have been directed at introducing precision requests and promises as an operating norm in business settings. In one real-world example, a team of designers uses computer-based commitment tracking as the basic management tool to record and track promises and requests made by team members to each other. The basic idea is to run the project entirely on the basis of explicit and public precision requests and promises and to track these in a computer database. The example below shows the computer-based format they use to store agreed-upon precision requests and promises.

The first field contains a brief description of the item, agreed to by both parties. The responsible person (RP) is the team member who has agreed to do the work. The requester (RQ) is the person who has requested the item. The item is further identified by a due date and a status indicator (Done, Promised, Failed, or Renegotiated).

This tracking of precision requests and promises is used as the primary project management tool. The database eventually grows to over 3,000 recorded requests and promises, similar to the one illustrated. Since the team is working in a networked computer environment, any of the 10 team members can access and update the

Item	RP	RQ	Due	Status
Operational workstation in my office	JW	DM	1-Jul-93	Promised

data at any time. Furthermore, any team member can see a view of precision requests or promises, selected and sorted by their needs. For example, a list of all precision promises containing one's own actions sorted by due date is essentially a to-do list. Alternately, team members can ask for a custom report showing all requests they had made of others, all uncompleted promises for which the due date is past, and so forth.

As straightforward as this may seem, the team finds that tracking precision requests and promises pertaining to everyday business interactions requires extraordinary attention to social and organizational issues in order to be successfully implemented in groups. One visiting manager, after viewing the system, said;

But this would only work for groups that actually wanted to get something accomplished!

As incredible as this example seems, it actually happened. People may resent making precision requests and promises, and they may worry that a permanent record of broken promises and missed deadlines may be used against them. One academic researcher came to the surprising conclusion that precision requests and promises are inappropriate in a business setting because people place a high value on ambiguity—that is, they do not wish to be pinned down!

However, real business experience suggests that if these issues are properly managed, the rewards in terms of team clarity, productivity, cooperation, and morale are extraordinary. The accompanying figure shows the number of accomplishments plotted against the number of precision requests made during a one-year period by a team that kept records of their promises to each other. Each point represents one month's worth of team activity.

The most striking observation about the data is the high correlation between accomplishments and precision requests in any given month. When team members made a larger number of requests of each other, the team achieved higher levels of accomplishment. When they made fewer requests, they accomplished less.

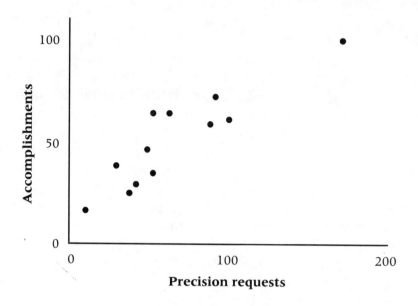

TO INCREASE YOUR PRODUCTIVITY, INCREASE THE NUMBER OF
PRECISION REQUESTS YOU MAKE.

You can use a similar system to track your own precision requests
and promises using a computer spreadsheet or even a paper-and-
pencil tracking system. Simply record everything you ask people to
do and everything they ask you to do that seems important enough
to record. In a few months, you will have an invaluable record that
will show you such things as:

- ⚙ The number of promises you actually keep.
- ⚙ What kinds of promises you tend to break.
- ⚙ The statistical likelihood that the people around you will keep
  their promises.

Such data can be an enormous source of information for self-
monitoring and self-improvement. We do not recommend using
this to track other people's performance without their knowledge or
permission. As a way to structure and accelerate your personal
accomplishments, however, it can prove very worthwhile.

IMPOSSIBLE REQUESTS

If your interest is in ultra-high-performance teamwork, you can use an extension of the idea of precision requests called impossible requests. An impossible request is a precision request that has no obvious or apparent means of execution. In other words, no one has any idea how to deliver the result. Making or accepting an impossible request forces people to go outside the boundaries of their current assumptions for the solution.

> IF ALL YOU EVER AGREE TO DO IS WHAT YOU ALREADY KNOW
> HOW TO DO, THEN ALL YOU WILL EVER ACHIEVE IS WHAT YOU
> ALREADY KNOW HOW TO ACHIEVE.

Impossible requests can turn divisions and entire corporations around in a year. A smaller division of a large corporation is losing money. For years, it has served its company by taking outmoded products from other divisions and giving them another life, finding new ways to prolong their usefulness as products and bring extra revenue into the company at minimal cost. But things are not going so well. The company plans to close the division unless the senior manager can make it profitable again. The manager pulls together a top-notch staff and makes to each one an overwhelmingly impossible request. "Jim," he says, "I am asking you to take this product and do whatever you need to do in order to sell a million of them by midyear." To the entire staff, he says, "Today our division shows no profit. But by this time next year, we will be making $4 million. I am requesting you to work as a team to make this happen. I will support you in whatever way I can, but it's all up to you." His staff has no idea how to go about creating a $4 million business, but they are excited by the challenge and actually complete the impossible request of their manager within a year. Their accomplishment fuels other impossible requests, so that today this single division accounts for over 60 percent of the profits of the parent company.

As this example shows, an ultra-high-performance team will

routinely make and accept impossible requests. However, in order to avoid burnout and exploitation, a manager must, along with members of the team, be committed to and unconditionally in support of the person or persons undertaking the impossible task. In particular, the group ethic must be designed in such a way that when a person fails, they receive more encouragement, acknowledgment, and support than when they succeed.

AUTHORITARIAN AND TRANSFORMATIONAL REQUEST STYLES

In workplaces based on the mindset of authority, no-nonsense managers attempt to achieve higher productivity by getting tough and issuing threats and orders. Failure is heavily penalized. The transformation-based work group using The Phoenix Agenda also strives for high productivity, but in the context of free choice. Impossible requests are routine, acceptance is always voluntary, and managers provide endless support for committed action and comfort in the instance of failure.

MANAGEMENT STYLE

Request style	Authoritarian Management	Transformational Management
Ambiguous requests	Yes	No
Orders, force, and threats	Yes	No
Precision requests	Sometimes	Yes
Impossible requests	Sometimes	Yes
Questioning authority	No	Yes
Freedom to decline	No	Yes
Support for failure	No	Yes

SAYING NO

In the same way that people in many business cultures are reluctant to voice precision requests, people are also reluctant both to hear "No" and to say "No" as an answer. In Japan, to put someone in a position where they have no choice but to say "No" is an extreme rudeness. It is variously associated with losing face, causing offense, hurting someone's feelings, and creating feelings of rejection.

And, yet, "No" is a precision promise. It is clear about what is going to be done: *Nothing*, and when: *Never*. Importantly, it leaves

COMMUNICATIONS TO SOURCE ACTION

Intent:	Drive action by making precision requests.
Appropriate grammar:	*Action request:* "I request that you enroll my staff in your strategy and grow the company into a $15 million business by the end of the year."
Work climate when you powerfully source action:	High levels of accomplishment, progress, results, and productivity.
Inappropriate grammar:	*Reality probe:* "Are you sure that's a good idea?"
	Status report: "We're not ready to do that."
	Transformational proclamation: "Let's refer that decision to a committee."
Work climate when you do not source action:	Nothing gets done, organizational paralysis, and buck-passing.
Practical steps to source action:	Drastically increase the number of precision requests you make, track requests and promises and the results they deliver.

the requester free to pursue another course of action, including asking someone else. The answer *Maybe* leaves the requester in an uncertain and awkward position.

Managers who fully embrace empowerment will, at some point, say to their people something like:

> *From time to time, I will ask you to do things. You are free to refuse to do anything I ask you, at any time, for any reason, or for no reason at all, and without fear of consequences from me.*

If there is to be empowered and free choice in accepting a request, then everyone must be free to say "No" to any request at any time for any reason and for no reason. If granting this kind of freedom to the people around you seems odd, ask yourself these questions:

- ○ Why are these people working with me?
- ○ Is it by their own free choice?
- ○ Have we created a vision together?
- ○ Do they honor, respect, and trust me as a leader?

The freedom to say "No" is crucial to ultra-high-performance teamwork. Without it, requests have an aspect of coercion. Any person who is forced to perform gives less than his or her absolute best.

TO IMPROVE PRODUCTIVITY, GIVE EVERYONE THE FREEDOM TO SAY "NO" TO YOUR REQUESTS.

6. Exploit Moments of Truth

GENERATE TRUST
UNCOVER CONTEXT
INVENT THE FUTURE
ARTICULATE STRATEGIES
SOURCE ACTION
✪ EXPLOIT MOMENTS OF TRUTH ✪
MAINTAIN AWARENESS
REALIZE RESULTS
CREATE WISDOM
TRANSCEND ADDICTIONS
COMPLETE THE PAST
ACKNOWLEDGE FREELY

BREAKTHROUGHS

Everyone knows that even the best-intentioned and well-planned actions run into obstacles and setbacks. Less well understood is that running into an obstacle *always* creates the opportunity for a breakthrough.

A group of four engineers on a critical semiconductor design project at Intel Corporation realize that they cannot meet their schedule the way their work is currently planned. This is a serious problem, because their project forms the basis for many other projects, involving hundreds of other people and tens of millions of dollars. Reluctantly, they approach their management expecting to be severely criticized and pressured. Instead, their manager says,

Fine, thank you for telling me. This is exactly the kind of timely information we need to manage effectively. I am not at all angry or upset. Quite the contrary. In fact, since you discovered the problem, I'm going to give you full authority to find a new solution. Revise the plans as you see fit and draw on whatever resources you need throughout the organization. The management team is here to help you in whatever way it can.

The group is astonished. People expected to be called on the carpet and to receive negative performance reviews and poor raises. Instead, they receive increased authority and resources. They dub themselves the "gang of four" and proceed with vast energy and enthusiasm to meet the schedule. The story of this example of empowerment in the face of crisis spreads throughout the organization and has a tremendous effect on morale. The "moment of truth," the crisis of the schedule slip, is turned to advantage, its creative and positive aspects successfully exploited.

DYNAMICS OF THE MOMENT OF TRUTH

Because exploiting moments of truth has the potential for massively and rapidly altering any given situation, it is one of the most powerful facets of The Phoenix Agenda. It is also one of the most dangerous in terms of backfiring and upsetting people. It requires careful design and management in order to be used successfully.

> The usual human reaction to crises and problems is to get angry, upset, sullen, aggressive, or despondent.

Any attempt to use moments of truth as a management tool to generate change needs to be accompanied by strong support and acknowledgment for both success and failure, by means of empowerment, unconditional trust, and the availability of expert coaching.

Unanticipated, unwanted, unexpected change can be one of the most unpleasant human experiences. It can also be by far the most productive. From a transformational perspective, change throws into bold relief and makes obvious the usually hidden rules of business as usual. Any drastic change faces us with a moment of truth—a decision point that makes clear that the way we have been operating is no longer adequate. At the moment of truth, we can choose one of two paths: collapse of the project or breakthrough to new results.

In the face of crisis, we have a free choice. One choice, toward "collapse," is to dwell in a mood of violated expectation, to be annoyed, fearful, hurt, displeased, irritated, angry, indignant, or even furious. We will, depending on our preference, direct these

DYNAMICS OF THE MOMENT OF TRUTH

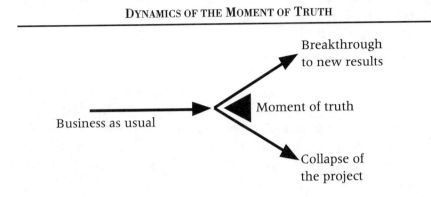

moods and emotions at ourselves, someone else, things in general, or perhaps even all three simultaneously. It is crucial to realize that these moods destroy communication and affinity, hinder learning, and collapse the future. When allowed to fester, they abort effective action, mask accomplishments and results, limit possibility, throw plans and strategies into disarray, harm recovery, spoil recreation, infect the present with past wounds, and mask the truth. In short, they are extremely nonproductive and inconsistent with The Phoenix Agenda. They are also deeply, fundamentally, and unavoidably human.

FACING MOMENTS OF TRUTH MAY BE THE *ONLY* MEANS OF ACHIEVING EXCEPTIONAL RESULTS.

The other choice, toward "breakthrough," requires courage and an act of will. For most of us, it also requires the sponsorship of someone else. The choice is to conduct an honest exploration, an inventory, an examination, an inquiry into the assumptions, viewpoints, and mindset that moments of truth expose. The manager at Intel who learns of the critical schedule slip explains his reaction to his own moment of truth:

I gulped and felt afraid. I imagined everything we were working for going up in smoke. Then I realized, hey, everybody's human. These guys probably feel terrible. Besides, they understand the project better than anyone else. Why not give them a chance to shine?

This manager chooses to keep open the possibility of recovering the schedule and thus empowers his team to generate a totally new strategy that could change the way they do business. The possibility he generates is one that, if successful, will mean faster time to market and higher revenue for his company. If he chooses to berate and belittle his team, he will only have a slipped schedule and damaged relationships.

The following illustration of impossible commitments in action is presented in some detail to show how the mechanisms of transformational scheduling work even in a "classical" industry with extremely well-established routines and procedures. The illustration involves a civil engineering company specializing in airport planning and environmental projects that has an opportunity to design a major hub airport. The undertaking is bigger than any project the firm has ever attempted, with an alarmingly tight schedule. The political impact of the project makes it a highly visible job that promises to provide good publicity for the company.

The management wrestles with the decision of taking on such a challenging yet golden opportunity. It is clear to all that this project is undoable within their current framework of assumptions and procedures. An unprecedented meeting is called of the entire company. The situation is outlined in full detail, including an assessment of risks and rewards. Everyone is asked (not told) if they would be willing to work together, to share both the risks and the rewards, and to come up with new creative ways of working that would make success possible. After dialogue, the company decides, as a whole, to say YES to the client, in full knowledge that they do not know how to achieve the goals of the project. Thus empowered, everyone gets to work.

The first step is to designate key engineers who have the expertise to work on the various aspects of the project. The head of the structural department remembers that there are two engineers in his department, one who had previously worked in civil airport engineering, and another whose original degree program had been in civil engineering with a focus in airport design, though she had then moved quickly into bridge design. These two, it is decided, can be brought up to speed and easily contribute to the design effort.

There exists enough overlap between airport planning and airport design and reconstruction that certain functions could easily be handed off to the planning department, thus freeing up the civil department to manage the rest of the project. The airport planners are also adept at handling the more sticky political relations with airport managers and federal agencies and so would assist in this capacity.

The drafting department has only one CAD (Computer-Aided Design) station for each drafter and no more. In talking to his drafting team, the department head finds that two of the drafters would rather work the "graveyard" shift than daytime hours, but this had never, in any engineering firm, been an option. Now it is a necessity. Two drafters who were laid off the year before are called. They wholeheartedly leap at the opportunity. But even with increased person power, there is a concern about the drafters being inundated by the design work that will be coming at them from all directions. One drafter suggests a new way of working. Rather than the drafters being given the work as it happens to come down from engineering, the work could be coordinated so that each drafter is designated for a specific function—i.e., one would do grading plans, two would do cross-sections, two could handle the detail sheets, etc. This way, also, each engineer working on his or her specific portion of the design would have designated one or two drafters, which would reduce miscommunications and thereby drastically reduce errors.

The project will call for about 140 drawings, about twice the number as the average civil project. The main obstacle here is the amount of time it takes to pen plot that many drawings for the final Mylar plots. The process has recently been greatly speeded up by the use of a thermal plotter for the many check plots during the design process, but the thermal plots lack the durability for a final record set. The thermal plotter can plot in four minutes a drawing that previously would have taken 40 or more minutes. One of the drafters has a brainstorm, and, on her own, takes a thermal plot into the print room. She runs the thermal plot through the print machine, printing, not on blueline paper, but on repro Mylar. A little adjustment of the speed, and the Mylar quality is perfectly acceptable. The plotting time has been cut by 90 percent.

The biggest obstacle involves the environmental assessment portion of the project. The environmental department is already overloaded with work. Two of the environmental engineers design on CAD and so can accomplish their work without calling on the drafting department, but highly experienced senior engineers are needed for the environmental assessment. With much discomfort, the head of environmental services suggests that they might place a phone call to their one major competitor to see if they might consider collaborating on this one special project. Hackles rise. This is unthinkable in normal times, but these are not normal times. Egos are put on the sidelines and a deal is arranged, without which the project would be guaranteed failure.

The deadline is met, the project a success. The employees have a sense of company unity and even greater loyalty than ever before. Many learn the pleasure of team spirit for the first time. Management is glowing with pride in the employees, not only for their hard work, but also for their creativity that took the company way outside the usual acceptable limits of how business is conducted. The "rival" environmental services company agrees that such collaboration may be useful at times in the future. Everybody wins.

Notice in this example that the commitment to impossible results produced a raft of innovations and breakthroughs in procedures and ways of working together, none of which would have happened if management had stuck to the rules of business as usual and had not taken the risk of accepting the project. By openly and honestly persuading every individual in the company to agree to an impossible project with an impossible schedule, management tapped a tremendous resource—the wholehearted commitment, enthusiasm, and specialized knowledge of all its employees.

How to Drive Action and Achieve Results

Intent:	Use the creative energy inherent in moments of crisis to generate innovation.
Appropriate grammar:	*Reality probe:* "What are we committed to? What new opportunities and insights are revealed by the crisis? Who can help us?"
	Status report: "We have a major breakdown here."
	Action request: "Realizing the urgency of this problem, I request that you and the product manager meet to resolve this crisis and get back to me by 3:00 P.M. today."
	Transformational proclamation: "Every crisis presents an opportunity. Let's not let this one get away."
Work climate when you skillfully exploit moments of truth:	Entrepreneurial spirit, flexibility, remarkable and unexpected achievements, courage, breakthroughs.
Inappropriate grammar:	*Reality probe:* "What jerk created this mess?"
	Status report: "We have a hopeless situation."
	Action request: "Don't bring me any bad news."
Work climate when you suppress or mishandle moments of truth:	Resistance to change, inability to seize the moment, constant fire drills, fear, blame, failure to achieve full potential, bitterness, and feelings of being a victim.

Practical steps to exploit moments of truth:	Seek out coaching, never punish for creating crises, only punish for concealing crises, deliberately create crisis but provide strong support for failure, be extremely open and honest in all dealings, make impossible requests, practice empowerment.

Moments of truth offer opportunity for exceptional achievement and the realization of seemingly impossible goals. Lost opportunity occurs, therefore, at the moment we choose to surrender to the fear, anger, and frustration that unexpected change creates, instead of being in action to manage that change for our benefit, our team, and our workplace.

7. Maintain Awareness

GENERATE TRUST
UNCOVER CONTEXT
INVENT THE FUTURE
ARTICULATE STRATEGIES
SOURCE ACTION
EXPLOIT MOMENTS OF TRUTH
✺ MAINTAIN AWARENESS ✺
REALIZE RESULTS
CREATE WISDOM
TRANSCEND ADDICTIONS
COMPLETE THE PAST
ACKNOWLEDGE FREELY

SHOW OFF YOUR PROJECTS

To maintain awareness means to express and reinforce thoughts and images—to put them on display. At the world-class garment manufacturing plant in Singapore, displays are numerous and potent. Each small team of people on the garment fabrication line has its own display on the wall. These displays look like poster displays at a school fair. Teams have names, such as the "Can Do Kids" and the "Tiger Team." The poster features pictures of the team members, colorful artwork, and a list of the manufacturing process improvement suggestions that members of each team have made, together with an illustrated story and a dollar estimate of the value of implementing the suggestion. The facility's training manager explains that these posters are an essential part of the plant's continuous improvement program. You sense an air of excitement and purpose about the plant. When you catch the eye of a worker, he or she returns your smile.

PLANS, ACTIONS, AND BREAKTHROUGHS MEAN NOTHING IF NO ONE IS AWARE OF THEM.

These lively and effective displays contrast sharply with the manufacturing productivity displays at another (later defunct) garment manufacturing plant in New England. A huge white board, squared off in a grid, shows production numbers by group. The display is colorless and dusty, and evidently has not been updated in many months. The graph lines on the white board are made of narrow black vinyl strips that are now peeling off and dangling from the display. Workers shuffle sullenly about their business and ignore you.

DESIGN ALL ASPECTS OF AWARENESS

Experience in general and spoken language in particular have an evanescent, impermanent quality. After something is said, it literally vanishes into thin air with no physical trace unless it is recorded. For example, have you ever had the experience in a business meeting of hearing and sensing that agreement was reached and that the group had clear strategy and goals, only to find by the next meeting that nothing had been done and that everyone seemed to forget whatever it was that was agreed to at the previous meeting?

If communication creates and defines reality itself, then recording and displaying of past communications become the embodiment and preservation of that reality. Maintaining awareness, in the sense of getting the word out, making things public, and displaying them is absolutely central to having any impact at all on the workplace. Display, in this broad sense, includes and is not limited to the printed word. To display is to take any action that has an impact on the awareness of others.

For example, at a job interview, you display yourself in many ways. Your inquiry letter and résumé are written forms. Visual forms of display include your dress, physical appearance, the way you move, and your facial expressions at the interview itself. What you say at the interview is of extreme importance and is a series of communication acts. All physical trace of your speech publications disappear as soon as you have said them, but you can design written publications such as follow-up and thank-you notes to increase the impact of your total presence in the experience of the interviewer. An awareness strategy involves coordinating, matching, and timing all of these aspects of display to form a coherent, comprehensible, and memorable total image.

The public or shared aspect of awareness is crucial. Conventional interpretation has it that declaring a project publicly (such as a project to stop smoking, for example) motivates you by the threat of public shame if you fail. A less moralistic interpretation is that the act of publication itself gives the project life and existence (since we have assumed that all reality derives from language).

COMMITMENTS, GOALS, AND PLANS ARE MUCH MORE LIKELY TO
BE REALIZED IF YOU DECLARE THEM PUBLICLY.

Publication can support the implementation of all the other facets of The Phoenix Agenda. For example, once a group has settled on a vision or a mission, it is often helpful to create and display a written or graphic representation of the vision in a place where the team members can see it. Some high-performance teams create special war rooms where continually updated materials are on display—progress charts, the original project manifesto, photos of the team members, tables and white boards where cooperative work is done, and so on. The room itself becomes a symbol, an active remembrance device for the entire project. People get excited, motivated, and want to come to work.

AUTHORITARIAN OBSTACLES TO AWARENESS

A remarkable case of obstacles to display involves a team that is trying to introduce a new product to market. The design team wants to find out what the customers want and so arranges an ambitious series of trips and interviews all over the United States to speak with prospective customers about their needs and desires. They have collected a massive amount of information, interview materials, and ideas to analyze and think about in determining the new product engineering and marketing strategy. On returning to the plant, they conduct a Quality Function Deployment (QFD) exercise—a two-day group working session in which the team writes up 400 to 500 ideas and pieces of engineering, marketing, and customer information on yellow Post-its, sorted and organized by relevance and relationship to known engineering and marketing factors. This array of Post-its, containing information vital to the new product development, needs a 40-foot running wall for display. The team invites people from engineering, sales, marketing, and product management to participate in organizing, categorizing, and sorting this massive collection of information in order to boil it down to a workable engineering and marketing plan. This type of group display requires a large physical wall space so that everyone can see the whole picture, participate in sorting the Post-its, and see and appreciate the input from the people in the other departments. The 40-foot wall display *is* the pith of the project.

The facilities maintenance people, however, take a dim view of 40-foot-long walls containing the Post-its in an otherwise neat and orderly plant and demand that the display be removed. Line management is either too busy or too uninterested to intercede. And so the project is lost, literally destroyed, never to be built.

The facilities people, of course, are only doing what they perceive to be their job, to keep things neat and orderly. The need for massive, parallel, visual, interactive, manipulatable, and accessible displays of information is simply not recognizable from the authoritarian mindset behind the work ethic of that organization, as reflected in its policies, procedures, and daily work practices. In the transformation mindset, the transforming context (in this case, the plans for the proposed product) itself must be brought to awareness and displayed. This sometimes requires 40-foot wall displays. Under the authoritarian mindset, which focuses on the atomistic, the particular, the linear, the sequential, and the orderly, the need for massively parallel displays is simply less available to conscious awareness. The workplace mindset drives reality down to the very design of office arrangement and work practice.

Modern computer tools and display devices, to say nothing of white boards, flip charts, and hand-drawn matrices, make possible extremely effective awareness and display presentations for group work. The linear language tools of old-fashioned management meetings are inadequate, outmoded, and insufficient for dealing with the complexities of today's business.

A SPOKEN SENTENCE SAYS ONLY ONE THING AT A TIME. A
DISPLAY ON THE WALL CAN SHOW HUNDREDS OF THINGS PLUS
THEIR INTERRELATIONSHIPS AT A TIME.

SHARED AWARENESS

Computer technology, or even large white boards, can be used to create displays that can be seen and worked on by many people at once. For example, Delta Airlines has a room, with an enormous wall display, showing the exact location and repair status of every airplane in its fleet. This board is constantly updated as new information comes in. At a glance, managers can see the entire repair situation and also focus down on the details pertaining to any single aircraft.

How to Drive Action and Achieve Results

At the Volvo automobile plant in Gothenburg, Sweden, engineers in charge of the manufacturing process can see every detail of that process on a huge computer display. The display is immensely detailed, interactive, and directly linked to events on the factory floor. Thus, a group of engineers can consult and have right in front of their eyes every piece of information relevant to their decisions. They can ask the computer to simulate the effects of various changes to the manufacturing process, see the results immediately, and discuss the implications with the group. They can also issue computer-based commands that are immediately implemented on the floor.

Computer-based systems now exist to support ordinary business meetings. One company, Collaborative Technologies Corporation, has a system designed to focus a team's goals, support simultaneous brainstorming of ideas, analyze possible solutions, and take immediate action—all right in the meeting room. The key element is a wall-sized computer display in the meeting room that everyone can see and interact with.

These three examples show the power of shared awareness—allowing a group of people to see and work on the same information simultaneously. Naturally, for such systems to succeed requires teamwork, shared vision, and trust.

A DRAMATIC AWARENESS STRATEGY

It is actually helpful not to distinguish between the medium and the message. In a transformational world, the message has no existence independent of the medium. Practically, this means that when you design publications, consider the medium to be used as an integral part of the message itself. For example, a corporate researcher applied for a $250,000 research grant to study the relationship between technology issues and people issues in computer-supported business meetings. The review board was composed of outstanding and highly experienced computer engineers who had little background in or sympathy for the social sciences. During consideration of the written proposal, one engineer commented:

> *Business meetings, ha! The only good meeting support tool is a two-by-four.*

He was referring to a two-by-four-inch piece of construction lumber that the meeting coordinator could use to hit unruly meeting attendees over the head. So the researcher knew he needed a dramatic publication strategy to save the proposal. What he did was to bring an actual length of two-by-four lumber to the presentation before the board. He held it up, slammed it on the table, and said,

> *I understand that you might feel this is the only useful meeting tool. Perhaps I can show something more modern,*

and turned to the computer-based meeting room projection system that was the heart of the proposal. Fortunately, the august board laughed, the review went well, and the funding was granted. It was very clear that the piece of lumber saved the proposal. As a piece of publication strategy, it was physical, unorthodox, mildly sensational, and salient. The medium and the message were designed together. Of course, the strategy was also high risk (it could have easily caused offense), but the researcher had little to lose since the board was negatively disposed to the proposal from the outset.

AWARENESS AND DESIGN

Even if something exists in written form, it still may not create the desired results. For example, in one Fortune 100 company, it is traditional for groups to leave the plant, perhaps once a year, and hold intense, informal meetings to discuss issues such as the group strategy, missions, and roles in the corporation. Many such meetings are productive, engaging, fun, and produce genuine insights. Often, the output is a written statement or manifesto about the

How to Drive Action and Achieve Results

COMMUNICATIONS TO MAINTAIN AWARENESS

Intent:	Find creative ways to make goals, plans, commitments, and accomplishments visible and memorable.
Appropriate grammar:	*Transformational proclamation:* a group mission statement embodied in an elegant visual display.
Work climate when you maintain awareness:	Fame, recognition, constancy of purpose, clarity, accurate records.
Inappropriate grammar:	*Reality probe:* "What was it we decided at the last meeting?"
	Action request: "Take down those unsightly posters!"
	Status report: "That information is only available on a 'need to know' basis."
Work climate when you deny awareness:	Anonymity, lack of recognition, forgetfulness, constantly shifting priorities, slipped commitments, "out of sight, out of mind."
Practical steps to maintain awareness:	Write things down, use multimedia computer-based displays in meetings, empower workplace groups to create names and logos, market yourself and your group within the corporation as well as with customers, invest in high-quality graphics, design, and printing.

group's core ideas and action plans for the coming year. What is remarkable is how little these meetings affect everyday work. A few days after the meeting, it is as though it had never happened. Someone files the manifesto, on paper or electronically, and the team members rarely, if ever, look at it again. Why? Clearly, neither the content nor the medium is substantive or hot enough to maintain people's interest or attention on return to the business-as-usual world.

As an additional example, another company festoons their cafeteria ceilings with hundreds of brightly colored mobiles, each bearing the message

Work smarter, not harder.

The employees, far from being inspired by this, seem embarrassed by what they described as a tacky and superficial approach to the problems of corporate productivity.

Effective publication, then, is a matter of sophisticated design and craftsmanship—an art, not a science. The design disciplines such as graphic arts, publication, image consulting, media arts, communications, computer display and interface design, and public relations, all have an enormous amount to contribute here, and you should consult frequently with people from these disciplines in designing personal, group, or corporate awareness strategies.

8. Realize Results

GENERATE TRUST
UNCOVER CONTEXT
INVENT THE FUTURE
ARTICULATE STRATEGIES
SOURCE ACTION
EXPLOIT MOMENTS OF TRUTH
MAINTAIN AWARENESS
✿ **REALIZE RESULTS** ✿
CREATE WISDOM
TRANSCEND ADDICTIONS
COMPLETE THE PAST
ACKNOWLEDGE FREELY

RESULTS ARE FLEETING

Business strives for results and holds them up as the only worthwhile thing. Results are, supposedly, what all plans and actions are designed to achieve. Strange, then, that results, when they actually happen, have little tangibility or permanence.

How to Drive Action and Achieve Results

ONCE RESULTS ARE ACHIEVED, MOST OF US COMPLETELY
LOSE INTEREST IN THEM AND DEVOTE OURSELVES TO THE
PURSUIT OF NEW RESULTS.

Therefore, that which is at the heart of no-nonsense management, namely, "getting results," is actually something valued only in the anticipation, never for long in the actual achievement. Whenever we say of someone, "He gets results," we refer not so much to his past track record as to the expectation that he will get us results in the future. Yet, when he does get results, the focus is again not on these results for their own sake. Instead, the focus is on the still-unrealized results we expect he will bring. Imagine that you are introduced to two men and you are told,

Tom and Bill are known for getting results. Tom is joining our group tomorrow and Bill is retiring.

You will hold Tom's and Bill's results in entirely different lights.

The importance of results has to do with the quality of experience they create rather than the results themselves. In the following two statements,

You'll be pleased with the results and *You'll get the results, but you won't like them,*

the results themselves could be identical. In both cases, you value the results as a means to satisfaction or dissatisfaction. So the results themselves, in some objective sense, are not important. What is important is how you embrace or interpret them.

The phrase "realizing results" can be interpreted in two ways: realizing, in the sense of achieving and attaining, or realizing in the sense of perceiving or appreciating. Achieving results is largely a matter of setting goals, devising plans, driving action, and evaluating the outcome to modify the goals and improve the plans.

Achieving results consistently and intelligently and in the face of change requires awareness of and sensitivity to process.

Appreciating results is quite different. First, it requires becoming aware of them, or even of selecting a context for awareness. Next, it involves acknowledgment and awareness, in the sense of making other people aware. Ultimately, it involves declaring satisfaction in the accomplishment.

WHO ACTUALLY PRODUCES RESULTS?

For many of us, accounting is a kind of business bedrock. Accounting procedures get at the bottom line, show the assets and liabilities of a business, and supposedly paint a true picture. Yet, accounting practices are themselves a relatively arbitrary set of rules and distinctions. Ultimately, they refer to no objective reality. The accounting statement at the conclusion of a corporate annual report, for example, contains no guarantees of truth. Rather, these statements refer to "established accounting procedures" and "in our opinion" as the ultimate justification and certification for the financial information presented. Often a business's primary assets simply do not have any representation at all in the context of established accounting procedures. For example, intellectual property, whether measured by trade secrets, copyrights and patents, or simply the creativity of a company's research division, is not an accepted category according to standard accounting procedures. Such things never appear on the corporate balance sheet. However, they can have enormous financial value, as, for example, in the case of the Xerox photocopying patents. In fact, savvy stock analysts regularly factor in the financial value of intellectual property in their estimates of corporate worth, even though accountants may not.

In large computer companies, when a mainframe computer is sold, the question arises as to who should get credit for it. This is important since groups who get the most credit for sales are in a better position to receive budget increases. Should manufacturing, which actually built the computer, get the most credit? Or perhaps the salesperson. What about the salesperson's manager? Of course, no one would buy a computer if it had no software, so perhaps the group that built the operating system should get credit. Operating systems themselves do nothing useful for the customer, so perhaps the credit should really go to the groups that coded the payroll software that delivers the functionality that the customer really wants. On the other hand, no customers would have ever heard of the computer system if not for the efforts of the marketing department. And what about the documentation, service, and telephone support groups?

> IN ANY WORKPLACE, WHO ACTUALLY PRODUCED THE RESULTS
> CAN NEVER BE PROVEN SCIENTIFICALLY. INSTEAD, A POLITICAL
> PROCESS DETERMINES WHO GETS CREDIT.

What actually happens is that all these groups and more claim credit through a Byzantine political process that results in an internal accounting of dollars up to 20 times the amount of the actual sale. This accounting has little if anything to do with the realities of who made the largest contribution to the manufacture, sale, delivery, and service of the computer system. It has everything to do with the political skills of the competing groups. It is a political process masquerading as an orderly accounting procedure. As such, it breeds dissension and competitiveness when what the organization needs most for success is cooperation.

Most employees of large corporations are eager to know that they are making a contribution to the company's success. In a large corporation, few people have any concept of whether they make a difference. There is simply no way to trace an individual's actions through to the bottom line. When the company is profitable, most people can feel a vague sense of contribution; when the company is not profitable, they feel a vague sense of failure and guilt. Indeed, elaborate conversations address the question of who contributes and who does not.

What have you contributed to my bottom line?

growled one vice president at the head of the organizational advanced development group. Actually, one may legitimately ask what contribution the vice president himself made to his own bottom line. If called upon to do so, what top executive could actually prove that he or she was, in fact, responsible for the performance of their division? This dilemma is poignantly illustrated in a letter sent out to his group by one vice president on the occasion of his retirement:

> *During the last 15 years at the company, I have personally been given credit for a lot of things I did not deserve. In actuality, the credit for all these accomplishments must accrue to all of you.*

This magnificent acknowledgment clearly shows the problematic nature of the conventional interpretation of results. Whose results were they? At the time of his employment, everyone spoke of them as his. Then, on his retirement, he said they were not, that they belonged to the team. Whose were they, really?

SHARING RESULTS BY PROCLAMATION

At a world-class semiconductor plant in Malaysia, the teams on the production floor have poster displays proclaiming their accomplishments. Prominently featured are photographs of employees who have suggested process improvements, together with a dollar estimate of the money saved by implementing the suggestions. For example, one employee suggested that a supplier be requested to ship raw materials in packages that are less time-consuming to open and unpack. The manager passed along this suggestion and the supplier complied. The time savings from this innovation is estimated at 100 minutes per week, which translates directly into increased assembly line output. The employee and his team are given full credit, visible for all to see on the poster display. All along the assembly line, similar displays can be seen.

How to Drive Action and Achieve Results

Intent:	All workplace participants grasp their importance and contribution to organizational achievements and goals.
Appropriate grammar:	*Transformational proclamation:* "Your efforts contributed substantially to our organization's success."
Work climate when you realize results:	Goal-orientation, pride, involvement, employee participation, profitability.
Inappropriate grammar:	*Action request:* "It's budget time. Prepare a justification of your activities and plans."
	Status report: "The quality group does nothing but delay products."
	Reality probe: "What have you done for my bottom line?"
Work climate when you fail to realize results:	Lack of involvement, alienation, drudgery, "A bad day of fishing is better than a good day at work."
Practical steps to realize results:	Show people the ways in which their efforts contribute to the company's goals.

The manager at the Malaysia plant explains that all employees take an active interest in the business as a whole, including business plans, budgets, strategic forecasts, and fiscal planning. Managers share information, including decisions still under consideration and review. This information allows each employee to better see the role of his or her individual contribution and to make meaningful suggestions for improvements. These managers are astonished to discover that their American management counterparts are far less open with their employees about strategic, financial, and business issues.

How can the workers improve if they know nothing about the business?

the Malaysian managers ask.

TRUE LEADERS SEEK TO GIVE CREDIT FOR RESULTS,
NOT TO CLAIM IT.

Realizing results means involving everyone in the business and making sure that each workplace participant can understand and feel pride in their particular contribution to the organization's goals. Everyone wants to contribute, to be assured that their contribution is meaningful. With this assurance, work is meaningful and rewarding. The opportunity for leaders is to help employees realize the value of their contributions.

7

How to Make Work Rewarding

Communication, after all, is not so much a matter of intellect as it is a matter of trust and acceptance of others

—Stephen R. Covey, author

9. Create Wisdom

GENERATE TRUST
UNCOVER CONTEXT
INVENT THE FUTURE
ARTICULATE STRATEGIES
SOURCE ACTION
EXPLOIT MOMENTS OF TRUTH
MAINTAIN AWARENESS
REALIZE RESULTS
✪ **CREATE WISDOM** ✪
TRANSCEND ADDICTIONS
COMPLETE THE PAST
ACKNOWLEDGE FREELY

KNOWLEDGE AND WISDOM

Knowledge and wisdom are integral to the advancement of learning, self-esteem, and personal growth, both within and outside the workplace. When people use their knowledge to generate wisdom, a company's business advantage takes an enormous leap forward.

With respect to customer satisfaction, for example, how does a company provide excellent support for customers? For one company, serving the customer better means giving frontline employees at customer centers excellent procedures, guidelines, and training. When customers phone in with suggestions or complaints, each employee in the center knows how to handle the call with courtesy and speed. Unusual requests are then passed onto supervisors, managers, and technicians who have more authority and experience. In this approach, customer satisfaction is creating knowledge that enables employees to respond appropriately to a customer's problem.

Another company provides excellent frontline support and takes an additional step to focus on the learnings of the customer centers. Managers of the centers make presentations to groups throughout the corporation. Awareness of customers is elevated. With this new awakening, employees on the production line take as much responsibility in guaranteeing customer satisfaction as the frontline employees in the centers. The results are phenomenal. Defects that once went undetected now stop manufacturing lines until they have been resolved. Employees are empowered to make decisions that previously were handled by managers. Managers listen carefully and learn from employees. The entire company is actively involved in a commitment to deliver results to the customer. They work together, manager teaching employee, and employee teaching manager, to create the wisdom within the business that keeps the customer delighted.

As these examples show, companies that focus on knowledge as an end itself, as contrasted to those that use knowledge to create wisdom, function differently. Knowledge is the raw material of business. It can be gathered and accumulated over time and documented. Knowledge is acquired through learning and is a commodity that can be bought and sold. Knowledge exists in each and every product that a company ships, in the education, skill, and experience levels of its employees, and in the strategies and plans created to drive the business forward. Knowledge is tangible.

Wisdom is generated in doing business. It exists only when integrity, personal commitment, and involvement are present at all levels of a company. With wisdom, you, your managers, associates, and co-workers have the ability to create knowledge continuously.

WISDOM IS KNOWLEDGE TRANSFORMED BY INTEGRITY.

Commenting on the rapid economic and political restructuring taking place in America today, Peter Drucker states, "International economic theory is obsolete. The traditional factors of production, land, labor and capital—are becoming restraints rather than driving forces. Knowledge is becoming the one critical factor of production."[1] This kind of change requires basic rethinking in how a company guides its resources in acquisition of knowledge and learning, contrasted with investment in land, labor, and capital.

Yet, in today's fast-paced world, knowledge can become quickly obsolete. For this reason, it is important that you make learning and the acquisition of knowledge a continuous and lifelong endeavor.

WISDOM ARISES FROM RECOGNIZING THE NECESSITY FOR
LIFELONG LEARNING BY EVERYONE.

In a workplace that emphasizes results, you may find it difficult to justify the time you need to listen, inquire, and learn—indeed, to find a better way to do your work. If this is true for you, then consider looking beyond the shortsightedness of a "no time to learn" view and purposefully take the time to share your knowledge and create a workplace around you that values wisdom.

WISDOM AND INTEGRITY

The ability to create wisdom begins with integrity. If what you say and what you do are inconsistent, no one to whom you speak will believe what you say or will trust that you are being honest with them. The degree to which you demonstrate integrity in your communications is the degree to which you will be able to convince others to listen to you.

Imagine how the employees of a large corporation undergoing layoffs and severe cutbacks would feel if they knew that the newly hired CEO flies the corporate jet to Europe empty, while vice presidents and executive staff pay expensive airline fares to travel to the same destination. When that CEO sends a message to the company and speaks to excellence, individual contribution, personal sacrifice, and cost cutting, who will listen? Would you?

Because mindsets and assumptions lead us to hide our flaws as a way to protect our ego and identity, it is often difficult for us to recognize when we lack integrity. Denial comes easily and excuses are numerous. But there are ways to avoid blindness so that we can live our commitments.

Here is one suggestion. Make a list of everything to which you currently have a strong commitment, whether it is accelerating the growth of your company or fighting world hunger, and become personally involved in some activity that promises to realize a result you want.

Integrity is the key that opens the door to wisdom.

For example, you might declare that you are committed to realizing excellence in quality within your company and intend to be recognized for the achievement by winning the Malcolm Baldrige National Quality Award within three years. If you take your commitment seriously, you will inquire into the process and learn how to make your company more effective in quality management. You will become involved in promoting the Baldrige Award goals and participate in employee small group improvement activities in support of others. You will talk with employees and learn from them. You will teach, coach, and inspire others in their struggle to overcome obstacles. In short, you will do whatever is needed. The point is that if you believe in what you are doing, if you speak with intention to act, if you have the courage to do what is right, you are on the way to creating the wisdom that will ensure the success of your company's quality program and possibly the winning of the Baldrige.

The Baldrige assessment criteria for organizational excellence are themselves examples of business wisdom. The key indicators of quality excellence used as Baldrige criteria for determining "world class" status include "We can learn from everyone," managers as coaches, widely deployed readily accessible data, comprehensive training and education, flat organization, stretch goals, contact with customers, frontline empowerment, and much more.[2] The emphasis on personal leadership, team consensus and decision making, employee values, and quality are structured to inspire performance and self-development. They are designed to create wisdom.

If your goal is to create wisdom and success for yourself and others, for your work, your company, group, or project, be aware that wisdom does not occur at the time you are learning. Wisdom occurs in the doing and the teaching. It occurs at the moment in which you integrate the learning so wholly with yourself that you generate a new way of seeing or relating to that learning. In the following sections, you can look at the various sides of creating wisdom, including the aspect of learning.

MASTERY OF WISDOM

The personal involvement of senior managers in workplace activities is critical to creating wisdom. Managers have a wealth of experience and know-how that when shared with others, stimulates and motivates individual employees to higher productivity. For some managers, involvement may mean "getting" wisdom as well as "giving" wisdom. And part of "getting" wisdom is learning how to listen.

The new roles of managers as coaches, consultants, advice givers, and mentors require that managers be excellent listeners, that they spend a high percentage of their time in conversation with workers, share information, and inquire into problems in a way that provides others with new skills.

TEACHING IS AN OPPORTUNITY FOR MANAGERS TO TRANSFER THE SKILLS OF MASTERFUL MANAGEMENT TO OTHERS.

One of the best ways to create wisdom is to teach. By devoting time to training, mentoring, and teaching, managers empower the organization with a more broadly diffused skill base through the training of others. Teaching also allows managers to focus and systematically organize their own learning. It further supports a "learning" environment in which people at all levels in the organization can learn from each other and listen openly in support. Consider how the following example might happen in your workplace.

A new vice president comes to an ailing division of a company. He is unusual. He reads extensively, including periodicals such as the *Harvard Business Review*. He even sends photocopies of relevant articles to his staff. They grumble at first at the extra work. Then he tells them that he expects each of them to teach at least two seminars per year to their people. His unorthodox methods start to take hold. People learn new skills, and their supervisors notice a markedly improved change in the group's outlook for the future.

WE CAN LEARN FROM EVERYONE

Have you ever worked in an organization that placed its own products and inventions on such a high pedestal that the managers refused to see that there was another world swirling around them that might possibly have something to teach?

The year is 1988 and the Apple Macintosh, a revolutionary new style of computer, has been shipping for 12 months. It incorporates a fascinatingly new user interface approach, unlike any ever seen before, and its central features have interesting names—mice, icons, windows, and dialogue boxes. A group of software engineers and marketing people in a competitive company order new toshes for themselves with the intent of studying them and including the best ideas in their own future products. A vice president happens to see the new Macintoshes, still in their boxes, in the hallway, about to be delivered to people's cubicles. He orders them all sent back to the supplier.

In this company, we only use our own products.

Later, when the company begins to build its own new style of interface, most people have never seen mice, icons, windows, or dialogue boxes, despite the fact that racks full of computer magazines describing the new style of computers are on display at the shopping mall one mile from the plant.

Companies can stay competitive only if the people in them are willing to admit that they do not know everything, and are willing to improve on what they already have in order to make it extraordinarily better.

By contrast, another company—also an Apple competitor—sets up a special room that contains hardware and software from every known computer and software vendor. All employees are encouraged to visit this room, to explore the various offerings at their leisure, and to use any and all ideas to better inform their own work. Not surprisingly, this company goes on to become one of the marketplace leaders.

SHARPEN YOUR COMPETITIVE EDGE BY LEARNING FROM EVERYONE AND EVERYTHING.

Learning begins with listening. In a business setting, this means listening to both the external world that surrounds the business, such as customers, market, and competitors, and to the internal world that gives the business its heartbeat. This internal world is people working with people to realize the goals and purpose of the company. It is also people working with people as teachers, coaches, team members, and supportive friends; people involved with other people in open and freely shared commitments. Critically, the success of all of these relationships depends on the degree to which each person is willing to listen and learn from another. So simple, and yet so difficult.

SETTING THE EXAMPLE

The values of senior executives and managers permeate a workplace and contribute extensively to the assumptions of the corporate culture they oversee. Anything top management does, or fails to do, employees question and interpret as a model for expected behavior within that company. For this reason, it is important that senior managers understand and practice the values and business concepts that they expect their employees to follow. This may seem to be common sense, yet consider how few managers you know who have taken the time to think about their personal value systems and then committed to developing leadership skills that give their words and actions integrity. For those managers who do not think about their values and speak thoughtlessly, the consequences are devastating.

Take, for example, the message given to an employee who wants to switch his career direction towards management. He approaches his supervisor for advice about pursuing an MBA program. The manager responds:

Waste of your time. You learn this business through years of experience; not by reading books and taking courses.

As might be suspected, this manager has not taken a training course in 15 years.

But what happens when the message is louder and even more pervasive than the voice of one manager? Perhaps you have experienced the following. As another business cycle comes full swing and revenues slip downward, company management sends out a sternly worded memo about cutting costs:

How to Make Work Rewarding

Eliminate all unnecessary travel and training. All exceptions require vice presidential approval.

Months later, when revenues begin to cycle upward (as they usually do), management never officially lifts the ban. It simply melts away, as people gradually realize that applications for training are getting approved more easily.

How would you interpret this? The most rational explanation is that management disapproves of training, allowing it only under duress or when they do not have a sufficient excuse to disapprove it. As a result, many employees never submit proposals for training. Supervisors scrutinize training requests carefully, and speak sternly to those who exceed their allotted number of courses for the year. It is not difficult to see how communications such as these go beyond any single person to create workplace assumptions that discourage learning, innovation, and contribution at every level.

Companies that discourage learning, that focus totally on dominance of their products in the marketplace and restrict training budgets at the first sign of financial difficulties, cannot be competitive. Their best people, knowing that continuous self-improvement is essential to a contemporary career, will not stay. If learning is not valued, people do not feel valued.

Senior managers and executives must set the example. One effective way to promote continuous learning in the workplace is to become an avid learner yourself. This may mean reading extensively and broadly, attending courses, and systematizing learnings in the form of papers and presentations. Andy Grove, CEO of Intel, is an author, teacher, and journalist, who once contributed a regular column to the San Jose *Mercury News*.

Another effective way to create wisdom is for managers to spend time learning from the people who do the actual hands-on day-to-day work of the business.

Intent:	Listen and learn in a way that transforms valuable knowledge into wisdom.
Appropriate grammar:	*Reality probe:* "What have we learned from this experience?"
	Transformational proclamation: "I will maintain the integrity of my word in each action and thing I do."
Work climate when you create wisdom:	Learning, integrity, continuous improvement, personal involvement, and partnership.
Inappropriate grammar:	*Transformational proclamation:* "This is a business. We've got no time for anything not directly related to profits."
	Action request: "Give me a detailed justification for why you want to attend that conference."
	Status report: "Profits are down. We've got to cut the training budget."
Work climate when you fail to create wisdom:	Failure to learn from others, repeating old mistakes, reinventing the wheel, devaluation of history, resting on laurels.
Practical steps to create wisdom:	Teach others, make strong commitments and become involved, write articles and papers, read extensively, value training and learning, listen and learn from everyone.

Managers can learn from employees. Employees can learn from managers.

This includes a commitment to work with others in shared understanding and communication, to become personally and actively involved in the activities that make shared work meaningful, and to create wisdom and vision as part of this collaborative learning. This requires that you be open to learning and alert to opportunities where you can remove workplace obstacles.

Openness and reciprocal learning have another advantage. Both foster integrity. A loss of integrity, by contrast, can lead to workplace addictions, the topic of the next section.

10. Transcend Addictions

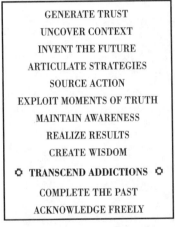

GENERATE TRUST
UNCOVER CONTEXT
INVENT THE FUTURE
ARTICULATE STRATEGIES
SOURCE ACTION
EXPLOIT MOMENTS OF TRUTH
MAINTAIN AWARENESS
REALIZE RESULTS
CREATE WISDOM
✪ TRANSCEND ADDICTIONS ✪
COMPLETE THE PAST
ACKNOWLEDGE FREELY

ADDICTIVE WORKPLACE BEHAVIORS

Recently, authors Anne Wilson Schaef and Diane Fassel advanced the idea that a workplace itself can assume the properties of an addictive substance. Severely addicted persons experience a loss of freedom, integrity, and vitality that those outside the clutches of the addiction can see but that is hidden from the addict due to the self-concealing dynamics of the condition.

> Anything can be addictive when it becomes so central in one's life that one feels that life is not possible [without it].[3]

> When loyalty to the organization becomes a substitute for living one's own life, then the company becomes the addictive substance of choice.[4]

Schaef and Fassel list symptoms and behaviors, common to addictive workplaces, that they have seen in consulting with hundreds of clients.[5]

- Raging or other forms of abusive behavior on the part of key management figures.
- Physical health problems, such as high blood pressure, ulcers, and other stress-related illness.
- Psychological malaise such as loss of joy in working, sullen attitudes, resignation, fear.
- A culture of hidden expectations—people are "in favor" or "out of favor" for reasons that are spoken of only behind closed doors, never openly.
- Inability of people to formulate and follow long-range strategies and goals.
- Crisis-driven behavior that always responds to the perceived needs of the moment.
- A reward system that is neither comprehensible nor geared to the organization's long-term health.

In any addiction, all interpretations support the maintenance of the addiction. Suppose, for example, that the addiction of a key manager is to power, status, and position. Anything questioning that power will be dismissed, even if the power that this key manager holds is ruining the company. Authority-based systems with few checks and balances, where top management is isolated from employees, are especially prone to this particular form of addiction.

THE OVERRIDING GOAL OF POWER IS TO MAINTAIN POWER, NOT TO DO WHAT IS BEST FOR THE BUSINESS.

Schaef and Fassell go on to say that addictive organizations, in their view, will experience the following results unless a program of recovery is successfully undertaken:

- People in organizations cannot solve their problems; instead the situation become worse as more dangerous addictive solutions are attempted.
- They become less ethical and more ruthless.
- Their best people leave.
- They eventually bottom out.

How to Make Work Rewarding

Many organizations foster addictive patterns of behavior and addictions to themselves. In his account of events at Data General, author Tracy Kidder[6] relates an employment interview in which the pressures of the job are explained to an eager young applicant:

You're gonna die, but you're gonna die in glory.[7]

The four workplace mindsets, introduced in chapter 2, lend themselves, in extreme cases, to particular forms of addiction. The authoritarian mindset can degenerate into an addiction to power and control, for its own sake. The mindset of orderly stereotyping can become an addiction to order—bureaucracy gone mad. The mindset of broad understanding can become an addiction to indecision—forever postponing judgment and referring matters to endless committees. And the mindset for continuous transformation can degenerate into an addiction to constant change and constant novelty.

COMMUNICATIONS THAT FOSTER ADDICTION

Addictions are initiated and held in place by types of communications. Foremost among these is the empty, unfulfilled, and unattainable promise. A promise that is always in the future hooks people into pursuing it, much as a donkey pursues a carrot on a stick. When reviewing an individual's performance, one manager is fond of saying,

Well, you're getting there

as his highest acknowledgment, no matter how extraordinary the individual's performance. With this manager, no one ever actually gets there.

In the black-humor war novel *Catch-22*,[8] the bomber pilots are constantly terrified for their lives, in fear of being shot down. As a hope, as a promise for the future to keep them flying, command sets a limit of 20 missions that are required before they can go home. As the main character approaches 20 missions, command sets the limit higher, to 25. As he approaches 25, they raise it to 30 missions. Schaef and Fassel characterize an addictive company promise as:

If you live up to what the company promotes, you may even be liked, and "belong"[9]

someday. In certain high-growth companies, as the employee population swells and gains seniority, the top job titles get filled. Personnel then simply adds more job titles and classifications on top of the ones that previously were the top. No one actually ever arrives at the top.

The purpose of such unfulfillable promises is to distract people's attention away from the embarrassing problems in the present. This is different from an invented, inspiring future that empowers people and gives them free choice. Yet, even when empowering, corporate missions and visions can become addictive promises. This is the dangerous side of empowerment, of the quest for ever-higher levels of achievement, service, and quality. When the pursuit of excellence turns from free choice to obsession, addiction sets in. Some authors even advocate obsession.

Even a pocket of excellence can fill your life like a wall-to-wall revolution. We have found that the majority of passionate activists who hammer away at the old boundaries have given up family vacation, little league games, birthday dinners, evenings, weekends and lunch hours, gardening, reading, movies, and most other pastimes. . . . Excellence is a high-cost item.[10]

The end result of this type of obsession is burnout, loss of meaning in life, and death.

Addictive communications are often manifested in reward systems. In many personnel organizations, it is common to speak of giving someone a large raise as

Giving them a good hit.

How to Make Work Rewarding

A "hit" is slang for an injection of a narcotic, and the choice of term is deliberate in this context. The metaphor signals the underlying ideas of addiction, dependency, and manipulation that are the operative concepts behind many corporate personnel systems.

MISGUIDED REWARD SYSTEMS THAT HAVE NOTHING TO DO WITH THE ORGANIZATION'S LONG-TERM BEST INTERESTS ARE A STRONG CLUE TO ADDICTION.

Most personnel organizations publicly espouse the philosophy that the better someone performs, the greater should be the reward. In practice, however, workplace rewards rarely work this way. Corporate middle managers are typically asked to prepare a salary plan a year in advance. This means estimating not how well people have done, but how well they are expected to do in the coming year. These estimates become part of a budget. The manager will be evaluated, not on how well people do in his group, but rather on how closely he stays within his budget estimates. Therefore, when it comes time to actually give raises, the manager sees no choice but to award increases on the basis of the past year's estimates—not on how well people actually did. Someone exceeding expectations cannot receive a commensurate reward because that would disrupt the budget that was planned the previous year. Thus, when an individual or a team strongly exceeds the expectations of the manager, this creates a situation that is actually unwelcome, undesirable, and disruptive.

This approach to rewards might even make some sense to people, except that administrators generally do not explain it. It is considered secret, privileged information that would be disruptive for employees to know. As a result of this approach, some people go unrewarded for extraordinary achievements, and others receive undeserved rewards for poor performance. Over time, people come to realize that their raises bear no discernible relationship to their performance. This again might be understandable if it were openly discussed. For example, administrators could be quite open with people about how the reward system actually works and explain that it is not, in fact, tightly related to performance, due to the limitations of operating within a centrally planned corporate economy. Unfortunately, the authorities in the typical workplace continue to speak as though people are being paid for performance, even though everyone realizes they are not.

The net result is a loss of integrity by managers and a loss of trust and confidence by employees with respect to management and personnel. The entire system is held in place by taboo and secrecy, another hallmark of an addictive system in operation. The addiction here is to secrecy, to the illusion of power that secrecy provides. In the transformed, addiction-free organization, every aspect pertaining to the reward system is open and public knowledge.

All addictive systems are characterized by secrecy and rules of silence. In a dysfunctional family, for example, it is forbidden to openly discuss the dysfunctions of the family and its members. Similarly, workplaces with addictive communication patterns maintain secrecy.

Secrecy is a clue to addiction.

LET PEOPLE GO

The opposite of addiction is openness and freedom. Most organizations, and even relationships, have elements of coercion.

Any attempt to manipulate people prevents them from doing their best. This is because manipulation always contains an element of deception and if people are deceived, they have neither the context nor the trust to do high-quality work.

Manipulation is disempowering.

For the high-performance, transformed organization, then, the ideal is complete openness of information and complete freedom for people to come and go. Every organization wants the best possible people. The best possible people are those who are also in high demand elsewhere. The acid test of a manipulation-free, addiction-free organization comes when valued individuals decide to leave.

How to Make Work Rewarding

THE ADDICTION-FREE ORGANIZATION PROVIDES ITS PEOPLE WITH
AS MUCH SUPPORT FOR LEAVING AS FOR STAYING.

This is far from the norm in today's corporate culture. Instead, when a valued employee leaves, the history of that person's contributions are sometimes rewritten.

Fred's a great consultant. He pulls in top billable hours and the clients like him

becomes

I always had doubts about Fred

after Fred leaves.

Most organizations have a policy of not forwarding former employees' mail. Such policies have various convoluted rationales, but the general effect is to imbue the current employees with a manipulative fear that they will cease to exist if they decide to leave the company. Since working for a corporation occupies much of an employee's waking life, it is not surprising that the values and worldview of the workplace become the employee's own. A competent and skilled senior manager, popular with employees and customers and admired by his peers, says,

I'd like to go out on my own, but I'd probably starve.

These are not the words of a man in an empowering environment. These are the words of a workplace addict. As Schaef and Fassel say:

Because the organization was so primary in their lives, because they were totally preoccupied with it, they began to lose touch with other aspects of their lives and gradually gave up what they knew, felt, and believed.[11]

TOOLS FOR TRANSFORMATION: THE PHOENIX AGENDA

In a world of commerce that is fast-moving, where technologies and entire industries change radically every few years, it is absolutely vital to have a workforce that is alert to trends and is aware, that takes an interest in life and in society generally, and that is perceptive, self-confident, and bold. None of these things are true of workplace addicts whose world narrows down to the tiny slice of reality provided by their particular corporate culture.

Today's flat organizations benefit from people who can quickly learn new skills, who can leap into new groups and situations and be effective quickly, who are valued for their broad knowledge, and

COMMUNICATIONS TO TRANSCEND ADDICTIONS

Intent:	Break out of self-defeating patterns and habits.
Appropriate grammar:	*Reality probe:* "Is there anything in our behavior that is not serving our own best interests?"
Work climate when you transcend addictions:	Restoration, renewal, rebirth, salvation, freedom, transcendence.
Inappropriate grammar:	*Transformational proclamation:* "My job is far and away the most important thing in my life."
	Action request: "Don't ever talk to me about that."
	Status report: "For their own good, we mustn't tell the employees about this."
Work climate when you maintain addictions:	Continual crisis, out of control, excessive work, glassy stares, abuse, raging, refusal to talk, eventual total organizational collapse.
Practical steps to transcend addictions:	Be open to coaching, use outside perspectives, use meditation and other forms of relaxation.

who have the self-confidence to chart their own career paths. These are precisely the sorts of people who have the greatest mobility in the job market at large. Rigid, hierarchical organizations discourage people with these same qualities.

THE FLUID, FLEXIBLE, ENTREPRENEURIAL WORKPLACE OF THE '90S AND BEYOND NEEDS EMPLOYEES WHO VALUE FREEDOM. SUCH EMPLOYEES NEED NOT AND WILL NOT STAY IN ADDICTIVE, AUTHORITARIAN ENVIRONMENTS.

Workplace addictions are held in place and maintained by patterns of communications. Similarly, they can be broken by altering communications. It is instructive to note that the most successful personal recovery program in the world, Alcoholics Anonymous, works entirely by people talking to people—no drugs, operations, or shock treatment—just by talking, openly and honestly. The communications are highly designed, refined, and structured, to be sure, but they are just words and they work.

Addictions thrive on secrecy, concealment, and denial. They cannot exist under conditions of complete honesty and integrity. Therefore, the more honest and open a workplace, the less chance for addictive thought processes and behaviors to take hold. Free inquiry as a probe into reality is the weapon of choice against workplace addiction.

11. Complete the Past

GENERATE TRUST
UNCOVER CONTEXT
INVENT THE FUTURE
ARTICULATE STRATEGIES
SOURCE ACTION
EXPLOIT MOMENTS OF TRUTH
MAINTAIN AWARENESS
REALIZE RESULTS
CREATE WISDOM
TRANSCEND ADDICTIONS
✪ COMPLETE THE PAST ✪
ACKNOWLEDGE FREELY

PUTTING THE PAST TO REST

What does putting the past to rest mean and how could it be relevant to business? What is a project or undertaking like with a past that has not been put to rest? You and other team members may have a sense of being stuck and unable to move forward. You may experience regret or even yearning about the past—a looking back—rather than a looking forward. You find yourself reliving a conversation or event over and over again, waking in the silence of the night to rethink it once again. Perhaps there are open wounds and animosities. You may feel angry and uncentered. All of these things point to a need to complete the past.

Without completion of the past, no progress is possible. When you lack a sense of acceptance and serenity about what is past, no matter whether that past is glorious or catastrophic or somewhere in between, you become obsessed with what the past represents and cannot move beyond it.

Have you ever made a promise to someone, a report that you would write, a luncheon date that you were going to have, or something similar, that for some reason you failed to carry out? Then you see the person in the hall and experience a little sense of unease; you avoid speaking to them. And then, as the days and weeks go by, your uneasiness becomes greater so that at some point, you may actually try to avoid the person because you know that you have broken a promise that you do not want to acknowledge. Does this sound familiar? What may be missing is a communication about the past that would put it to rest. For example, you might go up to the person and say,

Look, I promised that I would do this thing for you and I didn't and I'm sorry. Is there anything that we can do now?

That would be a simple and clean communication about the past.

THE PRICE PAID FOR A LACK OF COMPLETION ABOUT THE PAST IS A LOSS OF VITALITY.

When completion is missing, you may experience a sense of exhaustion, tiredness, and emptiness in life. Similarly, when things are brought to a compelling, significant, accepting, and reconciling completion, you experience the ability to move forward into new projects and new futures; you feel freed to create something new.

One useful thing to notice in society is the powerful historic connection between endings and ritual. Many of our more elaborate and long-lived rituals are rituals of completion. Consider the funeral ritual at the close of human life itself. At its best, a funeral is a celebration of a person's life and accomplishments. It is a way for the people left behind to come together in significant and meaningful tribute to the deceased person and also to begin to create for themselves a new future and a sense of life ongoing.

A group of managers in Holland is responsible for a 700-person organization of software developers and support people. This group has for years been a part of Philips Information Systems Division and has been acquired by Digital Equipment Corporation a few months previously. Many of the managers have 20 or more years seniority with Philips. What is immediately striking about the office building is the amount of display and remembrance material pertaining to Philips. A huge sign that reads "Philips" sits on top of the main building. The halls are plastered with Philips posters proclaiming various, now defunct, programs and initiatives. All the office stationery, pads, desk sets, and other memorabilia bear the Philips logo. When several of the managers are asked if these artifacts mean anything, if the group has been able to put the Philips past behind them, they reply,

Oh, yes, no problem.

Perhaps this is maturity, hardheaded business thinking, and an example of the famous Dutch stoicism. But when they hear about the idea of completion, of putting the past to rest, they are riveted. One manager suddenly and loudly proposes mounting an immediate expedition during lunch to scale the main building and tear down the Philips sign! Another man organizes a campaign to remove all the old Philips posters and stationery forthwith. After a brief discussion about completion, these professional, reserved, and highly capable men (they are all men) arrange to hold a wake for Philips, for all the memories—successes and disappointments— that their rich past holds for them. It is very clear to them that this is an essential step to take before joining Digital with full enthusiasm and getting on with their new future.

COMPLETION AND RITUAL

Another example of a completion ritual is the academic graduation or commencement. Those two words are revealing because graduation implies an ending, whereas commencement implies a beginning. Graduations, or commencements, are for the most part very upbeat events. Few people are sad about graduating, few people have a sense of loss or regret. Mostly, they are excited about getting on with their lives, finding jobs, or going on for further education. But it is an event that marks the completion of a significant achievement or a significant step in life.

In American business, ritual is rare. While there are some rituals, such as a farewell luncheon for a departing employee or a "first product ship" party, for the most part these events are infrequent and isolated and do not draw on any richly developed body of practice or rules.

WISE WORKPLACE LEADERS PAY ATTENTION

TO COMPLETION RITUALS.

COMPLETION AND LAYOFFS

The early 1990s are a time of large-scale layoffs at many companies in many industries. In some of these, it is common practice, once the decision has been made to terminate someone, to have a security guard go to their office, stand by while they pack up, and then escort them out the door, quickly, to be sure they don't have a chance to speak to anyone. This policy is based on a legitimate business concern; the distraught employee might commit sabotage at the workplace or might speak to others in a way that would spread dissension. On the other hand, the practice denies any kind of completion for both the employees and their colleagues. One woman, for example, spent a week weeping in her apartment. This is cruel and unnecessary, and returns to haunt the perpetrators.

IF YOU DENY SOMEONE COMPLETION, YOU CREATE AN ENEMY.

LARGE COMPANIES THAT LAY OFF EXTENSIVE NUMBERS OF

PEOPLE IN UNPLEASANT AND THOUGHTLESS WAYS ARE INSURING

FOR THEMSELVES A BODY OF ENEMIES WHO WILL, IN TIME, RISE

AGAIN AND SEEK VENGEANCE.

For example, one laid-off purchasing manager from a particular company soon found employment in another firm. For the rest of his career, he saw to it that the new company never gave business to his former employer. Thus, it is extremely poor business practice to lay people off in a way that denies completion. It is wise to consider termination policies that both allow completion for the people involved and also protect the company's interests.

As an illustration of how to handle layoffs well, here is how one enlightened senior manager handles them. She, the firing manager, meets face to face with the people affected. She apologizes on behalf of herself and the company for what is being done. She praises and thanks the employees for their past contributions, explaining that the termination is no reflection on them, that business conditions and poor management practices have gone to the point that the company can simply no longer continue to exist in its present form. Also, she offers to write the strongest possible letter of recommendation and explanation of the circumstances on behalf of the individuals to prospective employers. She ensures that mail will be forwarded indefinitely and that recommendations are kept on file. She asks if there is anything they need or want to say, anyone they need to say good-bye to. In short, she acts with integrity. Many of the people thank her, and even later write to say what a huge difference that interview makes. It also makes a difference for the company. By handling a difficult episode with honor, when the company eventually returns to profitability, valuable former employees can be easily hired back. And, in the meantime, they do not become enemies. Communications for completing the past work in both directions.

CONTINUOUS COMPLETION

These examples may give the impression that completion is a rare event—something that is only done with an elaborate celebration or ceremony at the end of a long project, career, or life. But completion does not have to come only at the end of lengthy projects. It can actually be something that is generated continuously.

IT IS POSSIBLE TO CREATE A WORK LIFE THAT CONSTANTLY
PROVIDES A SENSE OF COMPLETION.

For example, consider the job of taking phone-in catalog orders from customers all day. It is possible to consider the job as drudgery and approach it as a mindless chore. It is also possible to do the job with commitment to quality and a commitment to ongoing closure. That will look and feel like each individual phone order as it is taken and answered is the whole universe of work to you. At the moment of a single call being finished, that call feels like the best-handled call in the whole world. To create this state, try saying,

That was the best-handled phone order in the whole world,

as you finish a call. Better yet, say that to a trusted partner who is watching you and ask them to verify it. You may find you have generated a whole universe of meaning by a simple act of communication. You may also find that as each call is finished there is a sense of completion accompanied by a sense of moving gracefully on to the next call. Now imagine what work would be like if every task that you undertook had a commitment to quality and had an end that was in some sense perfect. Completion and quality are intimately linked.

So it is not necessarily the case that completion has to come just at the end of lengthy projects. It can be generated moment by moment in an ongoing way. You could, for example, imagine what a sense of completion at the end of each working day would be. You would feel an acceptance of what you achieved, and walk out of the building with peace of mind, satisfaction, a sense of putting business to bed for the night. You could go home free to enjoy family, friendship, the evening meal, sleeping, and so on. And then, of course, you would start up again the next day. The opposite of that would be leaving work with a sense of everything up in the air, everything jangled, nerves frayed, nothing having been achieved, just problems and worries with more of the same to come tomorrow.

Good leaders know about completion and will find opportunities to generate it. For example, when you facilitate a meeting, speak powerfully and appropriately at the end to bring about completion. How many meetings have you attended that simply peter out? The discussion winds down, people get up and leave, no one is thanked for a contribution, and there is no summary of what was accomplished or what the next steps will be. What is missing is completion.

TRY COMPLETING YOUR NEXT MEETING IN A POWERFUL AND ACKNOWLEDGING WAY.

To give a meeting completion, spend the last three or four minutes of the meeting acknowledging participants, reviewing the accomplishments of the meeting, and setting the stage for the next meeting. People will walk out of the meeting with the satisfaction that there was purpose to their being there, that they contributed something, and that they were acknowledged. And, of course, they will want to come back and contribute to the next meeting.

COMMUNICATIONS FOR COMPLETION

One very rich and fertile area of opportunity for generating completion is in any situation where something is left unsaid, left hanging, or where something from the past never got resolved. You may want to go up to that person that you worked with five years ago and did not treat very well, who you know is angry with you, and you may want to apologize. Who knows what that might bring? Your willingness to approach this person may well provide you with an opportunity to create a new work relationship and renew a once vibrant friendship.

You might want to design a completion conversation for the end of the day that allows you to go home with a sense of satisfaction and peace. If you're nearing the end of a major project, a major phase of your life, a major phase of your career, you might want to design a more ambitious completion conversation. What would an office party be like that was actually designed from the point of view of meaningfully acknowledging people's contributions and of giving a *powerful* sense of completion?

You need completion on anything to move beyond the past. It is one of the few facets of The Phoenix Agenda that points both to the past and also to a liberating future. You cannot generate tomorrow's project by looking in the rearview mirror.

COMPLETION CLEARS THE WAY FOR A FRESH COMMITMENT
TO THE FUTURE.

You can invent completion conversations that are quite appropriate in the face of what most people call failures. An example would be a canceled project. Usually, when things do not go well, everyone slinks away, and the pain of the failure remains for a long time. Finding a way to speak into that pain and acknowledging a team creates a path by which the team can complete. Giving a team the chance to speak publicly about their own personal commitments and issues around a canceled project also heals.

I remember a canceled advanced development project that I learned a great deal from and was able to carry forward into other projects. Management disbanded the group with no ceremony and no thanks. A year later, I had the opportunity to say publicly, in a staff meeting attended by the old project leader, that I really appreciated the work that he had done on that canceled project, that I learned from it, and that it allowed us to create our own next-generation venture. He came up afterward, quite moved, and said that no one had ever said anything like that to him before and that he had never heard praise for a canceled project in his entire business career. This individual would grant me a significant business favor tomorrow or even 10 years from now. Completion can create lifetime relationships.

Communications to Complete the Past

Intent:	Free up energy to construct the future. Declare victory and heal old wounds.
Appropriate grammar:	*Status report:* "I am proud to announce that the ASAP project was completed successfully on schedule."
	Action request: "I ask that, if you can find it in your heart, to please forgive my stupidity. What I did was thoughtless, and I will do anything to make amends."
	Transformational proclamation: "We declare this project complete. We achieved great things, learned a lot, and treated each other well. Even though some things we hoped to do, others will now have to carry on, we can all proceed to our next adventure with pride and confidence. We did our best."
Work climate when you complete the past:	Freedom, moving on, forgiveness, closure, and vitality.
Inappropriate grammar:	*Reality probe:* "How could this have happened? Who is to blame?"
	Action request: "Forget about that project. It's history!"
	Status report: "This project isn't over."
Work climate when you leave the past incomplete:	Pain, endless rehashing, old agenda, hatred, revenge, aimlessness, and inability to commit to new projects.
Practical steps to complete the past:	Arrange a ceremony at project completion, forgive people who have wronged you, ask forgiveness from those you have wronged, make a list of positive achievements and past learnings, and actively maintain past friendships and associations.

12. Acknowledge Freely

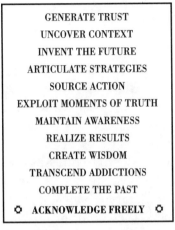

GENERATE TRUST
UNCOVER CONTEXT
INVENT THE FUTURE
ARTICULATE STRATEGIES
SOURCE ACTION
EXPLOIT MOMENTS OF TRUTH
MAINTAIN AWARENESS
REALIZE RESULTS
CREATE WISDOM
TRANSCEND ADDICTIONS
COMPLETE THE PAST
✿ **ACKNOWLEDGE FREELY** ✿

ACKNOWLEDGMENT HONORS PEOPLE

Acknowledgment is basically telling the truth in a way that honors and supports others. Acknowledgment reinforces trust. Acknowledgment at its deepest expresses our fundamental interdependence and interconnectedness. While it can be given in many different forms, the most powerful form is public acknowledgment.

A retiring vice president sent the following magnificent message to his people on the occasion of his retirement:

> . . . at the end of November, I will leave the group and the company. More importantly, I will leave you. This has been one of the hardest decisions of my career.

> I believe you constitute the most capable and professional group at the company and probably in the world. We have worked hard to create this, and I believe we have succeeded. . . . The challenge to apply this in the ever changing software world will be up to you. [The senior vice president] will decide on his organization and management before I leave. I am confident that any future decisions and management setup will insure your overall success as the company builds for the future.

> During the last 15 years at the company, I have personally been given credit for a lot of things I did not deserve. In actuality, the credit for all these accomplishments must accrue to all of you.

In terms of The Phoenix Agenda as a whole, this acknowledgment contains many powerful elements. It builds trust through self-disclosure, documents results, creates a new future by issuing a challenge, identifies a shift in context, endorses a network of support for this moment of truth, completes an era, and expresses deep acknowledgment. Powerful acknowledgments, such as this, make the speaker vulnerable and speak specifically to the inner resources that the people being acknowledged had to draw upon in order to achieve the results.

In business as usual, powerful acknowledgment is rare. In many organizations, the needs of acknowledgment are met through reward and recognition programs delivered only after evidence of extraordinary performance or delivery of results. Every year, a group of middle managers raise the issue of rewards. Every year, the team brainstorms a list of ways that, in their words, expresses their appreciation to people for the good work they are doing. The ideas cover such things as promotions, small monetary rewards, a public announcement, a plaque, or a citation in the monthly progress report to higher management. In their discussions, they are quite explicit that the purpose of the rewards is to get the employees to work even harder. In the back of their minds, every year, is the nagging thought that all of these things are not hitting the mark quite right, that they are somehow hollow, almost phony, and are being received as the carrot end of a manipulative management carrot-and-stick approach. In actuality, of course, the management team owes all their success, status, and position as managers to the good efforts of their people.

The issue troubling this management team is the difference between self-serving favors, given in expectation of return, and true acknowledgment that springs from generosity and trust. Contrast the following two statements of acknowledgment:

Jim, you've done a good job. Keep it up.

Jim, you've done a good job—much better than I ever could. I know what this project cost you—how hard you had to work and what you had to give up to achieve it. If you like, I will work with you to find ways to achieve extraordinary results at less personal cost. I owe my own position and success to your efforts and to the efforts of your teammates. Thank you.

In the first case, the manager is not even in the picture. It is manipulative in that it suggests that future acknowledgments will be contingent on further heroic performance. In the second case, the manager speaks the truth about the relationship, what it means and who benefits, and casts the appreciation in personal terms. Given that it comes from integrity, the second acknowledgment is likely to be heard profoundly.

ACKNOWLEDGMENT IS FREE

While everyone appreciates financial rewards, these alone buy only an unstable and deficient loyalty, especially in an affluent and mobile society. Above and beyond the impact of giving money, any communication that conveys a sense of belonging, a sense of meaning, relatedness, and purpose is highly acknowledging.

One manager discovers that virtually every employee prizes and keeps a file of acknowledging letters and memos. He prints a collection of these to give people ideas about how to write acknowledgments. The collection is a sellout.

Why do we interact with each other at all? The deepest acknowledgment may be one that recognizes our fundamental interconnectedness as human beings, sometimes called love. A good product or service acknowledges this truth, this interconnectedness. Have you ever sensed, through a product that really delighted you, a gratitude and appreciation for the men and women who created it, even though you had no idea who they were? By the way, the vice president's retirement acknowledgment, quoted above, ended with the words

Please know that I love you all.

Tools for Transformation: The Phoenix Agenda

Communications to Acknowledge Freely

Intent:	Powerfully and unmistakably recognize others for their contribution and dedication.
Appropriate grammar:	*Status report:* "This announcement from the vice president of sales acknowledges your success in selling the largest number of new licenses last year."
	Action request: "I request that you tell me immediately when you think that I have not properly acknowledged someone on the team for their hard work and ideas."
	Transformational proclamation: "You've done a wonderful job, better than I could have. You are a tremendous asset to the organization."
Work climate when you acknowledge freely:	Appreciation, gratitude, interconnectedness, loyalty, willingness to go the extra mile, and extraordinary teamwork.
Inappropriate grammar:	*Reality probe:* "It's time for your review. How do you think you did?"
	Action request: "Well, you did okay this time, but I expected more from you. Get with the program."
	Status report: "On a scale of 1 to 5, your performance rates a 2."
Work climate when you forget to acknowledge:	Jealousy, backbiting, scheming, rivalry, private agendas, disloyalty, and resentment.
Practical steps for powerful acknowledgment:	Acknowledge freely and often. Acknowledge who the person had to be to do what they did. Put it in writing. Praise someone immediately after they make a presentation. Do not mix acknowledgment with criticism.

PART III

Advanced Strategies for Workplace Transformation

Intelligent organizations have to be run by persuasion and by consent.

—Charles Handy, business author and teacher

Turbocharging the Agenda

*Survival is staying on the field, playing the game, learning
the rules, and beginning to grow.*

—Paul Hawken, entrepreneur

Benefits of Using The Phoenix Agenda

The Phoenix Agenda is designed to help you in all business and
workplace situations where you are working toward some result
that you have not yet achieved. If you make a serious effort to
master The Phoenix Agenda and apply it to all aspects of your
workplace life, you can expect the following benefits:

- Honor, integrity, and purpose in your workplace efforts.
- Unusual insight into the behavior of others.
- Ability to conceive projects and results that you and other
  people find remarkable.
- Capability to take on ever-larger, more impactful projects.
- Improvement and clarity in nonworkplace relationships.

This chapter contains a variety of ideas and conceptual tools to help you achieve these benefits. In part II, the 12 facets of the Agenda were presented one at a time. Real workplace communications and situations involve all facets at once, in constantly changing strengths and shadings. The examples and conceptual tools in this section are designed to increase your fluidity in using the Agenda in complex, everyday workplace situations.

Two Sides of Communication: Presentation and Reception

The power of The Phoenix Agenda to produce benefits derives from the view that language creates reality.

COMMUNICATION IS NOT ABOUT REALITY.
COMMUNICATION CREATES REALITY.

Orwell's dark classic, *1984*, describes a totalitarian world in which a sinister government seeks to maintain and extend control by not just censoring language, but by redesigning it as well. Words, phrases, and ways of speaking are obliterated, deleted from the dictionaries, workplaces, and schools. What remains is an impoverished form of communication in which it is not possible to say, or even think, negative or subversive thoughts about the regime and about its dictator, Big Brother.[1]

The purpose of The Phoenix Agenda is to achieve exactly the opposite. By providing an expansive system of communication, it enables you to create the reality and the results you want. You can not make things happen by wishing and hoping that everything could be different or by waiting for someone else to give you the answers. The key to getting the results you want in your workplace is your ability to listen and speak in a way that powerfully puts you and others into action. The Phoenix Agenda has, at its core, the view that all results are initiated and brought to completion through communication.

All communication requires a speaker (presenter of message) and a listener (receiver of message). When you speak, you speak to someone who, in turn, listens to what you say. We refer to the act of speaking and the context of that speaking as

presentation

and to the act of listening, including the context of that listening, as

reception.

Whatever reality is created in an act of communication is determined by intricate and strong interactions between presentation and reception. The presentation does not create reality in isolation from the person who is listening. Human beings as receivers take an extremely active role in determining what they hear. They can distort, tune in, tune out, or even alter the meaning of what they hear completely.

THE QUALITY OF THE RECEPTION DETERMINES THE QUALITY OF THE COMMUNICATION.

To realize this, imagine that you have five minutes to make a presentation to a large audience on a topic of extreme importance to you. The topic is one that you care about deeply, and you have prepared your remarks meticulously. You get up to speak and deliver the first few words. Murmurs, giggles, and titters move through the audience. You press on and someone shouts,

That's ridiculous!

Everyone starts yelling and booing. You try to continue, but people laugh, make rude gestures, motion you to get off the podium, and sarcastically paraphrase your remarks. You expect that at any moment, they will throw eggs, cabbages, and tomatoes.

Most people would find such an experience extremely trying and difficult. Advanced training courses in public speaking use this technique to strengthen the skills of their students. The experience is staged. The audience is instructed to be obnoxious and the speaker knows beforehand that people will boo and heckle her every word. Even so, many speakers find it impossible to continue speaking with any presence or conviction. Some find the experience devastating and traumatic, and leave the stage in tears. They learn painfully the critical role of audience reception and its relationship to their ability to present.

The most effective presentation and reception require an environment in which the communication that occurs is given respect. Without respect for the people who are speaking and listening, and for the words being spoken and heard, true communication is not possible. An example of this involves a down-on-his-luck movie writer who begs for an audience with the Hollywood producer who could give him a job for a new picture. After weeks of delay, the producer grants an audience. When the writer arrives at the producer's house, he is escorted to an enormous swimming pool. The producer is sunning in the middle of the pool on a rubber raft.

Well, there he is—speak to him,

the attendant says.

But I can't swim!

We know.

So the writer wades into the pool, but as he approaches, the producer paddles away toward the deeper end. Desperate to be heard, the writer wades farther in, until the water reaches his mouth. He tries to speak but can only gurgle. The producer paddles and suns himself. Finally, attendants haul the half-drowned writer out of the pool and boot him out of the house.

Turbocharging the Agenda

You've had your audience, now get lost.

Now consider your own listening, for example, when you give interviews or attend meetings. Are you generous, attentive, and supportive? Or are you cynical, unsupportive, and uninterested? The quality of your listening is completely correlated with the quality of what the other person is able to say. Presentation and reception are interdependent and support each other, either positively or negatively. Gifted, supportive listeners—that is, people who are receptive to your messages—give you the impression that they are hanging on your every word. They maintain eye contact and give you their full attention. Poor listeners cause you to wonder why you are bothering to speak.

As you can see, presentation and reception are inextricably intertwined. If you want to be heard, design your speaking in a way that takes into account how others listen and the reception they provide to you. For example, a director of the finance department, by virtue of her viewpoint, provides a different kind of reception to others than does a vice president of research and development. If you want your organization or team to be more productive and motivated, design and practice better listening and receiving skills first, better presentation skills second.

NINETY-NINE PERCENT OF YOUR POWER TO EFFECT
TRANSFORMATION IS IN YOUR ABILITY TO LISTEN FOR VALUE.

LISTENING FOR VALUE

When listening to people, we have the ability to consciously choose what kind of reception we provide. For example, in a formal technical review, the traditional reception, that is, the usual way of listening, is to analyze what is being presented in order to find flaws. At scientific conferences, it is the norm to listen intently for any possible error of logic, preparation, or judgment. After you find one, you are expected to ask highly intelligent and penetrating questions, which in the guise of revealing truth are potentially embarrassing and undercutting. Similarly, at many senior management corporate staff meetings, the reception that people provide for each other is cynical, suspicious, and self-serving:

Is he after my budget?

How will this affect my people?

How will this proposal affect my shot at a vice presidency?

Contrast this with the possibility of listening for value. Suppose a rival manager gives a proposal to increase his budget and resources. Can you find useful ideas in his presentation? How can the financial data presented be used to provide the critical insight you need for decisive direction? Setting aside your concerns for immediate turf issues, if the proposal were enacted, would it benefit the organization as a whole? Might there be some new role for you under the new allocation of resources he is proposing? It is an extremely beneficial exercise to practice finding and acknowledging the value in everything you hear.

PRESENTING SO THE MESSAGE CAN BE RECEIVED

This model of presentation and reception implies that presentations must be tuned to receivers in order to be heard. To speak effectively to people, you must know what they expect to hear and speak to that.

The following diagram illustrates the different possible relationships between presentation and reception. The diagram shows a large circle representing the sum total of what a person or audience is prepared to receive. Any communications inside the circle will be heard and any communications outside the circle will not.

The smaller circles represent three different presentations. The first (labeled 1) symbolizes a presentation designed to be totally within the area of reception. For example, a manager is expecting the monthly status report. You send it, on time, with a fairly dry

PRESENTATION AND RECEPTION AREAS

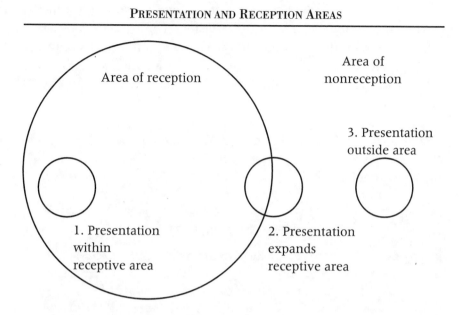

account of the month's events. Your manager's expectations are confirmed. The message has been received. No new actions result because the communication is purely routine and informational; it is just a status report.

If your presentation is far removed from the area of reception (as in circle 3 in the diagram), the message will either be rejected or not heard at all. The manager is expecting a monthly status report. You send it, including a complaint that some equipment that you need for your project has not arrived. You include no request and do not highlight your complaint in any way. Your manager takes no action. You fume for another month. The manager has completely missed your message.

PRESENTING TO ALTER THE RECEPTION

More advanced presentation strategies aim to alter and expand the receptive characteristics and tuning of the intended audience. Such presentation strategies are critical if you intend to make a difference, make a sale, advance a project, resolve a dispute, or interest others in sharing the creation of a vision. The trick is to design a communication that you position partially within and also outside of the audience's area of reception. This position, as shown by circle 2 in the diagram, has the immediate effect of expanding the area of reception.

To illustrate a communication designed to expand the area of reception itself, suppose that in your status report (which you know the manager will read), you include the following message, set in a different typeface:

EMERGENCY REQUEST

The compiler project is in danger of *slipping schedule* because we have not received requested supplies. Please sign the attached form today, so that we can place a new order. I will stop by your office at 5:00 P.M. to pick up the form. Thank you very much for helping.

This gets the necessary reaction from your busy manager. You use the status report as a communication vehicle because you know the manager will read it. You also use it in an unusual way by including a request for immediate action. This now primes the manager to expect further emergency requests via this route in the future. Your manager can tell you if this creates a problem. In fact, your action may point up deficiencies in the procurement system as a whole, which, if resolved, can lead to greater efficiencies across your organization. And it all began with your daring to expand the framework of communication between you and your manager by including an emergency request in a status report.

Design of Powerful Communications

LISTEN, INQUIRE, DESIGN, AND PRESENT

Whenever you desire something you do not have, be it higher profits, better service for your customers, satisfaction with your work, your next promotion, or the resolution of a bitter dispute, use The Phoenix Agenda to help you to effectively understand the problem and to alter it.

The first step in applying The Phoenix Agenda is to listen and be receptive to what is happening and being communicated around you. Listening with an open-mind and a sincere intent to learn is an essential and primary step to creating the clarity of insight necessary for transforming your workplace.

The second step is to compare what you find in your workplace with The Phoenix Agenda, carefully reading through all 12 of the facets and thinking about whether they describe patterns in your workplace or not. Ask yourself questions such as "Is there trust here? Do we ask the kinds of questions that uncover context? Do we listen to each other carefully and create the future of our projects together? Do we make precise requests and promises and commit openly to strategy and action? Do we do what we say and commit to results?" Use the tables in the previous chapter that summarize each facet to help determine which facets reflect your workplace and which are absent.

For example, if you sense that people are very busy in your workplace, and you see the same mistakes being repeated within each project and redundant work across projects, you might ask, "Do the people involved in these projects set aside time to learn from each other and teach?" In other words, does *create wisdom* occur within the project? "Do the members of the group trust each other and empower each other's work?" In other words, do they *generate trust?* "Do people freely express thanks and gratitude when they must depend on each other for help?" In other words, do they *acknowledge freely?* In this way, as you compare each facet to the patterns in your workplace, you can notice which of the facets are present and which are missing. Consider that it may be that one or more of the facets is always missing, or inadequately developed.

If in asking questions you discover that wisdom, trust, and acknowledgment are missing, then you might design one or more communications to *create wisdom, generate trust,* and *acknowledge freely.* The specific action you take after consulting The Phoenix Agenda is *only and always* to design and present a communication: make a phone call, attend a meeting, write a paper, pay a bill, issue an apology, make a request, write a letter, speech, report, or book. After completing the communication, you can use this same series of steps to inquire into other areas of work where you want results. As before, begin by listening.

This approach may be summarized as:

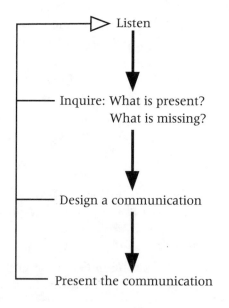

Listen

Inquire: What is present?
What is missing?

Design a communication

Present the communication

Turbocharging the Agenda

ACTIONS ARE *ALWAYS* COMMUNICATIONS.

ADAPT THE AGENDA TO YOUR CONTEXT

Design your communications to achieve the results you want in your workplace. It is possible to use The Phoenix Agenda to design all of your communications, whether formal or informal, including chance encounters in the office hallway or company parking lot. Try it. As with anything, practice makes perfect. The Phoenix Agenda is designed to be holographic. Holographic means that each facet of communication, while it stands complete and whole as a smaller unit of the full Agenda, also is essential to the complex interconnectivity that creates The Phoenix Agenda itself. As you design each of your communications, taking into account the specific context, objective of presentation, and area of reception for your needs, you are, in effect, changing the view from which you see the holograph. It is always the same image, but as you redesign and reuse the communication facets, you see a different emphasis. The intent behind the Agenda's design is to enable you to modify your communications and redesign them in a way that is appropriate to and effective within your particular business dealings and everyday concerns.

This means that your particular version of the Agenda can, and probably should, look quite different from the version presented in this book. As a stimulus to creativity, the diagram on page 208 shows one person's customized "Agenda," the Enrollment Management Model worked out by manager Peter Conklin.

Conklin's scheme is illustrated by the circle and the stages within the circle. In addressing a new project, Conklin always starts his management projects by considering Vision-Enrollment, and proceeds counterclockwise through the four quadrants of the circle. The italicized terms on the periphery of the circle show the mapping or correspondence to facets of The Phoenix Agenda. Notice that the correspondence to Conklin's Enrollment Management is close but

ENROLLMENT MANAGEMENT COMPARED WITH *THE PHOENIX AGENDA*

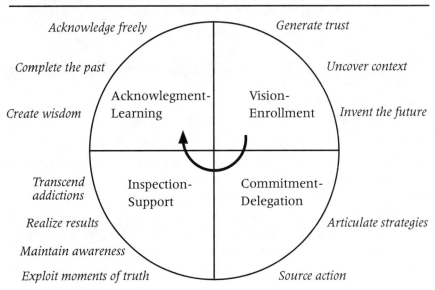

Acknowledge freely

Generate trust

Complete the past

Uncover context

Create wisdom Acknowlegment-Learning Vision-Enrollment *Invent the future*

Transcend addictions Inspection-Support Commitment-Delegation

Realize results *Articulate strategies*

Maintain awareness

Exploit moments of truth *Source action*

not exact. Conklin has chosen to represent his method as a cycle, whereas The Phoenix Agenda is designed to be thought of a holographic whole. Both approaches are legitimate and correct. One is not better than another. Conklin works in an engineering organization where people are accustomed to thinking of cycles and stages. Further, his background is in the operational aspects of business and hence gives inspection more relative emphasis. Similarly, you can work out a customized version of the Agenda, tailored to your own situation and background.

HAVE AN OBJECTIVE

Always have an objective in mind for any communication. In The Phoenix Approach, the objective is to present in an obvious and unmistakable way one or more facets of The Phoenix Agenda. For example, let us look at what happens when you forget to make a request.

Turbocharging the Agenda

A team of brilliant inventors, inexperienced in business, is determined to gain backing for their project. By perseverance and sheer good fortune, they are granted a 30-minute audience with a powerful CEO. He listens with interest while they enthusiastically describe their ideas and project. However, he seems confused about why they are meeting with him. At the end of the interview, he thanks them and the secretary shows them out. Only hours after the interview do the inventors realize that, while they succeeded in generating a future with this man and capturing his interest, they failed to make a request, such as:

Will you give us financial support this year?

The golden opportunity slips through their fingers for lack of a simple request.

Ambitious, long-term projects need to address all 12 facets of The Phoenix Agenda. Specific, limited encounters and brief communications can be designed to emphasize a few or only one. For example, if you and a co-worker quarrel, and you need to make amends, then a communication designed to complete the past must occur first.

In designing specific communications, it is helpful to consult The Phoenix Agenda and to write out or check off which facets seem most appropriate for the situation. In meeting someone for the first time, for example, it is almost always appropriate to speak in a way that generates trust. A way to do this might be to acknowledge the respect others show to this person for past accomplishments, team contribution, project results, and so forth. Acknowledgment and trust work well together.

Suppose your objective is to be accepted to graduate school. You know that the decision will be made by a graduate admissions committee. Who are the individuals who sit on this committee? What can you learn about them that will help you to build trust and acknowledgment for your work? For gaining admission to graduate school, an effective strategy is to research the published works of individual professors and to express an interest in working with them on their favorite projects. For being hired, an effective method is to find whatever problem is uppermost in the hiring manager's mind and to present yourself as a credible solution to that problem.

MAINTAIN BALANCE

As would be the case in gardening, emphasizing one or a few of the facets in The Phoenix Agenda to the exclusion of the others will lead to serious imbalances that undermine the entire system. To take a common example, most business people say that getting results is their highest priority. Constant preoccupation with results is expected as a norm. Employees are expected to be busy and constantly doing. In a company with an open-office plan where everyone can see each other, you might be embarrassed to have someone see you staring off into space at your desk, instead of writing, typing, or talking on the phone. Someone might even come up to you and tell you to get back to work.[2] In such a culture, the emphasis on quick results may be so great as to overshadow any other contribution you make in the office. You might need time to think about your own work, where your division can make a difference, and how you can improve the quality loop for your product. But as these results appear only slowly, you may feel guilty about taking the time to attend to them. It is not difficult to understand which facets of The Phoenix Agenda are missed as a consequence. You may be generating trust as a way to get results, but with no time to uncover context, you limit your ability to invent the future, to articulate strategy, or to participate in an iterative inquiry that creates wisdom. Action without strategy is often useless or even destructive, and strategy without wisdom is likely to be uninformed and flawed.

Attention to all 12 facets of The Phoenix Agenda is needed for effective action. Together, the 12 facets form a balance that naturally occurs as you use them. When the facets are used separately or in thoughtless combinations, your resulting actions have the potential to create problems that only a redesign in your communications can solve.

Turbocharging the Agenda

BE PERSISTENT

The facets of communication in The Phoenix Agenda share an important property. The real power of communication occurs in the moment of its being spoken and heard. In that moment of speaking, you create a new reality. Without your attention, effective communication occurs only by accident. For example, when you tell someone that you trust them, your word creates that trust. Without you saying this, random circumstances, and not you, dictate whether trust exists between the two of you. And unless you purposely regenerate this trust on a regular basis by saying it, you risk losing the trust you have created. What happens to your sales accounts if you do not call them for several months? What happens to your professional network if you never answer letters or calls? What happens to your marriage if you forget anniversaries?

So the reality created by communications in harmony with the facets of The Phoenix Agenda, such as trust, completion, results, and action, tends to vanish, to fall apart, to go to seed and weed over time. You cannot create it once and be done with it; rather, you must continually re-create this reality anew. Indeed, The Phoenix Agenda itself must be constantly created anew. It does not exist as a set of static points. It comes alive only in the act of you delving into each facet and searching for new expressions, new applications, and new designs as ways to bring them powerfully into your own projects and work.

In this respect, the facets of The Phoenix Agenda, by their very nature cannot be codified or written down but must be discovered and generated anew throughout life and across generations. Gardening makes a workable metaphor for appreciating the impermanent nature of these communications. No one would expect a garden to survive years of neglect or expect that someone could work a transformational miracle that would render the garden forever green without anyone ever having to tend it again. Just because you said something effective yesterday does not mean you need not say another effective thing today.

What's wrong with you? I told you you were a great employee two years ago! Isn't that enough?

If trust exists and is generated in the actual moment of expressing it, then to maintain trust you must continually express it in new and contextually appropriate ways.

HONOR YOUR WORD

Underlying the notion of committed speaking is the assumption that everything we say has the power to create a reality that was not there before. Obvious examples are: the minister pronouncing a couple as man and wife, the Congress declaring war, or someone announcing the beginning of a diet. Committed speaking is practicing, as a discipline, the art of speaking as though what you said actually created the condition that you are speaking about.

Ultimately, the power of your presentation depends upon your integrity as a person. Does it matter that you commit acts that violate your own integrity as long as they are secret and no one knows about them? Yes, in this world it does because in the creative act of launching a vision the only authority you possess is the degree to which you honor your word as yourself. Does this mean that you always keep your word? No, that is not given to mere mortals as a possibility. It does mean that the integrity of your word is a matter of deep and sacred concern for you. This does not mean concern in the sense of brooding privately about it. In fact, one of the best and quickest ways to heal a personal integrity issue is to publicly and honestly declare your lack of integrity. Launching and maintaining powerful visions require constant practice. Give your word, notice if you keep it, and take corrective action if you fall short.

DEVELOP CHARISMA

Charisma is mistakenly thought to be an innate, inherited gift. The dictionary defines it as a divinely conferred gift or power. In fact, it can be learned and used to excite and enroll others in your undertakings and projects. Charisma does not depend on polished speaking skills or on a magnetic personality. It is possible to stumble and stutter in front of an audience and still be charismatic.

CHARISMA DEPENDS ON COMMUNICATING WITH PASSION AND INTEGRITY ABOUT A FUTURE, MISSION, OR PURPOSE THAT IS LARGER THAN YOURSELF.

It can be difficult or even impossible to be charismatic if you have no vision for the future. The first step in developing charisma, therefore, is to develop a picture of the future that involves a strong element of contribution to others. The next step is to proclaim a deep commitment to that vision. In a sense, this means redefining yourself *as your vision*. For example, Ray Kroc, the founder of MacDonald's, is remembered not so much for himself as for his vision for hamburgers. People who knew him say he spoke about little else besides hamburgers. He had charisma and vision enough to launch and nurture a great international company.

CHARISMATIC MEN AND WOMEN BECOME THEIR VISIONS.

Examples of Using the Agenda

This section gives some specific examples of applying the Agenda to a range of workplace situations. In considering these examples, and applying them to your own situation, remember that The Phoenix

Agenda can be used to design any form of communication, from a chance encounter at the coffeepot lasting 60 seconds to a major project involving years of effort and thousands of people. In any undertaking, communications and actions relating to all 12 facets must be present and in balance in order for the project to be a success. If performance with respect to any single facet, or subset of facets, falls below a critical level, the project is in jeopardy. Further, without continuous and constant renewal through communication, the created reality may change over time in unwanted ways. This suggests continually regenerating each aspect of the Agenda throughout the project. This regeneration takes the form of committed, well-designed communication, that takes into account the current and ever-changing receiving characteristics of the project participants.

MEMOS THAT MATTER

Here is an example memo, quoted earlier in the book, written to obtain a meeting with a busy vice president. All 12 facets of The Phoenix Agenda appear in the memo as indicated by call-out numbers.

1. GENERATE TRUST
2. UNCOVER CONTEXT
3. INVENT THE FUTURE
4. ARTICULATE STRATEGIES
5. SOURCE ACTION
6. EXPLOIT MOMENTS OF TRUTH
7. MAINTAIN AWARENESS
8. REALIZE RESULTS
9. CREATE WISDOM
10. TRANSCEND ADDICTIONS
11. COMPLETE THE PAST
12. ACKNOWLEDGE FREELY

To: Bob Bellman, Vice President[12]

From: John Whiteside[7]

Re: Meeting about new markets[3] requested with you on March 31[2, 5]

Dear[12] Bob,

Congratulations[1] on your well-deserved[12] appointment to vice president.[11] All of us[2] learned[9, 12] from watching you. Now we might be able to apply what you have learned[9] to the challenge of a new market—we could double[3] the projected[3] profits.[8] My people and I have prepared a plan[4], code named Omega[7], that calls out a honed strategy[4], allows for rewards[12] for all involved, and has taken into account what is likely to go wrong.[6], [10] We're ready for your advice[2] and counsel.

May we meet with you at 10:00 A.M. next Friday, March 31, to present this?[5] The research people[1] and the presentation specialists[1] have put their heads together[9] to create something slick[7] that you'll enjoy[12] seeing.[7] Russ Farnsworth[1] can give you a 30-second endorsement and preview[1], if you'd like.[12] After the presentation[11], we'd like to take you out to lunch[5] to celebrate your latest achievement.[12]

Best personal regards[1], [12]

EFFECTIVE E-MAIL

Give the same careful thought to the design of E-mail communications as you would give to any important communication. E-mail communications are characterized by speed, large volume, and ease of forwarding and redistribution. This means that you have little control over who may ultimately see your message.

One busy and successful executive asks everyone who sends him E-mail to be very specific in the message header concerning what the message is about and what actions are requested of him. Try this yourself and observe the improvement in the quality of the messages you receive. Make a practice of being similarly clear in messages you send out. Also be brief. It is not uncommon for people to receive dozens or even hundreds of messages each day. By keeping your messages precise and brief, you increase the possibility that they will be read.

Because of wide potential distribution, the speed with which most of us write or read messages, and the limited nature of the medium, E-mail messages are a terrible place to express negative emotions. Save your criticisms or anger for other times and places. You will avoid a lot of pain. Be especially cautious about writing "flames"—that is, angry tirades intended for a large audience. Unless exquisitely designed and timed, these will hurt your reputation more than they help. One of the worst things you can do is to send an angry letter to a broad distribution list in an organization where you are not well known.

On the other hand, E-mail can be an excellent medium for simple requests, such as arranging a meeting or getting an approval quickly:

Please meet with us at 1:00 on Monday to set the date for field test.

Please approve by Friday my request for $1,500 to attend training.

As with any request, always say *what* you are requesting and *by when* you are requesting it.

MAKING PHONE CALLS COUNT

It is astonishing how many people answer the telephone with a tone of voice that suggests that the call is an unwelcome interruption. When this happens, it has the result of creating mistrust, incompletion, and lack of acknowledgment for the caller. Try encouraging people around you to answer the phone in an open, acknowledging way and to speak in a way consistent with sincere interest in what the caller has to say.

One never knows who might be on the other end of the line, as this next example shows. A harassed worker in the mailroom of a large corporation answers a late-night call:

Why the hell are you bothering us? Don't you know how busy we are down here?

This is the president. You're fired.

THE MAGIC MEGAPHONE

The magic megaphone is a design aid for developing a group mission, a start-up business, or a marketing campaign. Imagine that you have a message, something of value, that you wish to interest people in. By shouting, you can only attract the attention of a few people. If you use a megaphone, more people will hear you. If you use a magic megaphone that amplifies your message and makes all aspects of it coherent and mutually reinforcing, you can attract all the interest you need to achieve results.

As the following diagram shows, you speak your message into the metaphorical mouthpiece, or presentation end, of the megaphone. The message then travels from the presentation end as if through a series of amplifiers. As the message passes through each amplifier, it becomes louder and more coherent. When it finally comes out the other end, it is in a form that is tuned to the reception area of the audience that you intend to influence.

The amplifiers and filters inside the megaphone represent questions such as:

Presentation:

What is the objective or purpose of the presentation?

Vision:

What is the core philosophy or vision that gives coherency to the undertaking?

Attributes:

What concepts, characteristics, and properties derive from the vision?

Materialization:

What actual services and products would the customer receive?

Attraction:

What enticing messages will sell the undertaking?

Reception:

Who is the audience for the presentation and what is the audience ready to hear?

To use the megaphone as a design tool, answer the questions appropriate to each amplifier and fill in each compartment with ideas, using the magic megaphone diagram in this book.

Magic Megaphone

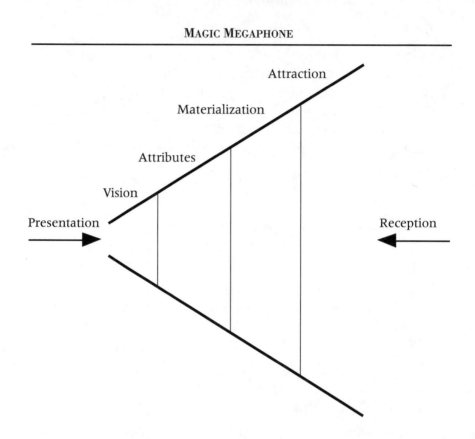

Turbocharging the Agenda

The magic megaphone works for a multiplicity of projects from community fund raising to devising corporate vision and leadership strategy. To show you how the megaphone works, we use the example of a small start-up business.

Suppose you and I are starting a modest family restaurant. We begin with vision, a simple statement of the core purpose and philosophy of the restaurant. In this example, let us use as a vision:

GOOD WHOLESOME FOOD FOR FAMILIES

From the vision, we develop a set of ideas, or operating principles that are consistent with the vision, such as:

- Family atmosphere.
- Fair, reasonable pricing.
- Popular menu choices.
- Fast service.

Next, we develop the ideas into materializations, that is, the actual product, benefit, or service that the customers will experience. This will be things such as:

- Chicken, beef, and lamb dishes.
- Smiling staff.
- Bright, clean tablecloths.
- Doggie bags.
- Free beer.

Finally, we have to attract people to our restaurant on opening day. This involves various advertising and marketing efforts. We might, for example,

- Place a newspaper ad in the Sunday funnies section.
- Hire a clown with a sandwich board.
- Have an outdoor display of balloons.
- Have kids stuff neighborhood mailboxes with a colorful announcement.

Magic Megaphone Filled In

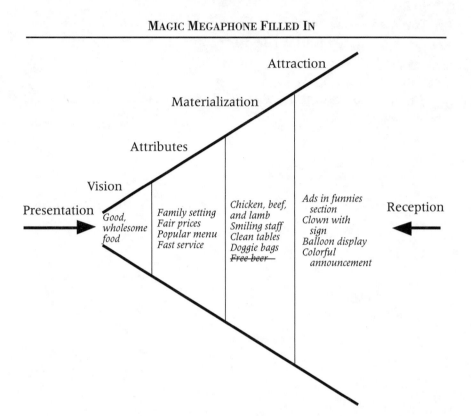

Placing all these ideas in the appropriate compartment of the megaphone lets us see if the entire package is consistent with the core purpose and philosophy. Looking over the megaphone, we notice that free beer does not seem to belong, so we cross it off.

The megaphone is in active use in large companies. It is especially useful in helping groups in corporations define and market themselves internally, as well as to customers. It is a simple tool that can be explained in a few minutes, yet it is sophisticated enough to help people visualize and coordinate a complex group mission.

Dealing with Communication Obstacles

NEGATIVISM

Some people give the appearance of being negative about every new idea or suggestion. They immediately react by pointing out flaws and pitfalls in proposals and suggestions. A useful interpretation to keep in mind when dealing with such people is that everyone basically wants to make a positive contribution and some people do not know how.

EVERYONE IS LONGING TO MAKE A DIFFERENCE.

When you encounter someone who lacks the skills to criticize constructively and compassionately, listen for the value in what they are saying and acknowledge and invite their contribution, as in:

CRITIC: That's a terrible idea!

YOU: Thanks for pointing out the difficulties. Do you have some suggestions?

INDIFFERENCE

If people are indifferent to your efforts and proposals, it means that whatever you are saying, proposing, or selling is falling outside of their area of reception. Consequently, to reach an indifferent person, change your communications.

THERE IS A KEY TO EVERYONE. IT IS JUST A QUESTION OF
FINDING IT.

In providing a product or service, an obvious piece of advice is "Know your Customer." That means research. Similarly, in the workplace, it pays to know your co-workers, subordinates, and managers. Clues abound. When you visit someone's office, for example, make a point of looking at how it is arranged and what sort of personal effects and posters are displayed. Noticing these things will give openings for conversation and trust building, as the following business anecdote shows.

A manager strives to keep a tight budget and scrutinizes all proposals carefully. He is free with criticism and rejects most proposals. Most people respond by trying to make their proposals even more down-to-earth, with elaborate justifications. He seems unimpressed. However, on his office wall are posters of fanciful achievements such as a vegetable garden under a glass dome on the surface of the moon. This clearly shows visionary tendencies. An observant team submits a proposal designed to be bold and risky, with an enticing, futuristic vision. He funds it enthusiastically.

In this example, the moonscape poster gave the team a vital clue as to which of the 12 Agenda facets the manager would be most responsive to: *inventing the future*. Most of his organization simply assumed, without looking for clues, that he would respond to the *articulate strategies* facet.

It is extremely valuable to discover which workplace mindset people tend to operate with: authoritarian, stereotyping, understanding, or transformational. Then your communications can be crafted in concepts and terms appropriate to that mindset. People who think in authoritarian or stereotyping ways, for example, are likely to be unimpressed by bold visions or anything "touchy-feely." They do respond well to proposals and analyses that convey order, rationality, and power.

POWERFUL COMPLAINING

A complaint may be legitimately made when someone breaks an explicit promise. An effective complaint contains a request to keep the promise or make amends. You reserve a table at a restaurant for 7:00 P.M. You arrive at 7:00 P.M., wait until 7:30 P.M. and are not seated. A weak complaint to make might be:

Turbocharging the Agenda

You promised us a table for 7:00 P.M. and we are upset.

A stronger complaint includes an action request:

You promised us a table for 7:00 P.M. and did not seat us. Can you now please give us a table for 8:00 P.M. and a complimentary meal at another time when you are less busy?

DIFFUSING COMPLAINTS

Complaining in the workplace is common, and corrosive. Complaints are a deficient form of speaking unless accompanied by a request for action. Usually, complaints are simply a request to be heard, a request to be acknowledged for the difficulties of workplace life. This can be effectively dealt with simply by acknowledging the complaint. If you want to stop a complaint, add a request or an offer of action to your acknowledgment:

COMPLAINER: I just don't think the marketing people are competent.

YOU: I hear what you are saying. I understand why you might feel that way given certain past experiences. What are you going to do about it? Would you like me to do anything about it?

COMPLAINER: No, nothing, thanks. I just wanted to get it off my chest.

HIDDEN AGENDAS

Straightforwardness is a rare and valuable workplace ethic. Many people operate from hidden agendas. Hidden agendas result when people do not voice problems and issues that are known but, for one reason or another, remain unspoken. Hidden agendas are often disempowering. Therefore, it is important to identify when a hidden agenda exists and to confront it as such. Because hidden agendas have unseen ties to human fears and apprehensions, it is important not to focus on blame or fault. An effective way to deal with this is to find out what the person is afraid of and promise to give support in overcoming the fear. This requires building trust. You could, for example, approach your manager directly:

> YOU: I know that there is something that is really bothering you. I sense this because you've taken on so much responsibility lately and seem frustrated and angry. You're a good friend and I want to be able to help you. Would you be willing to say what is bothering you? I promise to support you in whatever way I can.

> MANAGER: Well, between you and me, I think I've taken on more than I can handle and I'm afraid my people will begin to think that I'm incompetent.

> YOU: Is that why you sometimes come down hard on us?

> MANAGER: Yes, I guess so.

> YOU: I really appreciate you telling me this. It helps me to take what's happening around here less personally, and I promise to provide you with whatever support you need until you get this project moving again.

Such an agreement will allow both you and your manager to work more effectively and straightforwardly.

A hidden agenda is an example of a deliberately concealed context that, unchecked, can seriously undermine a workplace community. If something like this is getting in the way of a project for you, or is making things difficult in the workplace, one possible strategy is to create a moment of truth:

> *I request that we go around the room and speak frankly about our hidden agendas. If anyone is unwilling to speak, this meeting is concluded.*

This is an example of creating a moment of truth, accompanied by a conditional promise. As with any moment of truth, the result might be that people get upset or the result might be a genuine break-through in cooperation for the group. In the long run, either result is preferable to continuing to work under false pretenses. Presumably, the purpose of joint endeavor in a workplace is contribution and productivity, not the pursuit of hidden agendas. It is difficult to impossible to share accountability and trust with fellow team members if the problems you face are pitted with holes of secrecy and withheld information.

Putting It All Together

The examples in the previous section give some idea of the wide range of workplace situations to which the Agenda can be applied. Try adapting the ideas in this chapter to your own workplace. Notice how they work and make improvements and refinements. All the people who effectively use the Agenda treat it as a starting point, as a stimulus to creativity, not as a finished checklist or complete bag of tricks. The examples and conceptual tools presented here are intended both to be immediately useful and also to serve as a further spur to your own creativity.

Try, for example, using the megaphone to create a mission, action, and marketing statement for your group. See if it works. Practice making complaints until you get the result you want. Notice what happens as you begin to improve your listening skills. Use the Agenda to craft an important written request or proposal. Keep a journal of successes and setbacks and include new ideas and concepts that come to you. Invent your own conceptual tools. As you apply these ideas, you will notice unmistakable improvements in the results you obtain and in the way that others are responding to you. There will be mistakes and setbacks, but use these as an opportunity for further learning.

Above all, do not keep these techniques and ideas to yourself. The most powerful insights and results come when you share what you are doing with others.

9

Transformational Scheduling

There is chaos under heaven, the situation is good.

—Mao Zedong

Schedule and time are ever-present workplace concerns. This chapter presents a radically new approach to the classic problem of scheduling and managing massively complex projects. To illustrate the approach, a major success example is woven throughout the chapter—the story of the Alpha AXP project.

A Radical Approach to Schedule

To accomplish the largest project it has ever undertaken, a "bet the company" project, Digital Equipment Corporation throws out the entire rule book about managing schedules. At stake is the creation of fifth-generation computing:

. . . mobile, highly interactive computing that supports group work with algorithms that intelligently analyze, simulate, and synthesize in support of a wide variety of human endeavors.[1]

To realize the vision requires a massive, cross-organizational effort touching virtually every aspect of the corporation: engineering, manufacturing, product management, documentation, marketing, sales, third-party relations, and all of the support functions. The company's bottom line is affected at the rate of $1 million positively or negatively, for every hour gained or lost on the schedule. This huge project, code-named Alpha, involves the efforts of 2,000 people, reporting to dozens of different hierarchically structured organizations. The project is so vast and the entrenched organizational interests so strong that traditional management approaches are deemed hopeless from the start. Instead, the program management team, a mere eight individuals with no explicit authority, no staff reporting to them, and no budget, adopt an entirely different mindset toward scheduling and managing.

In rejecting a traditional, hierarchical approach, program manager Peter Conklin writes:

> In the classical organizational model, a hierarchical, or line, organization is formed, containing all the primary implementers. The problem with this approach to large programs is that it takes too long to form the organization. Staffing the teams and establishing operational procedures take longer than the market window and available technology allow. The result is grand visions and projects delivered years behind schedule.

In other words, an orderly organization, with all the categories and functions neatly assigned, is not the first priority for the Alpha management team; nor is applying pressure, as is typical under an authoritarian mindset. The team concludes:

> An alternative approach is to form small entrepreneurial teams and challenge them to work long hours to achieve the goals. . . . However,

when this approach is applied to large programs the result is that team members burn out without achieving the aggressive schedules demanded. Management becomes frustrated and tries again with different teams, but the results are no better.

Instead, Conklin and his fellow team members create and implement an entirely new system of large-scale management. Their radical approach, which they term enrollment management, makes no sense from within an authoritarian mindset but is a straightforward application of the mindset of continuous transformation. Its key elements are vision, precision requests, exploiting moments of truth, and free acknowledgment. The results are spectacular:

Digital met exactly the program's overall schedule to the month (i.e., date for high volume shipments), despite numerous setbacks along the way. The Alpha AXP system is meeting its original performance goals, and quality is excellent. Digital's Board of Directors has approved the full Alpha AXP program business plan and the investments necessary to capitalize on the Alpha AXP family's early successes. Initial reactions from customers have been favorable. Third parties have committed Alpha AXP support for their products in record numbers.

Underlying this success is perhaps the most difficult, yet potentially most rewarding, transformation possible for any goal-directed human endeavor—a transformation of one's relationship to time. To appreciate the Alpha management team's achievement, and to apply what was learned to our own projects, we must first consider time from the perspective of mindsets.

Workplace Mindsets Applied to Time

Time and its wise use is vital to any business. But what is time? Take the case that:

TIME IS AN INTERPRETATION, AN ARTIFACT OF ASSUMPTIONS AND VIEWPOINTS.

Creating, using, and designing the fabric of time then becomes an inquiry into the assumptions and viewpoints underlying time. To this end, the following four sections explore the different time realities that correspond to views of time under the four workplace mindsets presented in chapter 2. The main points are summarized in the accompanying table.

As you read, compare these different views of time with the personal interpretations you have for time and the degree to which these are shared or not shared with other people in your workplace. Examples to aid understanding are given throughout the following four sections, and each concludes by showing how each mindset does or does not characterize the Alpha team's approach.

SUMMARY OF WORKPLACE MINDSETS APPLIED TO TIME

Stereotypic time	Time, broadly understood	Authoritarian time	Transformational time
Sorting	Evolution	Driving to deadlines	Creative chaos
Accounting	Ebb and flow	Punctuality	Flexibility
Time clocks	Business cycles	Pressure	Speed
Billable hours	Healing	Consistency	Breakthroughs

AUTHORITARIAN TIME

The *authoritarian* workplace mindset views time as a fundamental, objective property of the universe, a measurable medium in which objects and actions coexist. Time is segmented, analyzed, and divided into units as critical increments of measurement. Objects exist as static entities in time, while actions occur within the continuum of time. Within the workplace, it is this analysis of time and its relationship to people and products (objects) and their work (action) that is most often measured and calculated as indicators of business success. Within manufacturing or office environments, it is an automatic managerial first step to study these and make decisions based on what is found. When the world screams for microchips, the manager's first reaction may be to allocate, but his immediate next step is to analyze the motions of his manufacturing line to determine how to produce more chips in a shorter time. As a result, complex project management seeks to divide work and projects into steps of time that analyze tasks and subtasks into ever-finer detail.

THE AUTHORITARIAN VIEW IS THAT IF THERE IS 100 PERCENT CONTROL OF ACTION AND TIME, RESULTS WILL BE 100 PERCENT PREDICTABLE.

This is a dominant business perspective today, and we can find many examples of where it works quite well. There are other examples where it seems not to work well at all. All knowledge work, for example, is notoriously unpredictable despite an impressive array of authority-based tools to plan, predict, and control projects.

IN THE AUTHORITARIAN WORLD OF TIME, WORDS SUCH AS *INTERVAL, DURATION, CAUSE AND EFFECT, LENGTH, SPAN,* AND *SEGMENTATION* PREDOMINATE.

Prediction and control goals are at the heart of the authoritarian mindset. A primary goal is to achieve prediction and control. This is an automatic, axiomatic commitment in this mindset. Authoritarians seek to define both outcome and means before the fact. For example, a project manager will plan out in fine time lines the exact number of tasks required on a per-person basis to complete a project. The predictability of the schedule depends on each person doing a predetermined task for an exact amount of time. Each day, she asks each person to give her the status. The outcome must be predictable. Schedules must be met. Plans must be understood and agreed-upon before they are undertaken. In each project, goals must be defined and deliverables clearly specified before management gives authorization to proceed.

To address schedule issues from this perspective, authoritarians look to the tools of force and action. They apply force to people (usually rewards and punishments) and engage in various forms of psychological manipulation to get people to do things. An authoritarian manager facing a tight issue would analyze the employees' activities in minute detail, not let them do anything that is not directly related to building the product, and institute short-milestone management. While this works, it works only up to a point.

Despite the seeming elegance of this approach, most industries face the following perennial problem:

MOST LARGE PROJECTS ARE LATE AND OVER BUDGET.

As an instance, in the 1980s, the central quality group at one large high-technology design and manufacturing company discovers that product development schedules are slipping an average of two days every week. In one large ($25 million per year expenses) software engineering group, an internal audit shows that not one single product has met its schedule over a three-year period. They also discover that it takes an average of four and one-half years to move from idea to delivered product, whereas leaner, meaner companies can do the job in one-half to one-quarter of the time. Experiences at Hewlett-Packard show that a six-month delay in getting a high-tech product to market wipes out, on average, all possible profits.[2] Clearly, something is badly amiss.

The problem is not lack of effort. The puritan work ethic fosters and rewards heroic effort. People willingly work themselves long past the point where family and health are jeopardized. Nor is the problem a lack of technical skill. The company boasts some of the finest and most experienced employees in the world. Nor is the problem lack of management attention. Enormous management pressure is always being applied to the teams to compress the schedule where possible, and not to slip. When things on a project get bad enough, the unlucky manager who must admit a schedule slip to his or her superior does so with the enthusiasm of a Japanese naval commander apologizing to the emperor after a defeat at sea. The most salient and feared word amongst the employees and their management is "schedule." Everyone is always painfully aware of schedule. Nor is the problem a lack of technologically sophisticated project management methods tools that they either have in abundance or develop themselves. Indeed, everyone agrees that time is a crucial problem, so much so that there is never enough time to think about it, much less to deal with it.

NO ONE EVER AGREES TO TAKE THE TIME TO STUDY THE
PROBLEM OF TIME.

People, realizing this, joke that they do not have the time to stop for gas. When they finally run out of gas and the schedule slips beyond recovery, 30 percent of the company's employees are laid off.

The Alpha team consciously rejects an authoritarian approach. Instead of seeking authority, such as to control budgets or to hire and fire, they deliberately choose to have no authority at all. No one reports to them. They have no budget. The only tool they have, or want, is the power of language, the power of open, honest persuasion.

STEREOTYPICAL TIME

Time and schedule are simply not a problem for people who work from the mindset of orderly stereotyping. The British administrators at the height of the colonial empire in the 19th century were primarily concerned with filling in forms and reports properly: so many battles lost and won, so many colonies in revolt with thus and such numbers subdued. The administrators were not concerned with understanding or acting upon the underlying meaning of these events. From this mindset, events such as schedule slips are simply things that happen. Operating within this mindset, everyone accepts this as inevitable, just as many corporations accept as inevitable that the vast majority of their products are late. Similarly, an accounting department or an auditing department is typically more concerned with reporting the facts than reporting the underlying meaning or implication of those facts.

STEREOTYPICAL TIME USES WORDS SUCH AS: *BILLABLE HOURS, DOWNTIME, TIME CARD, PRODUCTIVE TIME, TIME OF DAY, FISCAL YEARS, MEASURED TIME,* AND *QUARTERS.*

The time categories of an orderly, stereotyped world are rigid. What happens when we change the rules of this particular reality? A Japanese trade delegation mentioned that the single most productive step American companies could take is to abolish the use of fiscal quarters and to suspend quarterly reports to stockholders. This would, in their view, leave management freer to focus on long-term actions and solutions. The recommendation was rejected. But at what cost to American business?

Let us look for a moment at the hidden costs of the stereotypical time reality. In fact, quarterly reporting of sales figures as an act of measurement has a strong influence on the phenomenon it measures. It is a known fact amongst savvy customers of many corporations that they can get the best deals on equipment if they approach a sales person just before the end of the quarter when the sales department is under the greatest pressure to show strong figures. As a result, the customers wait until the end of the quarter, when they have the leverage to bargain for a reduced price. The discontinuity of the quarterly sales reporting and reward system, plus the sales person's tendency to react to the perceived need to boost sales immediately, before end of quarter, costs profits. The sales person perceives end of quarter as a deadline by which quotas must be met, and time as a data point on a graph that indicates success or failure in terms of his ability to do his job. By inquiring into the underlying interpretations of the stereotypical reality, we may be able to better understand this view.

Under the mindset of orderly stereotyping, time is an object to be named and categorized. In this sense, the various categories of time such as billable hours and fiscal years become entities with names that can be used to categorize other objects sharing the same characteristics. The name something receives, then, becomes crucial. For example, all things named "billable hours" are equal to one another.

IN STEREOTYPIC TIME, IT IS NOT IMPORTANT THAT ONE WORKER'S BILLABLE HOURS REPRESENT 10 TIMES THE OUTPUT OF ANOTHER PERSON'S BILLABLE HOURS.

Billable hours are simply billable hours. Things named the same are the same. In this way, everything is absolutely and rigidly ordered. It does not matter how many billable hours there are. What matters is that the form called "billable hours" is filled out and filed properly.

Time, in this mindset, is fixed and has no reason to be anything other than what it is. In a sense, everything is timeless. Time, as all things in the universe, is seen as belonging to one of a finite set of classifications and forms. It is a name. Those who view the world from this mindset see that time today is a certain way, that it has always been that way in the past, and will continue to be so for the future. Time is time. How can it possibly change?

The Alpha team absolutely rejected this view of time. They

needed a revolutionary and new way of creating and using time. They were prepared to do whatever was necessary to complete their project.

TIME, BROADLY UNDERSTOOD

From the perspective of broad understanding, time is the great unifying principle for growth and development.

KEY WORDS RELATING TO TIME UNDER THE MINDSET OF BROAD UNDERSTANDING INCLUDE: *CYCLE, PERIOD, SEASON, SPAN, STAGE, TERM, ERA, EON, EPOCH,* AND *EVOLUTION.*

Under this mindset, everything in the workplace is interrelated in the big system. Stages in the growth of groups, businesses, and other entities take place inexorably over time. Observers can create complex analyses of business from this perspective. The business cycle or the stages of evolution of a company from founding to growth to stability and finally to decline are two examples. Like all such analyses, these are descriptively rich and help one to know what to expect. However, they offer little to no prescription for action. Their value is in helping us to determine where to look for solutions. From the perspective of broad understanding, we might look to the total system of which the problem is a part, for example. We then might ask to what other aspects of the organization do "slipping schedules" relate? The organizational structure? The reward system? How we get input from the customers? In this way, it is possible to construct a variegated picture of a situation or problem that can then be used to support decisions for action.

Viewing time from the mindset of broad understanding helps spot trends and opportunities and helps keep in place a long-term view. The Alpha management team benefits from a broad understanding of their organization and a focus on a long-range goal. They see that this particular moment in history presents great opportunity because of the convergence of parallel and mutually reinforcing technological trends. The next leap in microprocessor technology (to 64 bits), availability of inexpensive computer memory capable of storing billions of bits of data, and the advent of faster, cheaper communications have all converged to make fifth-generation computing possible. They also understand that they are creating a computer architecture designed to last 20 years.

Important as it is to understand trends, however, this is not sufficient. One also must know how to take action.

TRANSFORMATIONAL TIME

In stark contrast to time viewed from the other three workplace mindsets, transformational time is completely fluid. The amount of time available has no necessary correlation to the amount of accomplishment possible. Approached in one way, a task might take a month, in another way the task might take five minutes.

> TIME CAN BE CONSIDERED AS A POSSIBILITY, AN OPPORTUNITY
> TO DO SOMETHING, RATHER THAN A FIXED, SCARCE RESOURCE.

Under the workplace mindset of continuous transformation, the focus is on the result to be achieved and the fluid nature of time is used to advantage.

> KEY WORDS AND PHRASES FOR TRANSFORMATIONAL TIME
> INCLUDE: *OCCASION, INSTANT, MOMENT, OPPORTUNITY, BREAK,*
> *CHANCE, CRACK, GAP, OPENING, SHOT, SEIZE THE MOMENT, RADICAL*
> *SHIFT,* AND *TRANSFORMATION.*

The danger of transformational time is its tendency to lapse into unpredictability and chaos. The Alpha management team faces this issue.

Management's inability to provide an overall plan induced a crisis of disbelief. The project managers threatened to revolt (or move to other projects).

However, a recently emerging branch of transformationalism called chaos theory, actually treats chaos as a natural state—powerful, desirable, and inevitable. This theory is presented by Mark Michaels, who applies chaos theory to organizations, Michaels teaches that the most successful organizations will be those that deliberately create and maintain a constant state of chaos.[3]

To cope with chaos, the transformational approach always seeks to redefine a problem in a more powerful way. This is done through inquiry, that is, basically asking a series of questions and then, from the inquiry, creating an interpretive shift that dissolves the problem. In inquiring into the problem of schedule slips, we might ask,

Why is schedule slipping a problem?

Perhaps because the engineers are overbuilding the products.

Why are the engineers overbuilding the products?

Because they have no input from customers and do not know what they want.

Why have they no input from customers?

And so the questions proceed. Eventually, an answer to the problem simply leaps out of the inquiry. Faced with schedule slippage, a solution might be to have the engineers talk to customers to find out what they want. Notice how this solution is unavailable from the authoritarian perspective, because under that mindset, time is a rigid entity with fixed beginnings and ends. In such a view, time spent with the customer is time wasted from the schedule.

Essential to the idea of transformational time is that the outcome of continuous transformation is inherently unpredictable. Using

Transformational Scheduling

Crisis	Initial Reaction	Creative Result
Executive challenge to accelerate schedule.	"Don't talk to me about crazy schedules."	Message that program is worth $1 million per hour.
Cannot choose the order of work.	Crisis of disbelief.	One-page master plan for entire project.
Lack of project management expertise.	Slip the schedule.	Project management training program.
Project slips.	Program disaster.	Formal inspection adopted.
Despair.	Fear, loss of morale.	Public "thank-you's" for hard work.
Broken dependencies (critical hardware slip).	Blame.	Selection of alternate hardware.
Incomplete assumptions concerning performance.	Performance will not meet goals, groundwork was shoddy.	Creation of a performance task force.
Shortage of prototypes.	Attempt to follow original plan for allocation.	Reprioritize allocation according to need.
Lack of quality metrics.	"Metrics are meaningless."	Creation of total quality metrics.

this approach, the Alpha program proceeds as a series of major transformations, crises, and redefinitions.

In each case, a crisis event generates an initial negative reaction, followed by a creative breakthrough. A total of nine transformations in the Alpha project are managed, using this model. These are described in the table on page 239.

Crises always reveal new possibilities, undreamed of before the crisis. The trick is to use the creative power of the crisis, as the Alpha team does, to generate new previously unimagined results, rather than to succumb to the initial negativism that inevitably shadows the first moments of crisis.

Change is hard. Organizational change is especially hard. Here is a way of thinking about time that is helpful if your objective is to spread a new idea, introduce a new product, or create a change in organizational procedures and values. The idea is to think in terms of an exponential view of change rather than a linear one. Suppose your problem is to alter the purchasing procedures in one part of the organization. It is difficult. People do not want to listen and have no idea what you are talking about. To make matters worse, the purchasing managers you speak with are very defensive about protecting their existing procedures. It appears to you that the effort required to change the procedures in even a single group is overwhelming, much less in the 100 groups across the entire organization. Under the linear view, you might assume that if it takes six months of backbreaking, unappreciated effort to convince a single group to try something new, then it would take 100×6 months, or 50 years, of effort to establish the change across the company. At this point, who would not despair and be tempted to give up?

However, if you assume that change proceeds exponentially— say, by an exponent of 10—then once you shift the first group, you are 33 percent done. If you can design an intervention whereby the change in the first group inspires 10 other groups to follow suit, each of which in turn triggers the change in 10 other groups, the process will be finished in 18 months, not 50 years. Now your design challenge is to put something in place that accelerates the rate of diffusion of the new idea, after you have the initial success.

Perhaps you can publicize the change that the first purchasing group makes through a well-crafted article in the company newsletter, or ask the vice president to mention it in a speech, or invite an industry consultant to write an article in a national trade magazine. Notice that in all these cases, you accelerate change and create awareness through language.

The Alpha management team exploits this view when they persuade a key group to commit to an "impossible" schedule. When this happens, many other groups follow their example quickly.

Time and Moments of Truth

The key to generating new and previously unimagined possibility exists within the moment of truth (presented in chapter 6). As a practical matter, access to peak transformational time dwells in prior commitment to impossible results. This means taking the risk of attempting something you have no idea how to achieve before the fact.

> AN IMPOSSIBLE COMMITMENT FREES YOU TO CHANGE THE RULES.

There are an infinite number of ways to get things done. In any organization, the context is artificially frozen to preclude all but a few methods. Altering the context always shifts the rules.

> THE KEY TO EXTRAORDINARY RESULTS IS THE COURAGE TO COMMIT TO THE SEEMINGLY IMPOSSIBLE.

Realization of this is also one of the cornerstones of success for the Alpha project. At first, when aggressive development schedules are proposed, a crisis of disbelief and confidence ensues. As Conklin describes it:

The project managers understood the rationale for this demand [to accelerate schedule] but could see no way to meet the aggressive schedule. The result was a loss of rapport between management and the technical staff with comments such as "Don't talk to me about crazy schedules" and "This is going to be a lot of hard work."

However, instead of applying authoritarian pressure, the Alpha management team designs a way of stating the importance of the project in a way the project managers can hear. They craft a brilliant communication that combines *inventing the future, maintaining awareness,* and *realizing results* into a single compelling message. This is the estimate that each hour of schedule improvement or loss is worth $1 million per hour, or $0.01 per hour on the fair market value of the company's stock. When presented with this compelling and carefully crafted message,

> . . . the key project managers were willing to consider new ways to tackle the program's challenge.

As a result, groups make the key leap into transformational time—they make a commitment to results before they have plans and knowledge of how to achieve them. In making this existential leap, one influential group says publicly,

We don't know how to achieve this, but we commit to finding a way.

As is always the case when making a commitment on faith, immediately upon doing so, new sources of assistance and possibility become available that were closed off before.

FACING UP TO MOMENTS OF TRUTH = CREATING TIME.

This idea has an analogy in modern views of the origin of the universe. The universe starts as a big bang, a completely unpredictable discontinuity, a state in which all the known laws of physics simply do not exist. Out of that singular event, time itself is created.

Transformational Scheduling

The influential group in the Alpha project that took the leap of committing to an impossible result attracts, by their courage, a top management consultant in the area of complex scheduling. This individual immediately shares his expertise, for which the team members, since they have freely chosen to be accountable for results, are now receptive and eager students. In addition, this series of actions starts an exponential effect throughout the organization so that all teams are trained in the tools necessary to achieve their "impossible" challenge, which they then meet.

In summary:

Don't talk to me about crazy schedules

is transformed into

The Alpha AXP program is the most complex program in Digital's history and has been delivered on schedule with high quality.

What It Takes to Create Time

The success of the Alpha project depends heavily on Peter Conklin's actions in the four years that preceded the project. Sensing that more powerful approaches to management were possible, he undertakes, in 1989, a courageous and lengthy inquiry into the nature of management itself, experimenting with new notions of management by open persuasion, abandonment of authority, and creative use of crisis. It is these investigations that allow the breakthroughs that the Alpha project experiences in 1992. However, in 1989 when he commences his experiments and investigations, his management is not supportive:

Peter's behavior is causing his management some concern.

His management cannot see the value and possibility in these management experiments and rethinking, even though they later create the new mindset critical to the success of the most massive and crucial project in the company's history. This resistance is because the experiments are outside the realm of business as usual at the time, outside the everyday concerns of those managers, outside their mindset. Fortunately for the company, Conklin has the courage to persevere.

> Anyone who undertakes transformation must have the courage to face resistance.

Transformational time is not given to you. Rather, you create it through proclamation. As a human being, you are the source of time. Individuals in organizations define the architecture of the organization's time. You create your own time and live out the ramifications and consequences of that designed or defaulted creation. Time is not given to you, you generate it.

> You are the source of your own time.

Through your word, you create the future. As such, you are responsible for the future you create and have the choice either to take an active role in the shaping and designing of it or to sit back passively and watch, leaving it to the hands of fate. In business, your choice to be an active participant or a passive bystander has important consequences for your company.

Transformational Coaching

No man is an island . . .

—John Donne, poet

Benefits of Coaching

One way to achieve ultra-high performance in business is to organize your life in such a way that you have a coach for every major project and undertaking that you carry forward. Many women and men would not dream of attempting a difficult project without organizing a strong network of capable and committed coaches. These people have freely chosen to lead ultra-high-performance lives in which their actions are driven by their commitment to something beyond themselves rather than by pettiness, delusions of self-sufficiency, or complacency. They realize that learning, striving, and mastering are lifelong processes, not end states. After they have fixed upon a commitment, they freely grant their coaches permission to be ruthlessly supportive in achieving that commitment.

TRANSFORMATIONAL COACHING IS AN EFFECTIVE METHOD FOR
ACHIEVING IMPOSSIBLE RESULTS.

Here is an example of a 30-minute transformational coaching session worth $9 million. A high-ranking manager in the semiconductor industry has a problem. He has contracted to produce a million chips at $3 apiece, and the cost of production is running at $12 apiece. He has to renegotiate the terms of the deal with his customer or else lose his shirt.

What does he do? He recruits a team of coaches, people he can trust, and takes on the role of their protégé. He invites them to a meeting and asks them to sit around a U-shaped table. He stands, alone, at the center of the U, exposed, vulnerable, and without any trappings of power and position. He explains his problem and asks for help. He acknowledges he has made a mistake—that he has struck a poor deal. The ground rules of the session are orderly and supportive.

The coaches are highly trained, though few of them know much about the details of the semiconductor industry. They listen, not so much to the specifics of the deal, but to the metaphors the protégé uses in describing the situation. The manager, a Texan, speaks in colorful cowboy terms about his relationship with the customer. Each, according to him, is trying to "hog-tie" the other, to "get the other person over a barrel," and to "whup" each other with "bull-whips." The coaches come to realize that their protégé is casting the entire relationship as a win-lose struggle. So they ask a number of leading questions designed to expose the possibility of using a different way of speaking, one that is less hostile and antagonistic, to describe the relationship.

As it turns out, the customer is not the final customer, but rather plans to resell the chip to add features to a line of consumer products. Would it be possible to work together to improve the ultimate value to the consumer of the features provided by this chip, and so increase the final market price, the coaches ask? The result is amazing. This manager, who had been stuck, hopeless, and anguished about this disastrous deal, suddenly sees the opportunity, rushes out of the room, calls the customer, arranges a new deal that includes investigating and adding value to the entire package from the consumer's perspective and so solves his unsolvable problem on the spot. Nine million dollars in 30 minutes.

This sort of high-leverage coaching and support, access to insight and empowerment, is available to any CEO, vice president, manager, and individual contributor in the corporate world. It is being used today to solve problems as diverse as:

- Transferring the engineering, business, and marketing expertise of an entire manufacturing division from the United States to Asia;
- Driving a major semiconductor design project on time and within budget;
- Creating and launching innovative financial instruments for the investment community.

The cost in money of finding a coach is trivial. The real price is a willingness to move away from the belief that you have to do everything by yourself.

Life without a Coach:
The Lone Ranger Syndrome

Most of us disempower ourselves in the world of work by working without coaches. We are surrounded by managers, co-workers, team members, and employees, and yet we keep a part of our identity private and concealed. Often this concealment cuts us off from what we most need to succeed in our work. Why does this happen? Some of us have a deep need to be the sole source of our own accomplishments. We may feel that in the final analysis, we as individual heroes must make the difference and make the project work. Others of us may hold the interpretation that our authority depends on an image of autonomous self-sufficiency. For example, in refusing to endorse a presentation that a group of marketing executives sought to make to their CEO, the CEO's gatekeeper confides:

I have built my career around being invisible to this man. He considers himself to be royalty and is absolutely closed to hearing suggestions from anyone in the company who is not in his inner circle. It would cost me my career even to broach your proposal.

Such attitudes prevent us from seeking help. To make matters worse, competitive organizational politics breeds the interpretation that our colleagues are, at some level, our rivals and therefore cannot be trusted in certain domains. All told, the business cost of this "Lone Ranger Syndrome" is very high.

To illustrate, consider the case of a senior manager, whose career hinges on his ability to direct his group through all sorts of witch hunts, power plays, corporate intrigues, project cancellation crusades, and market and technology changes. When he is asked,

To whom can you turn for trusted advice, dispassionate coaching, and honest appraisal?

he pauses and says quietly.

There is no one. I wish to hell there was.

The fate of hundreds of people depends on this man's judgment and there is no one for him to turn to. Eventually, his solitary skills prove insufficient and he loses his job in a round of corporate downsizing.

In the same company, a dynamic and brilliant vice president possesses strong vision and clarity of thought. His actions determine the careers and livelihoods of thousands of people. To whom does this brilliant man turn when he is over his head, to whom does he grant enough trust and permission to make him aware of his blind spots? According to his chief of staff,

Transformational Coaching

Roger doesn't need anyone—he's got it all together. . . . Well, he might confide in his wife now and then.

In the end, this vice president takes on too great a challenge. He fails and abruptly resigns, giving no one advance warning and seeking no one's help. His organization is stunned and directionless. Unable to support each other, 4,000 of his former people spend a fearful year getting laid off in successive waves because they cannot work together to create business success.

In a *Fortune* 100 company in an entirely different industry, an evening meeting includes a corporate vice president and also the chief expert on quality. The circumstances of the meeting are such that these men can speak more freely than usual. This vice president is a suave and dashing man with tremendous skill at working a room. The chief quality executive uses the opportunity to remind the vice president about the importance of quality.

I hope you're doing more about quality,

he says, eyebrows raised in hopeful yet hesitant inquiry. But the vice president's mind is elsewhere. He speaks of a painting in his office. It shows vultures wheeling over dismal tombstones chiseled with the names of his predecessors. The last grave site is freshly dug, open, and unfilled, and its tombstone bears his own name. The handsome vice president laughs, and his mind is on survival, not on quality. While his concern may have been justified, it certainly does not help him, for a year later he is asked to resign. His products are said to lack quality.

The three previous vignettes show the loneliness of power. Hierarchical, authority-based forms of organization encourage this lonely posture of self-sufficiency. People high in the hierarchy dare not seek assistance and compassion from those around them, especially in matters that reveal their own weakness. It is unthinkable, in most organizations, for managers to seek frank advice concerning their own areas of vulnerability from those who report to them.

That would undermine their own positional authority. Similarly, rivals might turn against and undermine those who sought their friendship and consolation in moments of vulnerability and need. And who would admit weakness to a superior, on whose good opinion one's raise and career directly depend?

All of this has the most unfortunate consequences for the good of organizations since it cuts leaders off from critical information for self-improvement, different perspectives, and a wealth of new ideas.

The Need for Coaching

Business today moves at a blindingly fast pace. Change is the only certainty. Rigid forms of organization cannot keep pace with rapid global communications, financial interdependency, and constant technological innovation. Management hierarchies have long played a role of coordinating and controlling, but today this form of control has become a bottleneck, a hindrance to progress and profits rather than a benefit.

Companies are experimenting with rapid-action, self-empowered teams that decide, execute, and implement business activities at the lowest levels possible. These teams still need the support, guidance, and sense of direction that management hierarchies were once able to provide. Where is the necessary support to come from?

Transformational coaching provides an approach and skill-building tools to fulfill the critical need for direction and support for individuals and teams at every level of the organization. Three aspects of coaching make it appropriate for these situations:

○ Coaching is a skill, not a job, position, or function. Most people, when trained, can be effective coaches, and members of teams can be trained to coach each other.

- Coaching fosters rapid, skillful action. People learn faster and build the set of skills and knowledge they need to get results through expert coaching from others.
- Coaching is always directed at empowering, not controlling, the individual. Growth of individual and teams through coaching builds self-esteem and provides a background for strong, self-empowering performance.

Organizations that can implement successful coaching have a powerful source of competitive advantage. Transformational coaching is designed for the problems and projects that people find difficult or impossible.

The change from authority-based to coaching-based organizations is a major mindset shift. Generations of managers have been trained in such a way that they consider coaching to be an anathema. These managers are currently losing their positions along with their market share. In the process of clinging to the old, authoritarian ways of running corporations, they will cause much damage. But the shift is inevitable.

Overview of the Coaching Role

As the ranks of traditional middle management collapse, many organizations are exploring coaching as a critical skill for creating high-performance, cross-functional work. This is a difficult transition for some. One manager, when asked to assume a coaching role, said:

What am I going to tell my family? I've spent my entire career getting to where I am in management. I'm the first in my family to make it past supervisor. Now you're telling me I've got to give all that up and be like a Little League coach in business?

Coaching can be, however, a deeply fascinating and rewarding task. In many areas of high achievement and performance outside of business, coaching is a critical and well-established function. Successful politicians, for example, are surrounded by coaches (who may be called advisers, consultants, or handlers) who work on everything from foreign policy decisions to media presentation skills. The role of coaching in professional sports is well known—so is the role of coaches in the performing arts. In all these cases, the coach closely observes the protégé's performance with the objective of providing focused and penetrating guidance on ways of improving. For some strange reason, though, coaching is quite rare in business.

It is the coach's job to speak and interact with the protégé in such a way as to bring forth the absolute best level of performance possible for the undertaking at hand. The coach may review past performance, not for the purpose of evaluation, but rather for the purpose of revealing insights that make future performance better. The coach will remind the protégé of commitments and goals as in:

> But it's cold and rainy and I feel miserable this morning. Besides, it isn't even light yet.

> You told me you wanted to win the race. If that's changed, fine, but meanwhile stop fussing, get out of bed, and hit the track.

Far from being irrelevant to business, coaching is sorely needed. It is the most potent tool for change in a transformational approach to management. A transformational coach basically manages the context through which their protégé views the world. Unfortunately, the English language does not have many synonyms for coach, and its everyday meaning is not accurate. Mentor and sponsor capture part, but only part, of the meaning and are also misleading in certain respects. The Confucian expression *zhong shi*, meaning a constructive relationship based on sincerity, purpose, and mutual respect, captures the idea more closely.

A master coach is professionally committed to the highest possible level of achievement for protégés, consistent with their own freely undertaken commitments. The coaching relationship depends on openness, trust, and permission. The transformational coach realizes that new assumptions and viewpoints can be invented, within which the protégé can access higher levels of achievement than she is currently capable of. The role of the transformational coach is literally to alter the interpretive framework, or mindset, of the protégé so that the previously impossible becomes possible.

Coaching someone else requires a special kind of speaking. As a coach, you need to speak in such as way as to allow the other person to generate and invent his own conclusions. It is rarely helpful to dictate information or conclusions, especially your own predetermined ones. In coaching someone, you provide the ground, the frame, or the opening for the solution to emerge spontaneously and creatively. The solution is rarely obvious, and both of you may be surprised at what it is.

In transformational coaching, do not try to identify a solution for the other person; rather make available a shift in the framework of interpretation (assumptions and viewpoints) so that the other person realizes possibilities for action that they did not see before. Usually, pushing your favorite solution diminishes the depth and permanence of any insight that the other person or group can achieve.

Practically, this means asking a lot of questions while remaining convinced and convincing, even if it seems hopeless, that a solution can be found. The solution may be unexpected and involve factors and twists of logic that are removed from the original statement of the problem. For example:

SALESMAN (morose, confused, and depressed): Paul, I'm in trouble. I'm just not myself. I'm missing meetings and not following through on things. I'm not happy about it. Can you help?

MANAGER-COACH: Sure. Can you think of an example?

SALESMAN: Yes, I missed a critical sales meeting yesterday. I thought it was next week, but it wasn't. I can't stop thinking about the customer, sitting there at the restaurant, drumming his fingers on the table, wondering where I was.

MANAGER-COACH: You're our best salesman. What seems different now compared to when things were great?

SALESMAN: I used to understand the products.

MANAGER-COACH: What's different now?

SALESMAN: They're so complicated. My kid knows more about software than I do.

MANAGER-COACH: Do you have any ideas about what to do?

SALESMAN: I'm not sure. I just don't feel motivated.

MANAGER-COACH: Could you do anything to feel more comfortable about the new products?

SALESMAN: I suppose I could take a course, but I'd have to take time out from my work.

MANAGER-COACH: So what? You say you're not doing such a great job anyway.

SALESMAN (pause): You'd let me take a two-week software course?

MANAGER-COACH: Sure.

SALESMAN (with excitement): This is great! I'll even be able to talk to my kid.

Notice a number of critical things about this interaction and the relationship it implies. First, the employee gives permission to be coached. He feels able to approach the manager with a serious problem because both have already established a relationship of trust in this partnership. Second, the manager never criticizes or belittles the salesman. She does not express anger at the missed customer appointment. Her one comment that could be interpreted negatively is phrased as an echo of the employee's own assessment. Third, the manager does not dictate solutions. She phrases everything as a question or suggestion. Fourth, neither the manager nor the employee has a clear idea what the underlying problem is, nor the solution, at the beginning of the session. Fifth, the employee invents the solution himself. Having done so, he is self-empowered to take action. Finally, the problem, missing a sales call, is removed from the solution—taking a software course. However, both are obviously (obvious after the fact, that is) related to a fundamental change in the nature of the products that he is selling. After this interaction, the salesman demonstrates a quantum leap in his ability to keep appointments with customers and to close deals.

Rules of Thumb for Successful Coaching

NEVER COACH WITHOUT PERMISSION

Coaching without permission is abusive and invasive. For transformational coaching to succeed, the person being coached needs to be open about all perceived weaknesses and fears. Coaching deals with deep levels of assumptions and interpretations, and with holding these open to question. This, at times, appears harsh. Everyone has secrets. To the extent that these secrets are not shared with others, the individual is weakened in some area of her life. At the same time, everyone has the right to hold secrets. This typically means that a coach waits to be asked, rather than offering or imposing services.

Coaching without permission looks like being a nag, being offensive, failing to mind your own business, intellectual abuse, or using the shield of your authority to criticize people without permission.

ASK A LOT OF QUESTIONS

Coaching is largely a matter of asking many questions and listening intently and creatively to the answers. It is possible to conduct a coaching session using nothing but questions. It is important to generate these questions spontaneously in the moment based on what the protégé is saying, rather than using a preplanned outline or checklist.

TRY TO DISCOVER THE MINDSET THE PROTÉGÉ IS USING

If the protégé operates from a recognizable mindset, then you can direct the coaching to focus on solutions that arise from an alternate mindset. For example, in an authoritarian mindset, many problem statements have a competitive, win-lose quality. A typical example is some variation of

> *How do I get those idiots in [marketing/sales/engineering] to do what I want?*

The tip-offs to the authoritarian mindset in this problem statement are:

How	This innocent-seeming word reveals an underlying belief in cause and effect, a hallmark of the authoritarian mindset.
idiots	Rude language that depreciates others is common for authoritarians.
get them to	This phrase reveals the desire to control and manipulate.

A coaching session on this problem could focus on any one of these three tip-offs. For example:

COACH: Is there anyone in marketing who isn't an idiot? Who might be the most receptive to your proposal?

PROTÉGÉ: Well, Hal is pretty good, but he's in a different department.

COACH: Is there anyone in the department you need that listens to Hal?

PROTÉGÉ: Yes, there is—Pam! Now if we could get her on our side, that would be great.

COACH: Does it make sense to talk to Hal?

PROTÉGÉ: Yes, I'll call him right away and ask him to talk to Pam. Thanks!

DO NOT DICTATE YOUR OWN SOLUTION, EVEN IF IT IS OBVIOUS

One of the hardest tasks for the transformational coach is to let the protégé discover a personal solution. The temptation to point out or impose your favorite solution can, at times, be overwhelming. But giving solutions is advising, not coaching. Even if your solution is correct, the protégé will not fully own solutions that he has not invented for himself.

NEVER BELITTLE OR CRITICIZE

A transformational coach generates the same degree of trust and respect as does a therapist, confessor, or trusted adviser. The greater the degree of trust, the more powerful and effective the coaching can be. Nastiness, belittling, coldness, and aloofness all diminish trust and have no place in a transformational coaching relationship.

NEVER ADOPT THE OTHER PERSON'S ASSUMPTIONS AND VIEWPOINTS

Most people can be quite colorful and persuasive in their defense of their way of looking at the world:

But my boss really is a jerk. And the marketing people really are impossible to deal with.

A friend might agree with these complaints. A coach will not. The idea is not to disagree, but to hold open the possibility of finding another way of looking at the problem. Negative assessments about other people with whom it is necessary to work are common in the workplace. These negative assessments never have an actual basis in physical fact. *Any* statement of this sort is a made-up interpretation. People tend to invent negative assessments of other people and then seek to prove them by getting other people to agree. The reward for this is that the name caller receives confirmation of his views. The penalty is a ruined and nonproductive relationship with co-workers.

Your value as a transformational coach lies in your access to a different perspective, a different viewpoint than your protégé. This value is lost if you buy into or adopt the assumptions from which the person is viewing the problem. This explains an otherwise paradoxical observation. The best transformational coaches are often people who know little or nothing about the technical details of the issue at hand. For example, in transformational coaching sessions, managers are often astonished that writers and secretaries are better able to coach them through tough business issues than are their management colleagues. This is true because nonmanagers do not share the same blinders that managers do. People who know the technical details of the subject matter are much more likely to fall, unnoticing, into the same mental bear traps that have the protégé stymied on the problem in the first place.

BE OPEN TO COACHING FOR YOURSELF

Coaching is a reciprocal, not a hierarchical, relationship. In fact, the best coaching occurs between people who coach each other. Taking a turn at being a protégé keeps fresh for the coach what a difficult and sometimes scary experience it can be. A pair or a team of people who coach each other builds a high level of trust, which makes not just their coaching, but also all of their work together, extraordinary. To tired corporate soldiers who have experienced only the one-sided relationships in authoritarian hierarchies, the experience of coaching and being coached can seem like a slice of heaven. This open way of working becomes so satisfying and productive that a return to the older way of working becomes unthinkable.

Being open to coaching means admitting, to your coach, that some area is a problem for you. Many people, especially in the authoritarian business world, have a hard time admitting to anyone that they have problems that they do not know how to solve. On the other hand, no one alive on earth is free of problems, including executives and managers.

NEVER COACH WITH A HIDDEN AGENDA

Effective coaching can be intense. Coaching, especially at deep levels, involves a sacred personal commitment. The coach and protégé need to have a relationship of openness and trust. The more difficult and impossible the problem being addressed, the more vulnerable the protégé will be. Therefore, it is both poor coaching and a personal violation for the coach to have a hidden purpose or hidden agenda.

For this reason, it is sometimes difficult for a manager to be an effective coach for people reporting to him or her. The manager may have a vested interest in people performing in a way that directly benefits the manager's position. Coaching with this background can become manipulation and exploitation.

ALLOW YOUR PROTÉGÉS TO INVENT THE SOLUTION FOR THEMSELVES

Coaching means allowing the protégé to invent a solution, not you showing the solution. Learning by inventing is deep, lasting, and profound. It leaves protégés enthusiastic about the resulting insights, because they created them. No matter how powerful and correct the solution you give to your protégé, the solution will not be internalized and acted upon on as forcefully as if she discovered it for herself.

A useful analogy to keep in mind is talking to a teenager. Young people often have extreme resistance to an adult's suggestions and dictates. An open style of interaction that allows the young people to work out solutions for themselves is much more likely to be effective.

NEVER ABANDON THE BELIEF THAT A SOLUTION IS POSSIBLE

Problems are only impossible due to the limitations and blind spots inherent within whatever mindset they are held to be problems. If some one can state a problem at all, as a problem, then a solution is possible. The only really impossible problems are the ones that everyone is completely unaware of, the ones that cannot even be articulated.

THE COACH DOES NOT HAVE TO KNOW THE ANSWER TO THE PROBLEM.

In transformational coaching, it is usually better if the coach does *not* have the answer. The coach *does* need to have an unshakable belief that a solution can be found.

ALLOW THE PROBLEM TO SHIFT

This sample coaching session, based on the common problem of getting budget approvals in a large organization, illustrates how the "problem" shifts as the dialogue proceeds.

PROTÉGÉ: We have a great business opportunity, but we can't get the funding.

Transformational Coaching

COACH: Why can't you get the funding?

PROTÉGÉ: Funding is tight. Everything now has to be approved by the vice president.

COACH: Can you ask the vice president?

PROTÉGÉ: No, I need to save that card for the day I really need it.

COACH: If you succeeded on this project, wouldn't that give you more cards?

PROTÉGÉ: Yes, but what if I fail?

Notice how the problem has now shifted from not being able to get the funding to being fearful of failing. This shifting of the problem statement during a coaching session is common. Continuing:

COACH: So the problem really is that you are afraid of failing. What would happen if you failed?

PROTÉGÉ: I'd get my legs cut off.

COACH: You'd get your legs cut off?

PROTÉGÉ: Well, not literally.

COACH: Seriously, what would happen?

PROTÉGÉ: Listen, I can't go up to the vice president and ask him to give me the extra $1.2 million I need. He's already made it quite clear through the layoffs that he's determined to trim us down. If I go tell him that I want more money, I'd get labeled a troublemaker and be given a black mark.

COACH: I've never seen a black mark. What does one look like?

PROTÉGÉ: A black mark is just another way of saying that they'd be sure to let me know I'd screwed up and had better straighten out my act fast.

COACH: What do you mean? What would actually, physically, happen?

PROTÉGÉ: You mean literally? My boss would slam me.

COACH: Slam? Would he hit you?

PROTÉGÉ: No, he'd fry me.

COACH: In a frying pan?

PROTÉGÉ: Oh, I see what you're getting at. Well, he would make it very clear in our one-on-one that I was not acting in the best interests of the company and might even attach it as a note to my performance review.

COACH: How much of a difference would that make on your raise?

PROTÉGÉ: Probably nothing. My performance rating is outstanding. My products already account for over 60 percent of the profitability of the division.

COACH: So what are you afraid of?

PROTÉGÉ: I guess there isn't anything to be afraid of, really.

COACH: So, will you talk to the vice president?

The problem statement has shifted several times during this coaching session. The protégé has mentioned many objections and reasons, supported by assessments that turn out to be exaggerations and fantasies. The questioning has allowed him to see that each of these is a fabrication with little or no basis in reality. At this point in the session, the protégé may well be ready to launch his proposal. If not, if he raises new objections, then the coach must go through the same general procedure to deal with them. In the end, either the protégé will see a clear way to obtain the funding, or will hit upon a problem so close to what he holds to be his identity that he will withdraw permission to be coached.

LOOK FOR MISSING INSIGHTS

Often, the protégé will simply lack the necessary insights or an appropriate framework with which to view the problem. In this case, the coach may suggest a framework or ask leading questions, as the following example shows.

The CEO of a *Fortune* 500 company commissions a task force to draft a new vision for their credit card business. They come up with:

GENERATE CASH FOREVER.

People sense, though they do not quite know why, that this somehow falls short of a powerful vision. People are giving lip service to the company's turn-around initiative, but not inspired efforts. One concerned employee recruits a coach.

PROTÉGÉ: I'm just not inspired by our divisional vision.

COACH: What are some examples of company visions that inspire you?

PROTÉGÉ: I can think of three:

A WORLD WHERE EVERYONE IS NOURISHED.

SHOEMAKER TO THE WORLD.

BETTER LIVING THROUGH CHEMISTRY.

COACH: What do they have that yours doesn't?

PROTÉGÉ: They seem more caring, more concerned about the customer, more selfless.

COACH: Do you think you can get the CEO to take another look at the slogan for our credit card division?

PROTÉGÉ: Yes! I'll send him a note tomorrow!

The protégé now has a new insight about corporate visions—that good ones often have a selfless, contributory quality. She proceeds to write a memo that gets her a rare meeting with the CEO.

COACHING IS A WIN-WIN GAME

The protégé wins by seeing and acting upon new, previously unavailable approaches to difficult or impossible problems. The coach wins by seeing the protégé succeed. The freedom and sense of empowerment and release that come from having a viable approach to a previously impossible problem can be amazing. The pleasure, joy, and sense of accomplishment in helping someone else succeed can be truly extraordinary.

BE PREPARED FOR COACHING TO RAISE PERSONAL ISSUES

One of the most striking and rewarding aspects of practicing coaching in a business setting is the degree to which protégés report benefits in their personal lives, even though personal issues are never explicitly discussed in the coaching sessions. The following comments are typical:

I can't explain it, but since we've been doing coaching, the quality of my marriage has improved.

I used what I learned to resolve an issue with my father-in-law.

These techniques worked with my teenager!

It may simply be that business relationships based on committed speaking, honesty, pursuit of meaningful shared goals, and open listening provide a decent model for relationships generally. The model for relationships suggested by coaching is in sharp contrast to the win-lose model provided by business as usual.

SUCCESSFUL COACHING INITIATES ACTION

A successful outcome of a coaching session *always* involves some specific action that the protégé agrees to take. This action is *always* a communication, an expression in language, that is related to one or more of the 12 facets of The Phoenix Agenda.

All results in business are achieved through joint activities of people. These activities are initiated, driven, managed, terminated, or supported through language. A manager does essentially nothing but talk to people and listen to people. This may be in meetings, memos, phone calls, individual sessions, presentations, sales calls, feelers, negotiations, papers, articles, speeches, or chance encounters in the hallway. Coaching seeks to improve and focus the design and execution of these communications so that they produce maximum impact and benefit. When a problem exists, it is always because some communication is weak, absent, or present in a destructive form.

For example, a CEO is worried that her company seems aimless and lacks direction for the future. What is absent is a communication called *inventing the future*. What sort of people are adept at such a communication? Perhaps people called visionaries and bold thinkers. Where might such people be found in the organization? Anywhere. But perhaps they are reluctant to speak out. Why? Perhaps they perceive themselves to be underappreciated in the organization, due to past practices. What is absent may be the communications called *complete the past* and *acknowledge freely*. The CEO might consider offering an apology.

In another company, the managers of engineering and of quality control do not get along. As a consequence, products are being inadequately tested. Customers are complaining. What is absent? Perhaps a communication designed to *articulate strategies* where engineering and quality control people can meet, have a frank and open conversation, and create efficient and workable procedures. Why is it that such a communication cannot take place? Perhaps because the managers mistrust each other and prefer name calling and finger pointing to cooperation. What is missing is a communication designed to *generate trust*. What can the CEO do to generate trust? Speak to the managers. What does she say? She communicates trust. How? Perhaps by vividly demonstrating trust herself.

The concrete outcome of successful coaching will often be that the protégé agrees to make a call, write a letter, hold a meeting, deliver a presentation, issue an apology, request an action, launch a proposal, request funds, or go on a sales call. A good coach will ask for specific details as to exactly what the action will be and when it will take place. The coach can then work with the protégé to design the activity. When the protégé dithers, or is distracted by other events, the coach is there to provide encouragement or even a call to action.

Managing, Consulting, and Coaching

Managing focuses on optimizing solutions to well-understood problems. Classical management is based on the mindset of authoritarian control. Transformational coaching is designed to solve problems that appear impossible. Both skills are valuable and necessary. Consulting, as a discipline, lies in-between these extremes. The following table summarizes these differences. Managers give direction and orders, consultants give analysis and advice, and coaches provide empowerment.

Coaching is best as a two-way street. For example, two managers in different organizations can coach each other. The coaching relationship does not depend on relative status or position on the organization chart. Some of the best coaching partnerships are between people far removed from each other in the organizational structure.

Transformational Coaching

A Manager:	A Consultant:	A Coach:
Directs and controls.	Analyzes.	Empowers.
Makes decisions.	Evaluates decisions.	Creates possibilities.
Imposes solutions.	Recommends solutions.	Helps you create solutions.
Orders.	Advises.	Questions.
Frequently criticizes.	Offers objectivity.	Never criticizes.
Maintains status quo.	Points out problems.	Deals with impossible problems.

When to Get a Coach

You may wish to consider seeking out transformational coaching under the circumstances outlined in the following table. You should not get a transformational coach when you are satisfied with the way things are, do not wish to be challenged, and want only to maintain the status quo.

CONSIDER GETTING A COACH WHEN:

You are attempting a seemingly impossible task.
You are striving for ever-higher levels of accomplishment.
You have a history of broken promises and commitments to yourself and others.
You are overwhelmed by the demands of everyday business and personal life.

For many of us, seeking help is synonymous with admitting deficiency, with admitting that there is something wrong with ourselves. The Lone Ranger does not ask for help. But the discipline of transformational coaching belongs to a different worldview, the view that all individual human beings are inherently limited in their perspective and knowledge and that they can mutually benefit by frank, yet compassionate support of one another. Coaching is not remedial. It is an opportunity for greater achievement by the already successful. However, the nature of coaching is such that it does tend to reveal character weaknesses that are getting in the way of whatever you want to achieve. This will threaten and anger the person being coached at times, especially if the task at hand demands much. To be coachable, one needs to be willing to face and work on whatever obstacles there are to improved performance.

A good coach will have extraordinary listening skills, be ruthless in holding the protégé accountable to freely chosen commitments, and yet simultaneously be compassionate toward the difficulty of the human condition in general and toward the protégé in particular. But a coach is quite different from a friend. A coach never commiserates on how difficult the task is or how overwhelming the obstacles are; a friend might. Friendship is for recreation and a sense of belonging. Coaching is for high performance.

The Dark Side of Transformation

For in much wisdom is much grief: and he that increaseth knowledge increaseth sorrow.

—Ecclesiastes

Warning

The power of the ideas and approaches presented in this book stems from the fact that they operate at levels that are deeper than human feelings and emotions. They operate at the level of redefining human nature itself. Though the insights underlying The Phoenix Agenda are potent, they can backfire in various ways. The methods can be deployed thoughtlessly, with damaging consequences. They can also be used for disruptive and sinister purposes. They can be used for transformation, or for brainwashing. A preoccupation with transformation, as with anything, can lead to addiction and burnout. This chapter warns of these dangers and concludes by reinforcing the critical role of coaching in avoiding these potential pitfalls.

Careless and Damaging Communication

Under the view that human communication does not reflect reality, but rather creates it, language is the key to all human power. Ultimately, it is communication that starts businesses, destroys them, opens new markets, attracts associates, motivates armies, persuades customers to buy, or turns customers away. Our use of language determines our success or failure, how far we will go in a career, and whether we in the end judge ourselves as a success or failure.

Language used as a tool is in itself ethically neutral. For business and workplace interactions we can use this power in one of three ways.

1. We can remain indifferent to the power of communication and ride the tide of consequences.
2. We can master the discipline of powerful and committed speaking to achieve results of benefit to ourselves and others.
3. We can deliberately undertake to use the tools of communication to undermine and defeat others.

Language, like any tool, can be used powerfully. The Phoenix Agenda suggests a set of inquiries that can help us to design our communications so that they have impact. But language, like any tool, can also be used in an unaware and thoughtless manner. This will, except by accident, have results analogous to the thoughtless and unaware application of any tool. Presenting and receiving communications in an unaware way is analogous to such things as using power tools, investing, and making career and marriage decisions on the basis of ignorance and naiveté. At the other extreme, one's language can be designed and expressed in a deliberate attempt to cause destruction.

The Dark Side of Transformation

CARELESS COMMUNICATION

Suppose for a moment that we really do create our world in the act of communicating and conversing. Then careless conversation creates a careless world. A World War I poster, displayed in public places around seaports, read, LOOSE LIPS SINK SHIPS. Careless speaking, then, is talking in such a way that the speaker is either not aware of or does not care about the effect that language has on what happens.

The opposite of careless speaking, in this view, is responsible or committed speaking. It amounts to having respect for the effect on the world of what one is saying. A common theme in folk lore involves being granted wishes by some magical power. The interesting part of such stories is the incredible care with which the wish must be phrased so as not to cause dreadful side effects. In one famous legend, an impoverished woman in Scotland is granted a magical wish and asks for a 1,000 pounds. The money soon arrives in the form of an insurance settlement on the life of her son who has been killed in a mining accident. Responsible speaking is speaking in such a way that you take seriously the effect of your words.

BE CAREFUL WHAT YOU SAY YOU WANT. YOU JUST MIGHT GET IT.

Consider the following statement, assumed to take place in the hallway at some place of business:

The manager of the finance group is incompetent.

From the point of view that holds that language is a description of an independently occurring reality, this comment could be taken as a statement of fact. We might accept the comment, look for evidence, or decide that the speaker was not telling the truth. In every case, however, we take as given that the utterance purports to describe some independently existing state of affairs.

Consider the statement from the point of view of language as creating reality rather than reflecting it. To the extent that such a comment was made in a maliciously skillful way and to the right person, it could literally have the effect of creating an otherwise excellent manager as incompetent in the mind of the listener.

Even under an objective view, where would we look for evidence of the truth or falsity of the statement? Essentially, the only place we could look, ultimately, is in the statements of people, including ourselves, about the manager. That is, our ultimate source of evidence would be what people said!

The reader who does not believe that speaking alone has the power to change the world is invited to think through the consequences of the following hypothetical experiment. Invent some highly undesirable characteristic about yourself ("I am incompetent," "I cannot be trusted," "I am a liar," and so forth) and announce it in a compelling way to a large group of your business associates. Were you actually to do this you would discover that you had succeeded in creating a new identity for yourself, merely through utterance.

DELIBERATELY DESTRUCTIVE COMMUNICATION

Whereas careless communication, under this view, is simply being irresponsible about what one says—that is, not taking it seriously one way or the other—destructive talk deliberately exploits language for purposes injurious to someone, as in the following incident.

Two professional rivals compete for years for the same promotion. Though they both work hard, at every opportunity they denounce and undermine each other's achievements. One day, one of them receives the coveted promotion, though this is not made public, so he schemes to break the news to his rival in the most hurtful possible way. At a break in a meeting with the rival, over the coffee and donuts, the newly promoted employee says, casually and with apparent friendliness, as though commenting on the weather.

The Dark Side of Transformation

Oh, by the way. I just got promoted to senior director.

The jealous rival sputters into his coffee in shock and jealousy. The comment, designed to hurt, has succeeded brilliantly.

Other instances of communications used in less than noble ways are evident in talking privately with top management of classically hierarchical and internally competitive companies. It is hard to escape the impression that the real work in the executive suite is the conduct of high-level political intrigue. Each executive tends to talk of the others as conducting complex and subtle plots to secure advantage for themselves and their organization. Rarely will an executive admit to being involved in such intrigue, but each one points to all the others as being involved. One gets the sense that a mysterious art is involved—the art of high-level corporate politics—conducted through language, and with the ultimate goal being control of more resources and personal advancement at the expense of others. Alliances, when formed, are alliances of opportunity and momentary advantage. When momentary personal advantage is no longer perceived, the alliance is broken.

The Art of Destruction

Power politics in Western companies is not a publicly admitted or publicly admired art, nor is it well systematized in courses and books.[1] However, in certain Asian cultures, a body of practice and knowledge codifies, in an extraordinary way, the art of power politics.[2] This body of knowledge is an ancient, widely read, and deeply embedded part of those cultures. It takes the form of 36 strategies designed specifically to disempower enemies and seize the advantage. All of the strategies rely on some form of deception and intrigue. The strategies are used in interpersonal encounters, business affairs, and even in national positioning and posturing. All of the strategies are implemented by acts of communication designed to confuse, disempower, deceive, and exploit opponents.

ADVANCED STRATEGIES FOR WORKPLACE TRANSFORMATION

A SAMPLE PLAN FOR DISCREDITING YOUR MANAGER

Strategy in Proverb Form	*How to Implement in the Office*
Beat the grass to startle the snakes.	Create an artificial office crisis for the purpose of seeing how your manager reacts to stress. This gives you valuable information on her weaknesses that you can exploit in refining the other strategies.
Take the firewood out from under the pot.	In private conversations, agree with the manager's complaints about the organization and amplify them for the purpose of undermining her morale. This will render the manager less effective and bold in carrying out her responsibilities.
Point at one to scold another.	Do not criticize the manager directly. Instead, criticize her projects, organization, staff, and policies.
Face the weary in a condition of ease.	Present your manager with difficult problems and crises when you are refreshed but when she is tired and her judgment is impaired. The quality of her actions and decisions will suffer, which will in turn be noticed by her superiors.

The Dark Side of Transformation

Scheme with an empty castle.	Appear to be without guile or power. Constantly speak about how little influence you have in order to hide your sinister plans.
Let them climb the roof, then take away the ladder.	Encourage your manager to take on commitments and assignments that she cannot possibly deliver on. Pretend that you are suggesting these things in her best interest. When she fails at these assignments, make sure that others in positions of power are made aware.

It is possible, especially in Western cultures where these strategies are not widely known, to design and implement a course of action that will devastate opponents in the workplace. Suppose, for example, that you decide that it is to your advantage to hinder or even destroy your current manager's career. Perhaps you see her as a rival, or perhaps you wish to take over her job. Here is an example of a course of action, based on 6 of the 36 strategies, designed to wreck your manager's chances of promotion, while at the same time appearing to be loyal.

Carefully and systematically executed, these strategies will have the effect of seriously undermining your manager's (or other opponent's) position, and if you are subtle enough, no blame or suspicion will accrue to you. Whatever our moral reaction is to strategies of this kind, in the short run, they actually work, especially against enemies who are not aware of them, who trust you, and who do not know the countermeasures.

All of these strategies depend upon establishing some level of trust and then deliberately taking advantage of that trust to cause harm. Most readers, on reflection, realize that they have acted and spoken in these ways with others, perhaps more out of thoughtlessness than by deliberate design. However, in the same way that powerful positive conversations can be designed and implemented as a matter of deliberate choice, so can powerful negative conversations. The plan for undermining your manager is a plan for creating a new reality for her, through your communications.

A word of warning for those intending to take the low road. This is not an area where halfway efforts and measures are appropriate. The strategies for disempowerment tend to backfire and to be addictive in the long run, especially if one's commitment to selfishness is less than complete.

To complete this litany of transformation gone wrong, we can restate The Phoenix Agenda in a dark parody or mirror image that serves to highlight, contrast, and emphasize the empowering version:

THE COUNTER-PURPOSE PHOENIX AGENDA

Extinguish trust.	Fog awareness.
Conceal context.	Waste results.
Surrender the future.	Squander wisdom.
Muddle strategies.	Maintain addictions.
Impede action.	Freeze the past.
Avoid moments of truth.	Acknowledge negatively.

In general, if individuals do not design their communications in a positive, constructive way, the results for the organization will not be neutral, but rather will be consistent with this negative version of The Phoenix Agenda.

Workplace Mindsets and Addiction

Unfortunately, most of us, most of the time, face an irresistible pull to act in ways that though they appear to deliver short-term benefits, also extract serious long-term costs. Under the mindset of authoritarian control, such things as controlling people, appearing right at the expense of associates and competitors, and having more status, power, or money than others appear to be desirable ends. This kind of authoritarian motivation has historically driven armies of conquest and today drives many business enterprises. The seduction of this viewpoint is that it galvanizes people into action, as, for example, in the case of Sun Microsystems and Digital Equipment Corporation, who compete vigorously with one another in the sales of expensive, high-powered personal computers. One of Digital's sales training and motivation programs involves dressing the sales force in combat aviators' flight suits and awarding "Sun Killer" medals to salespeople who successfully stop customers from purchasing the Sun equipment. In turn, the president of Sun gives sarcastic press interviews about the "low intelligence quotients" of Digital management. This hostile way of relating, with its underlying metaphor of war, motivates people to action.

The problem with any approach to life and to business that has at its core exploiting others, posturing as better than other people, and winning at others' expense is that it creates enemies. At a personal level, men who abuse and belittle wives and children achieve the intrinsic rewards of domination but suffer the consequences of impoverished and fear-laden relationships. A manager using insults and fear may get things done but pays the cost of stifling innovation, poor quality of work life, and organizational inflexibility.

Achieving and sustaining the dominant position in an industry, as a goal, may have its benefits and rewards, but it also has a dark side and may be ultimately unsustainable. In the 1960s, IBM and AT&T absolutely dominated the computer and telephone industries, respectively. At the time, it was unthinkable that either company's position could ever be challenged. Then the U.S. government initiated antitrust suits against both companies, who, naturally, defended against them with every means at their disposal. IBM won its antitrust suit and remained intact. AT&T lost theirs and was broken up. Today, IBM is unprofitable and in decline, surpassed in market value by Microsoft, a company that simply did not exist, even as an idea, in 1960. AT&T, by contrast, is a profitable and growing player in a competitive industry. With respect to this case, was the successful defense against the IBM antitrust suit indeed in the best interests of the company?

Most of us, most of the time, would rather be confirmed in our own beliefs and identity than have something larger than ourselves succeed. As a direct consequence, most of us are only rarely a part of a success larger than ourselves. A large, multinational financial services corporation notices that its market share is declining—the core of its business is eroding. Establishments are reluctant to accept its card, some even arrange a boycott. A top-level management team is assembled to create a new vision, a new future for the company—a fundamental shift in its business direction. But people's commitment to business as usual, to their positions and jobs as they know them, is so strong that the task force is handicapped by turf issues and cynicism.

Mindsets, whether in science or in business, have a grip so strong that they blind us to actions, even conceptions, outside their self-confirming frame. It is more important to us that our ways of thinking and living be confirmed than it is for us to succeed. Against the backdrop of a world that changes so rapidly that we ought to be shedding old mindsets the way reptiles shed skins, we can say that:

MOST BUSINESSES BECOME COMMITTED TO THEIR OWN DEMISE.

We can observe a fascinating and useful analogy between the nature of commitment to particular assumptions and addictions. Addictions—whether to alcohol, power, sex, or a particular belief system—are pervasive and powerful; in their grip, you have no freedom. The lack of freedom in the face of addiction is circular, self-reinforcing, parasitic, and insidious in its structure and function. An addiction is virulently self-referential and denies access to interpretations and actions that would undermine itself. The lens of addiction refracts reality in an aberrant way to render out of focus all open and free inquiry into itself. Closed systems of assumptions also have all of these properties and dynamics. Anything outside their scope or threatening to the foundational undergirding of their own self-maintenance is denied.

An example of this is alcoholic denial. The alcoholic identity has as a fundamental characteristic that it absolutely refuses to acknowledge itself as alcoholic. If you tell active alcoholics the truth about themselves, you will observe violent or evasive reactions, as though the identity were threatened.

In business terms, a company that has been highly successful for 20 years following a certain viewpoint on itself has an incredibly difficult time readjusting that viewpoint when times change and markets and profits fall away. All manner of changes and strategies may be tried except the most obvious—a fundamental reevaluation of itself as an entity. The survival of a particular view of itself is more important than its own survival as an entity.

Addiction theory is now being applied to corporations and organizations.[3] Organizations may become addicted to an image of themselves. This insight provides a rich new understanding and possibilities for action to address what previously have appeared to be intractable problems. Why do individuals and organizations so often repeatedly and helplessly engage in actions that are against their own best interests and fundamental goals? Folly is what historian Barbara Tuchman called this recurrent phenomenon in her historical analysis of governments and entire societies that repeatedly, doggedly, and deliberately take action to speed their own destruction.[4] The analogy to addiction gives clues and effective courses of action in the face of this baffling circumstance. Is the human race itself addicted to its own survival or, more accessibly, to the survival of its current assumptions about itself? Addictions unbroken are invariably fatal to their hosts. The model of mindsets as malleable offers effective action and hope in the face of these dismal conjectures.

Burnout

The tools and philosophy in The Phoenix Agenda are designed for ultra-high performance and for achieving seemingly impossible tasks. These tools work, in brief, by committing oneself to what appear to be impossible goals and then by altering the framework of viewpoints and assumptions in which the problem is held to be impossible until a solution emerges. However, for this to work without burnout entails a culture of absolute trust, acknowledgment, and support. Some managers throw impossible problems at their people and organizations with the intent of forcing creative, breakthrough solutions, but then do not provide the necessary support for failure or acknowledgment for success. As a consequence, they lead their people on a path to burnout, as in the case of ITT in the 1960s.

Harold Geneen, chairman of ITT, presides over a vast conference table with 60 chairs. Forty are filled with his staff people, trained in spotting fuzzy thinking and flaws in business plans. The line managers of Geneen's divisions and businesses come in, one by one, to present their forecasts. They hear:

> *You say you can do $10 million next quarter? I want $12 million and we'll be watching your every move.*

The line managers agree to Geneen's impossible requests like good soldiers. They receive no support at all from the 40 staffers—these are the watchdogs, not helpful resources. If a line manager fails to deliver, he is fired and a new manager brought in to replace him. Geneen goes through a lot of managers and a lot of people burn out. In time, there are few managers left who are willing to subject themselves to this, the approach is discredited, and ITT is a much smaller company today.

A burned-out individual or business is like a burned-out building. What is left is a hollow hulk or shell and inside all is emptiness

The Dark Side of Transformation

and destruction. Severe burnout involves an isolation from oneself and others and a loss of meaningful purpose for living and striving. A burned-out individual or business has no future, takes no pride in the present, and is bitter about the past. In burnout, all of the facets of The Phoenix Agenda are reduced to emptiness. For example:

GENERATE TRUST.

There is no possibility: "Why should I trust anyone? No one really cares about me or who I am. In doing X, Y, Z, I was abused and used—a victim. I believed in A, and I was told B, and was committed to supporting C, and I was used and lied to and here I am. Trust? Ha!"

INVENT THE FUTURE.

There is no future: "My work is in shreds. I gave so much and for nothing. I am tired and don't care what happens next."

EXPLOIT MOMENTS OF TRUTH.

There is no possibility: "I am miserable. Listen to me complain about what happened and how the company left me to twist in the wind."

In a true team environment, everyone is responsible for everyone else's success and welfare. Only in a culture of win-lose, a culture of domination, is burnout possible. The approach of setting impossible goals and making impossible requests will only succeed if these precepts are applied:

GIVE EVERYONE WHO WORKS FOR YOU THE FREEDOM TO SAY "NO" TO ANY REQUEST, WITHOUT EXPLANATION, AND WITHOUT FEAR OF ADVERSE CONSEQUENCES FROM YOU.

> WHEN A MEMBER OF YOUR TEAM FAILS TO DELIVER ON A
> PROMISE, THAT IS WHEN SHE REQUIRES THE MOST COMPASSION
> AND SUPPORT, NOT THE LEAST.

A popular story, now part of business folklore, illustrates the spirit intended by these precepts. A young executive is given responsibility for a $10 million project. After a year of effort, the project fails and all the money is spent with no return at all. The executive goes to his manager, dejected, and says,

Well, I guess you are going to fire me.

The wise manager replies,

Fire you! Hell no! I've just spent $10 million training you!

The Threat to Identity

Transformation, as a key to a more successful life or business, may be too inaccessible, too threatening, for some individuals and organizations. An IBM executive, his whole life oriented to enhancing his position in the corporate hierarchy, hits a roadblock. He is told that he will never advance beyond his present position. He drives to a wooded area in Upstate New York, thinks for a while about how he has neglected wife and family in pursuit of his now shattered corporate dream, puts a revolver to his head, and fires.

Shifts of identity, shifts of mindset, shifts of core assumptions are usually, almost always, preceded by soul searching and pain. Many people and businesses avoid this pain by never inquiring into who or what they are. Others, like the IBM executive presented with the necessity of deep inquiry, never make it past the pain. Any inquiry

The Dark Side of Transformation

into the nature of our own identities has the character of doing violence. We perceive an attempt to unearth, in a powerful way, the roots and wellsprings of our identities as a threat. But penetrating inquiry *is not* doing violence, it only *has the character* of doing violence. Something can only threaten the identity if we interpret it as a threat.

It can be costly to protect identity too closely. One company undertakes an ambitious effort to integrate many previously separate products. The market potential is huge. Years of effort, endless meetings, and many management initiatives are invested, with no positive accomplishment. One program manager with unusual insight and courage draws upon her experience to diagnose the problems and call for effective, radical action. The problem is that her analysis is too accurate! She has noticed and pointed at issues such as incompetence in the management hierarchy above her, engineers with obsolete technical knowledge, and high-ranking technical leaders with poorly developed collaboration skills. A sympathetic colleague draws her aside:

> *The things you are saying are right on. This is why the projects are not succeeding. But the level of pain hasn't reached the point where people are willing to hear your tough messages about themselves. So, instead, they are now down on you. There really isn't a place for you in the organization any longer.*

In other words, by attempting to penetrate to the core of why the organization's programs are not working and detailing what the necessary actions are, this particular program manager has been ostracized. The people involved absolutely refuse to even consider the possibility that their own weaknesses and blind spots might be responsible for the continuing failure of the product initiative. The program fails.

Advanced Strategies for Workplace Transformation

LEADERS OF ORGANIZATIONS ARE OFTEN MORE COMMITTED TO
CONCEALING THEIR OWN SHORTCOMINGS THAN THEY ARE TO THE
ORGANIZATION'S SUCCESS.

Initiating shifts of core interpretations of reality can be dangerous
work. In the history of science, paradigm (mindset) shifters were
often denounced as heretics and frauds. Many were tortured and
put to death. Today such people may be merely ignored, ridiculed,
fired, or have their funding withdrawn. On the other hand, the
world as we know it today owes much to the courage of such
women and men. Fortunately, insights into the power of language
offer us ways to shift core assumptions and mindsets and to include
the necessary support structures to deal with any negative fallout.

A prerequisite for transformation is taking a deep, soul-searching
look at the particular reality seen as official or true. This is best done
with the help of others in an open, free, and supportive environment. However, it usually requires a major disaster before most
people are willing to take this step.

It is a truism in the management consulting field that the level of
business pain has to cross a certain threshold before people will
consider serious change, especially if change requires taking a long,
hard look at themselves. In relatively slow-moving industries, perhaps this luxury of waiting still exists. In all industries affected by
rapid change, it does not. The markets and products change so fast
that by the time an organization is ready to face serious problems, it
is too late. The organization that ostracized its critic simply ceased to
exist 18 months after the incident described above.

THE PRICE OF TRANSFORMATION IS LOOKING CRITICALLY AT WHO
YOU ARE AND TAKING RISKS.

The Saving Role of a Coach

It is most difficult for people to see the limits of their own view-points and assumptions. Having a coherent mindset is what makes cogent thought and action possible at all. At the same time, any perspective has blindness and blind spots. A coach is someone who ruthlessly, but with permission, goes after these blind spots, uncovering everything that is in the way of the organization's success. The role of a coach is essentially to point out weakness, blindness, and areas for improvement, and to do so in a way that aids discovery of clear choices and empowers action.

Transformational coaching unleashed in an organization and deployed to its fullest will unearth the core reason that is preventing success, no matter how unacceptable that reason is to individuals in the organization. For example, suppose an executive, committed to the organization's success, engages a coach. It emerges that the single biggest obstacle to the organization's success is the executive's lack of knowledge about international finance, a shortcoming that he is reluctant to admit publicly. The coach's role is to point out, to the executive, that he has a clear choice between refusing to learn new finance skills and continuing on a downward path, or learning the new skills in order to drive his organization's success. The coach cannot make this choice for him, but can only present the choice in a compelling and obvious way. Of course, the executive can get upset and simply fire the coach.

The higher you rise in an organization, and the more people are dependent on your judgment and insights, the more your blind spots become a liability. Unfortunately, the nature of power and authority is such that the more of it you have, the less willing you are to admit blindness and weakness. For this reason, hierarchical organizations tend to breed leaders who rise for a time, reach a level beyond which they cease learning, and then drag the organization down in a effort to maintain power. It could be that the time to fire leaders is at the height of their success.

INDIVIDUAL ACHIEVEMENT IS A LONELY ROAD. TO ACHIEVE
GREAT THINGS, SURROUND YOURSELF WITH EXCELLENT COACHES
WHO WILL, WHEN NECESSARY, TELL YOU THE THINGS YOU LEAST
WANT TO HEAR.

Coaching is absolutely critical to the empowering use of The Phoenix Agenda, not just in pursuing success, but also in avoiding various pitfalls, disasters, misapplications, and lost opportunities. When a Roman general paraded to public adulation in the streets after a victory, he would be accompanied in the chariot by a slave who whispered reminders that all fame is fleeting. However, enough of dire warnings. The next and last chapter is about preparing for the parade.

12

The Phoenix Rises

If I don't manage to fly, someone else will. The spirit wants
only that there be flying. As for who happens to do it, in
that he has only passing interest.

—Rainer Maria Rilke, poet

The Three Themes of The Phoenix Agenda

TRANSFORMATION

The myth of the Phoenix is a fable of death and glorious rebirth, endlessly repeating. Transformation in The Phoenix Agenda refers to the passage from one mindset to another, from one interpretation of reality to another. It is not an end state to be arrived at, rather it is a continuing journey fueled through listening and language. The mindset of continuous transformation collapses completely if the efforts at transformation are ever stopped. The reality in the mindset of continuous transformation is in the constant openness to change, not in the result or end state. The miracle is in you

understanding your power as a human being to create and accelerate that change through your words and actions. As the world
around you changes, you change also, not as a bystander, but as a
full participant in that change.

LANGUAGE IS POWER

The interpretation that language is power is the lever that shifts
everything presented here from the realm of theory and philosophy to the realm of immediate, everyday, practical action. To review, the key aspect is to treat everything that you say, not as a
fact, but as a wish that is certain to come true. Speak as though
everything you say acts as a magical spell. If you want poor relations with your neighbor, tell people he is an idiot. If you want
good relations, tell people about his good qualities. If you want
your organization to succeed, speak success. If you want it to fail,
speak cynicism.

YOU MAKE THE DIFFERENCE

In the final analysis, it is always and only individuals who make the
difference. Though many of us disempower ourselves by buying
into society's interpretations about the limitations of our particular
position and status in life, it is possible to live guided by more
rewarding interpretations.

Many people make their livings forecasting, commenting on, and
predicting the future. Professional trend spotting is a popular and
lucrative pastime. But where do new trends, ideas, and possibilities
come from? Do mysterious superbeings in the sky introduce fash-
ions, novel product ideas, and world revolutions? Is our role as
people simply to comment upon and evaluate these innovations
after they have been introduced?

Not so.

The Phoenix Rises

Every innovation ever created, every product, every trend, every advance, every business, and every accomplishment starts from the openness to possibility and the courage of a single individual.

IT IS THE BIRTHRIGHT OF EVERY HUMAN BEING TO CHANGE THE COURSE OF HISTORY.

Putting the Agenda to Immediate Use

PROCLAIM A PERSONAL VISION

Just as companies reap enormous benefits from having a clear and attractive mission and vision, so, too, can individuals. Few things provide as much direction and power as having a clear sense of individual purpose and mission in life.

To the extent that this mission is self-centered, it may provide direction and energy and may also fall short in attracting other people, as in:

My vision is to make $1 million for myself.

If a personal mission is born from a sense of an injustice, a wrong that must be righted, that can be intriguing to some, but it also creates enemies and resistance because it is based on negating something that someone else feels is valuable. An example is:

My vision is to stop Fred from ruining the department.

However, a personal vision that includes others and is founded on positive contribution can powerfully attract the assistance and commitment of other people. For example:

My vision is a great day at work, one day at a time, for everyone.

The selection of your own mission and vision is a deeply personal matter. No one can or should tell you what the purpose of your life contribution is to be. A personal vision should ring clear and true to yourself, should speak first to you in an unmistakable way.

Trusted friends and coaches are invaluable in giving supportive feedback as you develop your personal vision. To be sustaining and potent, your personal vision needs to arrest and engage others. Try saying to another, perhaps at first a trusted friend, what your life's mission is. Use humor, charisma, seriousness, openness, brilliance, or whatever style of communication comes most naturally to you. Ask the other person if what you have said rings as a true expression of yourself. Is the person sufficiently moved by what you have said to sign up to support you? Keep at it until you are satisfied.

Strong personal vision clarifies, directs, and supports your life in the same way it does for a winning company. When things go wrong and you experience setbacks, the personal vision provides a rope of rescue from the descent into self-doubt and negativism.

It is possible to think of ourselves in many ways. Some of us in corporations think of ourselves as our business cards, as our positions and titles. The danger of this, especially today, is that once the business card disappears, we are left with no identity, no sense of self. Others of us may think of ourselves as a history of learnings and accomplishments, a résumé. While it is wonderful to have achievements, they are in the past and do nothing in themselves to create the future.

An empowering way to think of yourself is as a possible future that extends beyond your own life. In this way, everything you say and do becomes at the service of a possible future that goes beyond who you are now, beyond your own emotions and feelings and the petty concerns of the moment. It is actually possible to construct a personal identity based on the difference you are committed to make in the world at large, rather than on one distorted by self-referential emotions and feelings.

GET INTO ACTION IMMEDIATELY

Some people wait endlessly before taking steps to improve their circumstances. Please do not become one of these. While The Phoenix Agenda can be used to support major projects and undertakings, it can also be used and practiced in routine, everyday situations. Practice acknowledging someone for a contribution at a meeting. Sharpen up your next request by adding a precise time. Practice being a good receiver or audience for the person at your next one-to-one meeting. When you hear that next proposal, instead of immediately jumping all over the flaws and holes, take a moment to listen for the value, to see the vision for the project as the person proposing it must see it. Begin to notice the impact that your words have on those around you.

It is not necessary to have detailed strategies and plans. All that is required is a mission, and a first next step. Live your next day at work the way Conklin ran his Alpha project, as described in chapter 9. Notice moments of truth, exploit them, record the results, and learn from the experience.

Mastering the Insights That Empower Your Vision

INVOLVED PARTICIPANT OR DETACHED OBSERVER?

In a world of people conscious of cause and effect, are you a cause or an effect? That is to say, do you make things happen or do things happen to you? Before you give a factual answer, a status report, in response to this question, consider giving an answer as a transformational proclamation. It could be that it is entirely up to you to say whether your involvement in the workplace will be as observer or participant.

Observing is interesting and valuable. However, it rarely makes a significant difference. Workplace transformation requires participants committed to action. The future does not exist as foreordained. It is created, moment by moment, by actions that communicate meaning to yourself and others.

As Paul Hawken says in his book on growing your own business, when you expand your range of influence and meet more and more highly placed people in the world of affairs, an astonishing realization is apt to strike you.[1]

No one is in charge.

This insight provides an opening for you to exercise your own influence on the world.

ATTEND TO PAST OR FUTURE?

The Phoenix Agenda is designed to empower action and produce accomplishments. To fully use its potential, it is worthwhile to consider accomplishments from two different perspectives, as shown in the diagram. Looking at a past accomplishment means commenting upon it, reporting on it, assessing it, and attempting to understand it. This is the common, standard way of thinking about events and accomplishments. For example, virtually all news media, such as newspapers, news magazines, television news, and commentary, are written from the perspective of reporting on past events, of providing a view into the past. Reporting is giving a factual account. The form of speaking appropriate to reporting is the status report, as explained in chapter 4.

Another way to look at accomplishments is via the view into the future. From this perspective, you have not yet achieved the accomplishment, you do not know exactly how you will do it, or whether or not you will succeed. The appropriate actions, from this view, are transformational proclamations:

The Phoenix Rises

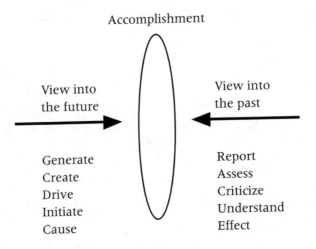

Accomplishment

View into
the future

View into
the past

Generate
Create
Drive
Initiate
Cause

Report
Assess
Criticize
Understand
Effect

This accomplishment will happen because I say so.

And requests:

Please do action X by date Y.

Unfortunately, most people in the workplace do not distinguish between past view and future view. Most of us use only the view into the past when we are trying to create some potentially new and exciting results. This severely limits the possibilities for genuine accomplishment.

THE VIEW INTO THE PAST HAS LIMITED POWER TO CREATE NEW
ACCOMPLISHMENTS AND RESULTS.

Making the shift of mindset from the view into the past to the view into the future is a simple matter of replacing, in your speaking, status reports with proclamations and requests.

THE VIEW INTO THE FUTURE GENERATES EXCITEMENT
AND ATTRACTION.

For example, suppose you are determined to re-create your eight-year-old marriage as exciting, wonderful, and new. It probably does very little good to comment, report, and criticize concerning what has gone poorly or even well during the past eight years. On the other hand, if you and your partner can create a clear and compelling vision of what the marriage will be like in the future, and then launch a series of explorations and initiatives to bring that about, the prospects for success are much brighter.

PROCLAIM YOUR FUTURE AS OPEN OR CLOSED?

From certain viewpoints, it appears that everyone's future is closed, that when each of us dies, that is the end of our particular story. And those around you who participate in this mindset, by viewing their lives within the finite boundaries of birth and death, foster interpretations that are disempowering.

From a transformational mindset, however, the future can be completely open. In the transformational approach, there is always the possibility that minor actions can have unlimited consequences. At some level, all of us know that this is the case. For example, many people buy lottery tickets in the hope that this will transform their lives. The problem is that most of us, most of the time, place the source of transformation outside of ourselves; we give it over to luck, the lottery agency, or fate, rather than trust in our own abilities to design the future the way we would prefer to see it.

Ethics of Transformation

From the viewpoint of continuous transformation, human nature itself is malleable. Many psychological theories say human nature is fixed in childhood, or is inherited, but this is not so. Though I have been thoroughly trained in psychology, I have also seen so many people transform their lives, and through imagination and courage overcome the most difficult of circumstances, that I no longer find compelling the notions of fixed traits, personality characteristics, and aptitudes as governing factors in people's lives.

Using this interpretation means that you can literally change and transform the lives of people around you. You can, through speaking powerfully, invite them to question the most basic assumptions that hold their identities together. Questioning can be an objective exercise and it can be a transformational experience. Depending on the depth of inquiry, it can also be extremely disruptive. The question then to ask yourself is:

Do any of us have the right to tinker with the architecture of each other's personal truths?

In resolving this dilemma, it may help to realize that by simply choosing to remain alive, each of us is choosing to take up space on the earth, consume resources, and influence other people. Simply by being alive we already impact others in irreversible ways. Every time we speak, we either cement an existing interpretation of reality or point the way to a new one.

WE ARE ALREADY DEEPLY INTERRELATED WITH OTHERS.

Coaching for You, the Reader

MINDSETS AND PEOPLE

When a mindset is active, it can be like a parasitic alien who controls our thoughts, and of whom we are not aware. In questioning a mindset, you are, in a sense, threatening the alien who is committed to maintaining her position as controller of the mind at all costs, even, in some cases, if maintaining control results in the death of the host. Thus, communications to shift mindsets must be designed with great care. The alien, sensing her position is threatened, will respond with an amazing variety of defense mechanisms: denial, indifference, hostility, evasion, anger, dismissal, and logic.

In essence, though, the message of The Phoenix Agenda is simple:

THE WAY IT IS IS NOT THE WAY IT HAS TO BE.

As human beings, we have been given the opportunity to construct our own identities, to design our rules of reasoning, be at peace with our emotions, and act, if we so choose, in ways that support our fellow beings. Or we can surrender these birthrights to the authorities and to the mindsets of the times that we happen to be born into. My concern is only that you recognize that you can have a free and fully informed choice.

RISK

Of the innumerable ways of structuring a life, two stand out in particular. One is a path of caution and minimization of risk. The other is to knowingly face the unknown, determined to make a difference in the world around you, consonant with a noble purpose. Many of us avoid the latter choice because we are afraid of risk.

Risk, as it turns out, is largely illusory.

SIMPLY BEING ALIVE MEANS ALREADY TO BE AT ULTIMATE RISK.

Disappointment, pain, and death are not risks. They are certainties—an unavoidable part of the package of life. To truly minimize risk would mean to be committed to nothing and to take no actions. One could avoid the companionship of fellow beings, never marry, never have children, never apply for a job, never try to make a difference in the workplace, and simply stay in bed. And even this approach is far from risk-free. One could still get depressed, sick, or go insane.

So, nothing in The Phoenix Agenda is concerned with minimizing risk. Rather, the Agenda acknowledges that we are already at 100 percent risk for everything in our lives. In the face of that, the question becomes, what are we going to do? A life of risk minimization is disempowering and not attractive to others. A life deliberately placed at risk in the service of a noble purpose is inspiring. We honor women and men who thus design their lives with statues, memorials, and public holidays.

EVERYONE HAS A FREE CHOICE TO ASPIRE TO GREATNESS,
OR NOT.

If you choose the path of continuous transformation, you may or may not succeed, but you *will* have worthwhile adventures. Along the way, you will discover glorious and inspiring relationships, unlike anything seen in the world of business as usual.

IF ANYTHING IS TO CHANGE, IT BEGINS WITH YOU

The Phoenix Agenda is written not for organizations, but rather for individuals who happen to work in organizations. You have not read phrases in this book such as

The organization must . . .

Top management should . . .

Organizations do not decide and corporations do not act. You *do* decide and act, always. Everything begins and ends with you. You have a free choice to aspire or not, to empower others or not, to drive your organization to greatness or not.

No one has the blueprint for the future. Even mighty corporations with all their resources, power, and wealth can be helpless in the face of the future. With insight, commitment, and skills in creating the future through committed speaking, you have as much right and opportunity to shape the world that you desire as anyone alive.

IF NOT YOU, THEN WHO? IF NOT NOW, THEN WHEN?

Notes

Chapter 1

1. Andrall Pearson, "Corporate Redemption and the Seven Deadly Sins," *Harvard Business Review* 70, No. 3 (May–June 1992): 62.
2. Peter Drucker, "The Coming of the New Organization," *Harvard Business Review* (Jan.–Feb. 1988), p. 45.
3. William Lareau, *American Samurai: A Warrior of the Coming Dark Ages of American Business.* (Clinton, NJ: New Win Publishing, 1991), p. 29, 30.
4. *Time*, "Can GM Survive in Today's World?" Cover story, 140, No. 19 (November 9, 1992), p. 42.
5. Peter Senge. Remarks presented at the 1992 Conference of Organizational Systems Designers. Washington, D.C., June 1992.
6. Managers in this organization, who control annual budgets in excess of $10 million, required their manager's approval for nonstandard item expenditures over $50.
7. William H. Davidow and Michael S. Malone, *The Virtual Corporation* (New York: HarperCollins, 1992).

Chapter 2

1. *Boston Globe*, February 13, 1992, p. 3.
2. Gregory Bateson, *Steps to an Ecology of Mind* (New York: Chandler, 1972), p. 320.
3. Descartes, the father of Cartesian coordinates and the modern scientific approach to life, actually conceived the core vision of his philosophy when he once sat for a long period in a heated baking oven!

Notes

4. W. Edwards Deming, "On Some Statistical Aids Toward Economic Production," *Interfaces*, 5, No. 4, August, 1975, p. 1–5.
5. Stephen Pepper, *World Hypotheses* (Berkeley: University of California Press, 1942).
6. "A Trade Mission Ends in Tension," *The New York Times*, January 10, 1992, p. 1.
7. Frederick W. Taylor, *The Principles of Scientific Management* (New York: Harper, 1911).
8. Peter Senge, *The Fifth Discipline: the Art and Practice of the Learning Organization* (New York: Doubleday, 1990).

Chapter 3

1. *Fortune*, "Invest or Die," Cover story, February, 22, 1993.
2. *Wall Street Journal*, August 12, 1991, p. 61.
3. Senge, *Fifth Discipline*, p. 4.

Chapter 4

1. This view of language is a modification of the work of John Searles as presented in *Speech Acts: An Essay in the Philosophy of Language* (Cambridge: Cambridge University Press, 1969).
2. Senge, *Fifth Discipline*, p. 4.

Chapter 7

1. Peter Drucker, *Wired*, "Post Capitalist," (July–Aug. 1993), p. 80.
2. Christopher Hart and Christopher Bogan, *The Baldridge* (New York: McGraw Hill, 1992).
3. Anne Wilson Schaef and Diane Fassel, *The Addictive Organization* (San Francisco: Harper and Row 1990), p. 119.
4. Ibid., p. 125.
5. Ibid.
6. Tracy Kidder, *Soul of a New Machine* (Boston: Little Brown, 1991).
7. Ibid., p. 66.
8. Joseph Heller, *Catch-22* (New York: Simon and Schuster, 1955).
9. Schaef and Fassel, *Addictive Organization*, p. 120.
10. Tom Peters and Nancy Austin, *A Passion for Excellence* (New York: Warner Books, 1985), p. 495.
11. Schaef and Fassel, p. 119.

Notes

Chapter 8

1. George Orwell, *1984* (New York: Harcourt, 1949).
2. In many Japanese companies, if you were seen staring blankly into space, it would be assumed that you were engaged in productive and creative thought and no one would dream of disturbing you.

Chapter 9

1. Peter Conklin, "Enrollment Management, Managing the Alpha AXP Program." *Digital Technical Journal* 4, No. 4 (Special Issue, 1992). All quotations in chapter 9 are from this article.
2. C. House and R. Price, "The Return Map-Tracking Product Teams." *Harvard Busines Review*, 69, No. 1, January 1991, p. 92–100.
3. Mark Michaels. Remarks presented at the 1992 Conference of Organizational Systems Designers. Washington, D.C., June 1992.

Chapter 11

1. An exception is Machiavelli's *The Prince.*
2. Thomas Cleary, *The Japanese Art of War* (Boston: Shambhala Publications, 1991).
3. Schaef and Fassel, *Addictive Organization.*
4. Barbara Tuchman, *The March of Folly* (New York: Knopf, 1984).

Chapter 12

Paul Hawken, *Growing a Business* (New York: Simon and Schuster, 1987).

Recommended Reading

Below is a list of recommended reading for those interested in pursuing the topics addressed in *The Phoenix Agenda* in more depth. Each recommended reading is accompanied by a brief review concerning content, relevance, and level of difficulty.

The books in Section 1 of this reading list deal from a business perspective with new forms of work and organization that are unfolding in the 1990s and with the trends and forces that are driving the corporate world. All are readily accessible to the well-educated layman.

The books in Section 2 are primary reference material for the still-developing theory of transformational management. Many are quite difficult reading. However, to paraphrase a recent Boston *Globe* article about philosophy's effect on computing said, "The future of management belongs to the philosophers." Reading and benefiting from all these books would be for someone willing to make an investment in their own career on a similar scale of effort to undertaking, say, an M.B.A.

Section 1

Paradigms: The Business of Discovering the Future
    Joel A. Barker
    HarperBusiness, 1993

A highly readable popularization of Kuhn's ideas about paradigms, applied to business.

Recommended Reading

Teaching the Elephant to Dance: A Manager's Guide to Empowering Change
James A. Belasco
Penguin Books, 1991

A corporate change-agent's manual with practical advice.

The Death of the Organization Man: What Happens When Economic Realities Change the Rules for Survival at Your Company
Amanda Bennett
Simon and Schuster, 1990

A realistic look at what to expect as corporate downsizing continues unabated. Read this if you need motivating to change and learn to insure your own future.

Workplace 2000: The Revolution Reshaping American Business
Joseph Boyett and Henry Conn
Dutton, 1991

If you believe the future belongs to the prepared, you should be familiar with these prognostications.

The Age of Unreason
Charles Handy
Harvard Business School Press, 1989

Highly recommended—a reasoned and careful look into the future of work. Intellectually powerful.

American Samurai: A Warrior for the Coming Dark Ages of American Business
William Lareau
New Win Publishing, 1991

A dismal view of the future for American corporations. Emphasizes individual survival skills. Strong on Deming and QC approaches and contains a strong call to action.

Thriving on Chaos: Handbook for a Management Revolution
Tom Peters
Alfred A. Knopf, 1987

Recommended Reading

A very readable popular guide to managing differently. Packed with examples, ideas, and lists of things to do. Even more applicable today than when it was written.

The Fifth Discipline: The Art and Practice of the Learning Organization
Peter M. Senge
Doubleday, 1990

Extremely good. Points to dialogue and systems thinking skills that are needed in close teamwork. Contains lots of possibilities for new approaches and markets for the visionary manager.

Section 2

Being-in-the-World: A Commentary on Heidegger's Being and Time, Division I
Hubert L. Dreyfus
The MIT Press, 1992

Though never mentioned in The Phoenix Agenda, *Heideggerian thought forms the intellectual basis for virtually every idea presented. Heidegger is proclaimed by some as the greatest modern philosopher, by others as completely confused. Dreyfus provides an introduction to Heidegger's extremely difficult-to-read work.*

Beyond Culture
Edward T. Hall
Anchor Books, 1981

An accessible work. Develops, through rich examples, the distinction between Western linear, mechanistic thought patterns and non-Western, contextual structures of interpretation.

Being and Time
Martin Heidegger
Harper and Row, 1962

This is a work of fundamental philosophy and difficult in the extreme. The concepts are, however, crucial to transformational thinking. You may wish to start with an introductory book about Heidegger, such as the one by Hubert Dreyfus.

Recommended Reading

Zen Action, Zen Person
  T. P. Kasulis
  University of Hawaii Press, 1981

  The relationship between Heideggerian existentialims and Zen is striking. Also provides valuable background insight into Japanese thought and approaches to management. Fairly readable.

The Structure of Scientific Revolution
  Thomas Kuhn
  University of Chicago Press, 1962

  The groundbreaking book that introduced the idea of paradigms and paradigm shift. You will have to apply the analysis to business. College-level difficulty.

World Hypothesis
  Stephen Pepper
  University of California Press, 1942

  This seminal work forms the basis for the idea of workplace mindsets used throughout The Phoenix Agenda. *This is a difficult work of philosophy, not of business. Pepper's terms for the mindsets are: formism, mechanism, organicism, and contextualism.*

The Reflective Practitioner: How Professionals Think in Action
  Donald Schön
  Basic Books, 1983

  An unconventional examination of the nature of professions, exploring the contextual and linguistic nature of the way professionals such as architects and psychologists work.

Speech Acts: An Essay in the Philosophy of Language
  John Searle
  Cambridge University Press, 1969

  The view of language presented in The Phoenix Agenda *is a modification of the framework presented in this important work on theoretical linguistics.*

Recommended Reading

Computers and Cognition
Terry Winograd and Fernando Flores
Ablex, 1987

Extremely important book for the ideas presented in The Phoenix Agenda. *One of the first books to apply Heideggerian philosophy to business, specifically to the computer and management consulting industries. The perceptive reader will see endless opportunities for major new lines of business in the 1990s. This book was extremely controversial when published.*

Index

Index

Index

Index

Index

Index

Index

Personal life
  mindset shifts in, 56
  mindsets in, 36–38
Philips Information Systems Division,
    completion rituals at, 183–84
Phlogiston theory of combustion, 36
Phoenix
  cycle of the, 5
  meaning of, 4
Phoenix Agenda, 77–78
  adapting to context, 207–8
  benefits of using, 197–98
  counter-purpose, 276
  definition, 93–94
  Enrollment Management Model and,
    207–8
  as holographic, 207–8
  immediate action for, 291
  implementing, 96–97
  power of, 198
  purpose of, 198–99
  put to immediate use, 289–90
  sample use of, 95–96
  themes of, 287–89
  vision for, 288–89
  see also Action and results, achieving;
    Projects, launching and sustaining;
    Work, as rewarding
Phoenix Agenda, examples of using,
    213–20
  E-mail, 215–16
  magic megaphone for, 216–20
  memos, 214–15
  phone calls, 216
Phone calls, Phoenix Agenda applied to,
    216
Phone-in catalog orders, sense of
    completion with job of, 186–88
Politics, in uncovering context, 108–9
Possible, transforming impossible into,
    113–16
Power
  authority-based systems maintaining,
    174
  language as, 288
  in uncovering context, 108–9, 110
Precision promises, 128
  commitment tracking of, 134–36
Precision requests, 90–91, 127–40
  authoritarian and transformational styles
    of, 138
  commitment tracking of, 134–36
  communication for, 139
  expectations and, 133–34
  handling objections to, 133

impossible, 137–38
  precision promises and, 128
  saying "no" to, 139–40
  vague requests versus, 128, 129–32
Prediction, in authoritarian control
    mindset, 231–32
Presentation and reception, 199–201
  to alter reception, 203–4
  listening and, 201–2
  magic megaphone and, 217, 218, 219,
    220
  model of, 202–3
  to receive message, 202–3
Presenting, for designing communications,
    206
Pressure, applying, see Authoritarian
    control mindset
Prestige, in uncovering context, 108–9
Priestley, Joseph, 36
Printed word, for maintaining awareness,
    149–50
Problem statement, coaching allowing shift
    in, 260–62
Proclamation
  of future accomplishments, 292–94
  sharing results by, 160–62
  transformational time created through,
    244
  see also Transformational proclamation
Projects, canceled, 189
Projects, launching and sustaining, 99–125
  see also Context, uncovering; Future,
    inventing; Strategies, articulating;
    Trust, generating
Promises, addictions maintained by, 175–76
  see also Precision promises
Publication, for maintaining awareness,
    150–51, 154–56

Quality
  Baldrige Award and, 166–67
  completion and, 187
Questions
  coaching using, 253–54, 255–56
  for designing communications, 205–6
  ethics of, 295
  of old assumptions, 28–30
  reality probe as, 87–88
  for uncovering context, 109–10
  see also Inquiring
Quitting, addiction-free organization and,
    178–81

Reality, language creating, 70, 198, 211
  see also Workplace reality

Index

Index

Index

Values of management, as example for
company, 170–73
Violated trust, 104–6
Virtual Corporation, The (Davidow and
Malone), 30
Vision
for charisma, 213
to invent future, 112–13
magic megaphone and, 217, 218, 219,
220
mastering insights empowering, 291–95
Phoenix Agenda put to use with, 289
proclamation of, 289–90
strategy separated from, 118–20
Volvo, shared awareness at, 153

Wang, 14
layoffs in, 25
Wisdom, creating, 163–73
communication for, 172
designing for communications, 206
integrity and, 165–67, 173
involvement for, 167–68
knowledge and, 163–65
listening and learning from everyone for,
168–73
management setting example for, 170–73
teaching for, 167–68
training for, 170–71
Work, as rewarding, 163–94
see also Acknowledging freely; Addictions;
Past, completing the; Wisdom, creating
Workplace mindsets, 34–57
addictions and, 175, 277–79
business-as-usual management
assumption and, 18, 19–23
coaching discovering, 256–57
comparing, 52–54
definition, 4, 34–35, 38–39
exploiting, 44–47
identifying, 44, 53–54

innovation versus fixed, 65–67
multiple contradictory, 45–47
principles of, 40
rigid, 19–23
transformations created by, 33
see also Authoritarian control mindset;
Broad understanding mindset;
Continuous transformation mindset;
Control-based management; Orderly
stereotyping mindset; Workplace
reality
Workplace mindsets, shifting, 34, 39,
40, 56
coaching for, 69
communication for, 69–70
difficulties in, 60–61
from excuses to action, 65–67
need for, 295–96
risks involved with initiating, 283–84
Workplace reality, 57–78
appreciation of other, 70–72
blindness to other viewpoints and, 59–61
breaking rules of, 67–74
business as usual management as, 60–61
filters and sieves and, 61–62
interpretations of, 57–58
language and, 82–85
metaphors as clues to, 67–69
negative attitude towards other, 63–64
rigidification of made-up realities and,
58–59
transforming, *see* Transformational
language
see also Workplace reality, new
Workplace reality, new
communication for, 74–75
freedom in, 74
possibilities of, 72–73
risk-taking for, 75–76
transformational language and, 83–85,
86